Jews, Confucians, and Protestants

Jews, Confucians, and Protestants

Cultural Capital and the End of Multiculturalism

Lawrence E. Harrison

ROWMAN & LITTLEFIELD PUBLISHERS, INC.
Lanham • Boulder • New York • Toronto • Plymouth, UK

Published by Rowman & Littlefield Publishers, Inc.
A wholly owned subsidiary of The Rowman & Littlefield Publishing Group, Inc.
4501 Forbes Boulevard, Suite 200, Lanham, Maryland 20706
www.rowman.com

10 Thornbury Road, Plymouth PL6 7PP, United Kingdom

British Library Cataloguing in Publication Information Available

Library of Congress Cataloging-in-Publication Data Available
ISBN 978-1-4422-1963-2 (cloth: alk paper)—ISBN 978-1-4422-1964-9 (electronic)

∞™ The paper used in this publication meets the minimum requirements of American National Standard for Information Sciences—Permanence of Paper for Printed Library Materials, ANSI/NISO Z39.48-1992.

Printed in the United States of America

~

Contents

~

Acknowledgments

I wish to express my gratitude to Stephen Bosworth, Dean of the Fletcher School, for his support and friendship of thirty years. I also want to record my thanks to Celia Campbell. Lupita Ervin, and Kate Taylor of the Fletcher staff for their interest and help.

Special thanks to the Smith-Richardson Foundation, John Templeton, and Sidney Swensrud Foundations for their financial support.

I also wish to express my gratitude to David Brady and William Ratliff of the Hoover Institution at Stanford University for their interest in my work, and to Celeste Szeto for her helpfulness.

The section on the Sikhs in Chapter 6 is largely the work of Narinder Kapany and his colleagues at the Sikh Foundation in Palo Alto, California. The section on the Mormons in Chapter 7 is largely the work of Jeremi Brewer, but reflects also the comments of Paul Comstock. The section on the Ismailis is largely the work of Pervez Hoodbhoy. I am most grateful for all of these contributions.

Several people made helpful comments on the manuscript: Michael Glennon, Ian Isaacs, Neil Isaacs, Lawrence Lederman, John Rohe, and Thomas Sowell. I am particularly grateful to Steven Pease, author of *The Golden Age of Jewish Achievement*, for his continuing interest, extensive comments, and encouragement.

I want to take special note of the interest of Erin Graham and Rob Tempio and their helpfulness in suggesting Rowman and Littlefield as the publisher. And I want to thank Jon Sisk, R&L vice president, for his interest and support; also Darcy Evans, Elaine McGarraugh, and Mary Bearden.

That Rowman & Littlefield is publishing *Jews, Confucians, and Protestants* appeals to both my senses of symmetry and nostalgia. My first book, *Underdevelopment Is a State of Mind: The Latin American Case*, was co-published in 1985 by Harvard University's Center for International Affairs and the University Press of America/Madison Books, whose president was Jed Lyons, whom I got to know quite well. Twenty-seven years later, in 2012, Jed Lyons is the president of the Rowman and Littlefield Group.

Although *Jews, Confucians, and Protestants* is dedicated to my friend and colleague Samuel Huntington, I also want to take note of my family: daughter Julia, her husband Jeffrey Grady, and their children Dylan and Georgia; daughter Beth, her husband Francisco Thébaud, and their sons, Max and Harry; and daughter Amy, her husband John Donnelly, and their children Megan, Jack, and Nora.

~

Introduction

I am convinced that the luckiest of geographic circumstances and the best of laws cannot maintain a constitution in despite of mores whereas the latter can turn even the most unfavorable circumstances and the worst laws to advantage. The importance of mores is a universal truth to which study and experience continually bring us back. I find it occupies a central position in my thoughts: all my ideas come back to it in the end.

Alexis de Tocqueville in *Democracy in America*[1]

That some cultures are better, much better, than others at realising the full potential of their members is not simply a conclusion of *The Central Liberal Truth*, it is a defining premise. White, Anglo-Saxon Protestants are a major beneficiary of this self-evident truth, but so too are Jews and anyone lucky enough to be born into a Confucian society.

—John Birmingham in *The Australian*, April 4, 2007

Culture matters. If the world needed to be reminded of that truth, George W. Bush's adventure in Iraq should serve the purpose. What were the chances of consolidating democracy—not just elections but also the full array of political rights and civil liberties—in Iraq, an Arab country with no experience with democracy and two conflict-prone Islamic sects, Sunni and Shia, and an ethnolinguistic group, the Kurds, seeking autonomy—all of this within an Arab world in which not one country has yet achieved democratic stability—the "Arab Spring" notwithstanding?

The Iraq adventure and a similarly frustrating experience in Afghanistan raise a question that will discomfit many around the world who are committed to multiculturalism—the idea that all cultures are essentially equal, if different. If cultural values, powerfully influenced by Islam and its divergent currents, are obstacles to the achievement by Iraq and Afghanistan of democratic stability, social justice, and prosperity—the goals of the UN Universal Declaration of Human Rights—then doesn't that explode the multicultural idea?

Moreover, as we shall see, the achievement of these goals is *facilitated* by the values, beliefs, and attitudes of other cultures, prominent among them Jewish, Confucian, and Protestant. (I place them in this order on chronological grounds: Jewish culture—values, beliefs, and attitudes—is roughly 4,000 years old;[2] Confucian culture 2,500 years old; Protestant culture 500 years old.) These and several other religious or ethnic groups, such as Ismaili Muslims, Basque Catholics, Sikhs, and Mormons, enjoy the fruits of a set of values that can be labeled "Universal Progress Culture," including, for example, focus on the future, education, achievement, merit, frugality, and ethical behavior. In geographic settings as varied as those of Sweden, Hong Kong, and the United States, this set of values produces the most successful societies, societies that have benefited from *cultural capital.*

Cultural capital adds another dimension to earlier concepts of capital:

- Financial/resource/property capital (Adam Smith and Karl Marx)
- Human capital—the quality of the workforce (Gary Becker)
- Social capital—the tendency of a society to encourage association of its members (Glenn Loury, James Coleman, Robert Putnam, and Francis Fukuyama)

Cultural capital, which is addressed in the first chapter of this book, is intimately linked to human and social capital; it can be viewed as a key facilitator of both. Human capital will be richer in societies that value achievement and education; social capital will be richer in societies that emphasize ethical conduct and trust.

The End of Multiculturalism

Since the 1960s, multiculturalism has increasingly become a dominant feature of the political and intellectual landscape of the West, particularly in the United States and Canada where immigration is significantly altering the ethnic and religious composition of both societies. It is noteworthy, and relevant, that during the past few decades, the level of trust in both the United States and Canada, as measured by the World Values Survey, has declined sharply.[3] Robert Putnam recently identified immigration as a major contributor to the decline: "The short run effect of being around people who are different from us is to make all of us uncertain—to hunker down, to pull in, to trust everybody less. Like a turtle in the presence of some feared threat, we pull in."[4]

Multiculturalism has also become a dominant theme in international development, for example in the World Bank, where economic historian David Landes's assertion at a World Bank conference in 2000 that some cultures are "toxic" for development shocked much of the audience.[5] And multiculturalism was strongly implied in the Bush administration's doctrine: "These values of freedom are right and true for every person, in every society."[6]

But multiculturalism rests on a frail foundation: cultural relativism, the notion that no culture is better or worse than any other—it is merely different. Anthropologist Ruth Benedict, author of the classic study of Japanese culture *The Chrysanthemum and the Sword*, wrote that all cultures are "'coexisting and equally valid patterns of life, which mankind has created for itself from the raw materials of existence.' In her view . . . each culture is self-contained, autonomous, separate but equal. Each makes sense in its own context, and all you have to do is know the context to understand what the people are doing and why they're doing it."[7]

That's doubtlessly good advice for cultural anthropologists doing ethnographic studies in the field. If one's goal is full understanding of a value system quite different from one's own, ethnocentrism can seriously distort the quest and the conclusions. But what if the objective is to assess the extent to which a culture facilitates progress toward democratic governance, social justice, and an end to poverty—the goals of the UN Universal Declaration of Human Rights? In this case, cultural relativism becomes a huge obstacle, because the assessment presupposes that some cultures are more nurturing of progress than others and challenges the very essence of cultural relativism.

Religious Relativism

Religion is a principal source of values, beliefs, and attitudes, the aspects of culture most relevant to the behaviors that powerfully influence the way a society evolves. Consistent with cultural relativism, there exists today a widespread presumption that all religions must be regarded as of equal worth, and in any event are not to be the object of comparative value judgments.

That presumption—let's label it religious relativism—is the dominant one in the West. However, when it comes to the relationship between religion and human progress, I find compelling evidence that some religions do better than others in promoting the goals of democratic politics, social justice, and prosperity.

Voodoo, the dominant religion in Haiti, is a case in point. Haiti is by far the poorest, least literate, most misgoverned country in the Western Hemisphere. Voodoo is a religion of sorcery in which hundreds of spirits, very human and capricious, control human destinies—the only way to gain leverage over what happens in one's life is to propitiate the spirits through the intervention of the Voodoo priests and priestesses. Voodoo is without ethical content and, consequently, a major contributor to the high levels of mistrust, paranoia, sense of helplessness, and despair noted in the anthropological literature about Haiti. The insight of Placide David, a Haitian in exile writing in 1959, is particularly poignant: "Our souls are like dead leaves. We live in indifference, are silently malcontent . . . the most flagrant violations of our rights and the most outrageous abuse of authority provokes among us merely submission."[8]

Voodoo's roots are in the Dahomey region of West Africa—today the country of Benin. The indicators of income, child malnutrition, child mortality, life expectancy, and literacy are virtually identical for Haiti and Benin.

The roots of much of the population of Barbados are also in Dahomey. But unlike Haiti, which won its independence from France in 1804 through an uprising of the slaves, Barbados gained its independence from Britain in 1966, at which time the descendants of the slaves first imported to the island in the first half of the seventeenth century dominated politics and a good part of the economy. During three centuries, they had so acculturated to British values and institutions that they are sometimes referred to as Afro-Saxons or Black Englishmen. The dominant religion is the Church of England.

Today, Barbados is a prosperous democracy, forty-second on the 2010 UN Human Development Index, just making it into the "Very High Human Development" category. Haiti is number 145 (of 169 countries). Culture matters. Race doesn't.

The Economists' "Relativism"

Cultural and religious relativism provide the principal intellectual foundation of multiculturalism. But economics also contributes a pillar. Many economists would like to ignore culture. As the former World Bank economist William Easterly, author of *The White Man's Burden*, wrote in reviewing my book *Who Prospers?*, "Maybe there is a lot to be said for the old-fashioned economist's view that people are the same everywhere and will respond to the right economic opportunities and incentives."[9]

That was in 1994. Today, Easterly sees the world quite differently: "I am far more open to the importance of social norms, individual values . . . in short, culture."[10] Much as I do, he has noted that in multicultural countries where the economic opportunities and incentives are available to all, some ethnic or religious minorities often do much better than majority populations, as in the case of Chinese immigrants in Indonesia, Malaysia, Costa Rica, and the United States, among others.

Why has the "Washington Consensus" prescription of free market economics (e.g., fiscal policy discipline; emphasis on education, health, and infrastructure; tax reform; trade liberalization; openness to foreign investment; privatization) worked well in India and poorly in Latin America, where socialism, even authoritarian socialism in the case of Hugo Chávez's Venezuela, appears to be alive and well and where only Chile has been able to achieve transforming rates of sustained economic growth? Cultural factors are not the whole explanation, but surely they are relevant. (In Chile's case, the disproportionately large segment of its population of Basque antecedence is a key to Chile's exceptionalism.)

Alan Greenspan got it right when he said, in 1997, "Much of what we took for granted in our free market system and assumed to be human nature was not nature at all, but culture."[11]

Foreign Policy Implications

If culture matters, then, by influencing the degree of receptivity of a society to democratic institutions and the degree to which the society produces and encourages entrepreneurs, what are the implications for a foreign policy, a fundament of which was the doctrine "These values of freedom are right and true for every person, in every society," a doctrine suffused with multiculturalism and with roots going back at least to Woodrow Wilson? The Bush administration staked huge human, financial, diplomatic, and prestige resources on the doctrine's applicability in Iraq. It is now apparent that the doctrine is ungrounded.

Moreover, it is increasingly apparent that the Iraq experience is relevant to Afghanistan, a traditional society in which, in the period 2000–2004, 43 percent of males and 13 percent of females were literate, according to United Nations International Children's Emergency Fund (UNICEF) data.[12]

Francis Fukuyama argues that in the long run, all human societies will converge on the democratic capitalist model because it has proven itself to be the most successful way of harnessing human nature to produce progress.[13] I agree, even in light of the battering that capitalism has taken in the current economic downturn. But what about the short run? What are the chances of consolidating democracy in Iraq and Afghanistan—not just elections, which can be arranged in just about any country, for example, Haiti—but also the full array of political rights and civil liberties?

To assess the possibilities of a successful promotion of democracy in Iraq, we might start with an assessment of the condition of democracy in Arab countries more generally. Freedom House's 2006 rankings, in which 2 is best and 14 is the worst, produce an average of 11 for fifteen Arab countries. By contrast, most First World countries are ranked 2 by Freedom House. In those same fifteen Arab countries, the *UN Human Development Report 2004* presents data on literacy that average out at 77 percent for males and 57 percent for females. More than half of the females were illiterate in Iraq, Egypt, and Morocco. In Yemen, 70 percent of males and 29 percent of females were literate.

Although stable democracy may not depend on high levels of female literacy, as demonstrated in India, where female literacy is about 50 percent, it must surely be enhanced by literate women, particularly since women play the lead role in child rearing. The data on gender literacy underscore the subordination of women to men in contemporary Islam.

If nothing else, the Iraq adventure demonstrates the enormous risks that attend a foreign policy predicated on a multicultural worldview. But it also underscores the need to appreciate the role culture plays in all aspects of foreign affairs, as well as cultural competence on the part of all foreign affairs agencies, including the Department of Defense.

Multiculturalism and Development Assistance

Development assistance institutions, both multilateral and bilateral, have thus far failed to address cultural change chiefly because culture-blind economists, and anthropologists and other social scientists committed to cultural relativism, have dominated policy. That some cultures are more prone to progress than others is a message that goes down very hard in development circles, evidence to the contrary notwithstanding. This obstacle is magnified by the politics of the international institutions, where both donors and recipients have a voice, and where it is much more interpersonally comfortable, and less threatening to self-esteem, to view the countries lagging behind as either the victims of the more successful countries or as having failed thus far to find the proper content and mix of policies, incentives, and institutions.

Representative of this intellectual–emotional obstacle is the negative reception in some Arab circles to the four courageous UN Development Programme's Arab Human Development Reports (2002–2005), cosponsored by the Arab Gulf Programme for United Nations Development Organizations and written by Arab experts. All four focus on the need for cultural change; the 2005 report promotes gender equality.

Symptomatic of the multiculturalist environment at the World Bank was an encounter I had after having made a presentation on culture at a World Bank Poverty Reduction Conference a few years ago. (I assume that I had been invited to speak because of the popularity of *Culture Matters* at the World Bank bookstore. I had had several prior contacts with the World Bank that had sensitized me to the institutional hostility to anything that challenged cultural relativism.) During the question and comment period, an African employee of the World Bank said, with some fire in her eyes, "I thought we had put 'blaming the victim' explanations behind us long ago."

I can only hope that the persistent, widespread dissatisfaction and frustration with the sluggish pace of progress in most poor countries will cause development assistance institutions to ponder the message of *Culture Matters, The Central Liberal Truth*, and this book. The considerable intelligence, creativity, and dedication of development professionals over the past half century have not succeeded in transforming the large majority of poor, authoritarian societies. Where transformations have occurred, they usually either have been nurtured by cultures that are progress prone (e.g., the Confucian societies of East Asia) or have been cases where cultural change has been central to the transformation (e.g., Spain, Ireland, Quebec).

Multiculturalism, Race, and Immigration

The foundation of multiculturalism is the idea that all cultures are essentially equal. But what if they aren't? What if African American subculture, not racism and discrimination, is now the principal obstacle to progress by black Americans? And what if Ibero-Catholic culture, not imperialism, colonialism, or dependency, is the principal reason that Latin American countries are poor, unjust, and authoritarian by comparison with Anglo-Protestant Canada and the United States (and Barbados)? What if culture is a key part of the explanation of black and Latino underachievement in the United States—and what if some of the people who believe that to be true are themselves Latin Americans, Hispanic Americans, Africans, and African Americans?

Two prominent Latin Americans, Argentine intellectual Mariano Grondona and Cuban exile columnist Carlos Alberto Montaner, believe that

Iberian cultural traditions like fatalism, authoritarianism, a narrow radius of identification and trust, and disdain of economic activity have impeded Latin America's quest for democratic prosperity. So do Nobelist authors Mario Vargas Llosa and Octavio Paz; former Costa Rican president Oscar Arias, winner of the Nobel Peace Prize[14]; and former president of Ecuador, Osvaldo Hurtado.

In *The Americano Dream*,[15] Mexican American Lionel Sosa argues that the same value system is an impediment to the upward mobility of Latin American immigrants in the United States. So does former US congressman Herman Badillo, a Puerto Rican whose book *One Nation, One Standard*[16] is both an indictment of Latino undervaluing of education and a call for cultural change. And so does Mexican American Ernesto Caravantes in his three books: *From Melting Pot to Witch's Cauldron: How Multiculturalism Failed America*[17]; *Clipping Their Own Wings: The Incompatibility between Latino Culture and American Education*[18]; and *The Mexican-American Mind*.[19]

In his article "Know Thyself: Latin America in the Mirror of Culture,"[20] President Hurtado concludes,

> The relationship between Latin America's failures and its culture is a difficult subject to discuss. It is not politically correct, and it evokes awkward emotion, especially when raised by outsiders. Most of the observations I have made here would be overwhelmingly affirmed by Latin Americans speaking privately, but these same people would be very reluctant to voice them in public, particularly in mixed cultural company. Moreover, it is virtually impossible for scholars to quantify culture, and so these days it is easy for them to ignore it. Above all, cultural analysis points to challenges for which there are no quick fixes.
>
> Yet we must tell the truth about Latin America, and not just in private confidences, or we will handicap all of our efforts to improve the situation. Certainly, changing any culture is not easy. It takes time. But until Latin America's best thinkers and opinion leaders overcome their prejudices and acknowledge cultural issues, Latin America will not change. Yet it must change, and it can. Cultural values are neither immutable nor inherent to a particular race, religious group or social class. They can be transformed through political and juridical actions, through economic and social reforms, through the efforts of enlightened political leaders, and through the power of education in schools, churches and the mass media. And perhaps beneficial outside influences can help too—even from Spain and the United States.

In his final book, *Who Are We? The Challenges to America's National Identity*, Samuel Huntington stressed the centrality of Anglo-Protestant culture to America's success. Among the elements of that culture are rule of law;

fair play; individual rights; limits on governmental authority; a blend of individualism and sense of community; freedom, including freedom of religion; an ethical code that breeds trust; work ethic; and a commitment to human progress, importantly through education. These values are substantially shared by most advanced countries of the world, for example, the countries of northern Europe. But they are not commonly found in the countries of the Islamic world, Africa, and Latin America.

Hispanic Americans, poorer and less educated than African Americans, now form the largest US minority and are projected by the Census Bureau to constitute almost one-third of the US population in 2050.[21] Their experience in the United States recapitulates Latin America's culturally shaped underdevelopment. For example, the Hispanic high school dropout rate in the United States is alarmingly high—25 percent or more (see Chapter 9); it is a good deal higher in Latin America, where education has had a much lower priority than in the United States and Canada. And Latin America's sluggish economic growth reflects in part an entrepreneurial shortfall influenced by the cultural factors that Lionel Sosa and others highlight.

The progress of Hispanic immigrants, not to mention harmony in the broader society, depends, then, on their acculturation to the values of that broader society. Efforts—for example, long-term bilingual education—to perpetuate Latin values in a multicultural salad bowl work against acculturation to the mainstream and upward mobility and are likely to result in continuing underachievement, poverty, resentment, and divisiveness. So does the willy-nilly emergence of bilingualism in the United States—no language in our history has ever before competed with English to the point where one daily hears commercial enterprises responding to telephone calls with, "If you want to speak in English, press 1; *Si quiere hablar en español, oprima el botón número dos.*"

Highly relevant are Samuel Huntington's words in *Who Are We?*:

> Would America be the America it is today if it had been settled not by British Protestants but by French, Spanish, or Portuguese Catholics? The answer is no. It would not be America; it would be Quebec, Mexico, or Brazil.[22]

The Structure of This Book

Chapter 1 provides the conceptual framework for what follows. It elaborates on the idea of cultural capital, employing a value-belief-attitude typology in which twenty-five factors are viewed very differently in cultures prone to progress and those that resist it.

Chapter 2 presents an analysis of the performance of 117 countries, grouped by predominant religion, with respect to ten indicators of political, social, and economic achievement. Taken together, the typology and the 117-country analysis document the idea of a Universal Progress Culture, shared by Jews, Confucians, and Protestants and several other religious or ethnic groups.

Chapter 3 reviews the history of Jewish achievement and traces it back to the sources of Jewish values, starting with the Ten Commandments.

Chapter 4 examines Confucianism and other sources of East Asian values, beliefs, and attitudes—and behaviors—like Taoism, Buddhism, and ancestor worship.[23] It then reviews the East Asian economic "miracles" and the achievements of Chinese, Japanese, Korean, and Vietnamese immigrants in various geographic settings.

Chapter 5 first examines the significance of the Reformation—I consider it the most important progress-promoting event of history. It then focuses on the strikingly different post-Reformation courses of Scotland and Ireland, both originally Celtic, and Lutheranism as the common denominator of the "Champions of Progress": the Nordic countries—Denmark, Finland, Iceland, Norway, and Sweden.

Chapter 6 discusses two high cultural capital groups that form minority populations of a nation or nations: the Basques, who are Catholics; and India's Sikhs.

Chapter 7 discusses two other high cultural capital minorities: the Mormons; and the Ismailis, who are Muslims. The chapter concludes with a section addressing reform of Islam, based on the Ismaili experience.

Chapter 8 addresses the shortfalls of Catholic countries, especially those of Latin America, in contrast with the Protestant United States and Canada. The chapter concludes with some comments about reform of the Catholic Church.

Chapter 9 reviews the performance and condition of Latino immigrants in the United States. The evidence—high school dropout rates, low self-employment—of slow acculturation and slow upward mobility of Latino immigrants is alarming, especially in light of the Census Bureau projections for 2050.

Chapter 10 addresses the two principal explanations—racism/discrimination and cultural obstacles—for African American underachievement and discusses the impact of the election of President Barack Obama.

Chapter 11 concludes the book by (1) urging countries that have fallen behind to seek cultural change that moves them toward Universal Progress Culture through the following:

- Modifying child-rearing practices
- Religious reform/conversion
- Education reform
- Increased responsibility on the part of the media
- Economic policy modifications
- Culture-tuned development programs
- Increased sensitivity to cultural factors in the private sector
- Leadership committed to cultural change

and (2) reviewing the experience of the Cultural Change Institute during its first four years of operations.

CHAPTER 1

∼

Cultural Capital Defined

Cultural capital is a set of values, beliefs, and attitudes that drives societies toward the goals of the UN Universal Declaration of Human Rights:

- democratic governance, including rule of law;
- social justice, including education , health care, and opportunity for all; and
- elimination of poverty.

These values, beliefs, and attitudes have been disaggregated in the "Typology of Progress-Prone and Progress-Resistant Cultures."[1] As we review the typology in this chapter, it will become apparent how cultural capital powerfully influences human capital and social capital.

I have found helpful a diagram in the book *Cultures and Organizations* by Geert Hofstede and colleagues that presents the three fundamental forces that motivate human behavior as three slices of a triangle: the base is human nature; the apex is individual personality; and in between lies culture (Figure 1.1).[2]

Pierre Bourdieu and Cultural Capital

The distinguished French social scientist philosopher Pierre Bourdieu is often identified as the person who originated the concept of cultural capital in his 1973 article, with Jean-Claude Passeron, "Cultural Reproduction and Social Reproduction."[3] However, his focus is on the individual rather than

Three Levels of Uniqueness in Mental Programming

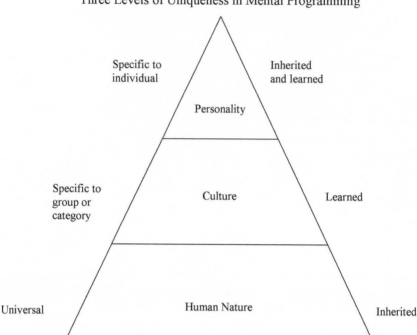

Figure 1.1 Three fundamental factors influencing human behavior.

society as a whole. "Cultural capital [consists of] forms of knowledge, skills, education, and advantages that a person has, which gives [him or her] a higher status in society. Parents provide their children with cultural capital by transmitting the attitudes and knowledge needed to succeed in the current educational system."[4]

In Bourdieu's "The Forms of Capital,"[5] he identifies three subtypes of cultural capital—embodied, objectified, and institutionalized:

- **"Embodied cultural capital** consists of both the consciously acquired and the passively 'inherited' properties of one's self (with 'inheritance' not in the genetic sense but in the sense of receipt over time, usually from the family through socialization, cultural exposures, and traditions)." Linguistic capital—mastery of language—is a form of embodied cultural capital.
- **"Objectified cultural capital** consists of physical objects that are owned, such as scientific instruments or works of art. These cultural goods can be

transmitted both for economic profit . . . and for the purpose of 'symbolically' conveying the cultural capital whose acquisition they facilitate."

- **"Institutionalized cultural capital** consists of institutional recognition, most often in the form of academic credentials or qualifications, of the cultural capital held by an individual."

Although these are all valuable insights, Bourdieu did not establish structures that would facilitate comparative assessment of different cultures, at least as far as I've been able to tell. Fortunately, however, someone else has.

Disaggregating "Culture"

In 1999, the Argentine scholar and journalist Mariano Grondona published a book titled *Las Condiciones Culturales del Desarrollo Económico* (The Cultural Conditions of Economic Development).[6] Grondona is a columnist for *La Nación* (a leading Buenos Aires newspaper), a professor of government at the National University of Buenos Aires, and the host of a popular weekly public affairs television show. He has also taught at Harvard University.

Over several years of thought and observation, Grondona evolved a theory of development that is captured in a typology of cultural characteristics that contrasts cultures that are favorable to economic development (high cultural capital) with those that resist it (low cultural capital). In his words, drawn from a chapter in *Culture Matters* that derived from his book

> Values can be grouped in a consistent pattern that we may call a "value system." Real value systems are mixed; pure value systems exist only in the mind, as ideal types. It is possible to construct two ideal value systems: one including only values that favor economic development and the other including only values that resist it. A nation is modern as far as it approaches the former system; it is deemed traditional as far as it approaches the latter. Neither of these value systems exists in reality, and no nation falls completely within either of those two value systems. However, some countries approach the extreme favorable to economic development, whereas others approach the opposite extreme.
>
> Real value systems are moving as well as mixed. If they are moving toward the favorable value-system pole, they improve a nation's chances of developing. If they move in the opposite direction, they diminish a nation's chances of developing.[7]

Four of Grondona's colleagues contributed to the expansion of the typology to embrace political and social, as well as economic, development: Irakli Chkonia, Ronald Inglehart, Matteo Marini, and myself.

I want to reemphasize Grondona's characterization of the typology as "idealized." It is also highly generalized. There is no monolithic culture; all cultures have crosscurrents to their mainstreams, and that is as true of the Argentine/Latin American culture that served as the model for the progress-resistant column of the typology as it is for US culture, the model for the progress-prone culture. This is an extremely important point. As Boston University anthropologist Robert Hefner reminds us, "this theme [of variety within cultures] allows us to recognize that even in relatively progress-unfriendly cultures, there are alternative streams at work, some of which may contain bits and pieces of progressive values."[8]

Ronald Inglehart, president of the World Value Survey, has tested the twenty-five elements of the typology with data from the World Values Survey; I will make reference to his findings as I review the typology. In general, "these empirical findings tend to support the 'Progress Typology'—sometimes very strongly."[9] Of the twenty-five factors, eleven receive "strong confirmation" from the World Values Survey data; three receive "moderately strong confirmation"; there is "no significant support" for two; and no data are available for the others. As Inglehart stresses, "the World Values Survey was not designed to test the Progress Typology. But it was designed to provide a comprehensive exploration of all important realms of human values, and consequently it does tap most . . . of the domains included in the Progress Typology."[10]

The sections that follow describe the categories identified in the document "Typology of High Cultural Capital and Low Cultural Capital Societies," based on the original structure of Mariano Grondona with inputs from Irakli Chkonia, Lawrence Harrison, Ronald Inglehart, and Matteo Marini, as shown in Table 1.1.

Table 1.1. Typology of High Cultural Capital and Low Cultural Capital Societies

Based on the original structure of Mariano Grondona with inputs from Irakli Chkonia, Lawrence Harrison, Ronald Inglehart, and Matteo Marini

Factor Capital	High Cultural Capital	Low Cultural Capital
	WORLDVIEW	
1. Religion	Nurtures rationality, achievement; promotes material pursuits; focus on this world; pragmatism	Nurtures irrationality; inhabits material pursuits; focus on the other world; utopianism
2. Destiny	I can influence my destiny for the better.	Fatalism, resignation, sorcery
3. Time orientation	Future focus promotes planning, punctuality, deferred gratification	Present or past focus discourages planning, punctuality, saving

Factor Capital	High Cultural Capital	Low Cultural Capital
4. Wealth	Product of human creativity, expandable (positive sum)	What exists (zero-sum)
5. Knowledge	Practical, verifiable; facts matter	Abstract, theoretical, cosmological, not verifiable; debate matters
VALUES, VIRTUES		
6. Ethical code	Rigorous within realistic norms; feeds trust	Elastic, wide gap twixt utopian norms and behavior = mistrust
7. The lesser virtues	A job well done, tidiness, courtesy, punctuality matter	Lesser virtues unimportant; love, justice, courage matter
8. Education	Indispensable; promotes autonomy, heterodoxy, dissent, creativity	Less priority; promotes dependency, orthodoxy
ECONOMIC BEHAVIOR		
9. Work/achievement	Live to work: work leads to wealth	Work to live: work doesn't lead to wealth; work is for the poor
10. Frugality	The mother of investment and prosperity	A threat to equality
11. Entrepreneurship	Investment and creativity	Rent-seeking
12. Risk propensity	Moderate	Low; occasional adventures
13. Competition	Leads to excellence	Aggression; a threat to equality—and privilege
14. Innovation	Open; rapid adaptation	Suspicious; slow adaption
15. Advancement	Merit, achievement	Family, patron, connections
SOCIAL BEHAVIOR		
16. Rule of law/corruption	Reasonably law abiding; corruption is prosecuted	Money, connections matter; corruption is tolerated
17. Radius of identification and trust	Stronger identification with the broader society	Stronger identification with the narrow community
18. Family	The idea of "family" extends to the broader society	The family is a fortress against the broader society
19. Association (social capital)	Trust, identification breed cooperation, affiliation, participation	Mistrust breeds excessive individualism, anomie
20. The individual/the group	Emphasizes the individual but not excessively	Emphasizes the collectivity
21. Authority	Dispersed: checks and balances, consensus	Centralized: unfettered, often arbitrary
22. Role of elites	Responsibility to society	Power and rent seeking; exploitative
23. Church-state relations	Secularized; wall between church and state	Religion plays major role civic sphere
24. Gender relationships	If not a reality, equality at least not inconsistent with value system; should also apply to gender preference	Women subordinated to men in most dimensions of life; gays/Lesbians are discriminated against
25. Fertility	The number of children should depend on the family's capacity to raise and educate them	Children are gifts of God; they are an economic asset

WORLDVIEW

1. Religion. Religion can be a—in some cases *the*—major force for progress to the extent that it nurtures rationality and objectivity, encourages accumulation of wealth, and promotes ethical behavior. The foregoing statement captures the essence of the Protestant ethic to which Max Weber attributed the rise of capitalism. It reverberates in many of the subsequent typology factors, for example, destiny, ethical code, education, work, frugality, entrepreneurship, and innovation.

Religion—in the case of the Confucian countries, an ethical code—is a principal source of values, and the values may persist long after religious practice has gone into decline; witness the case of the Lutheran Nordic countries. Those values can be either nurturing of or resistant to democracy, economic development, and social justice. In Democracy in America, Alexis de Tocqueville notes "[the British settlers] brought with them into the New World a form of Christianity which I cannot better describe than by styling it a democratic and republican religion. This contributed powerfully to the establishment of a republic and a democracy in public affairs; and from the beginning, politics and religion contracted an alliance which has never been dissolved."[11]

If a religion nurtures irrationality, inhibits material pursuits, and focuses on the other world, its adherents are likely to be indisposed to economic development. But they are also likely to be susceptible to a passivity, a resignation in which authoritarianism and injustice thrive.

With the great early centuries of Islam in mind, Bassam Tibi wrote, "In reading the Qur'an and studying its precepts . . . I . . . find in Islam a deep commitment to rationalism and achievement as well as to the pursuit of worldly affairs . . . but I miss this spirit among contemporary Muslims."[12]

As Haiti is prototypical of a progress-resistant society, Voodoo is prototypical of those religions that nurture irrationality.

Inglehart makes an interesting observation in linking the typology to his World Values Survey data: "Strong emphasis on religion is negatively correlated with progress [America's exceptionalism in this respect notwithstanding]. Societies in which religion is linked with rationality, material pursuits, and a focus on this world tend to attach much less importance to religion."[13] In these words we find a loud echo of the words written by John Wesley more than two centuries ago:

> I fear, wherever riches have increased, the essence of religion has decreased in the same proportion. Therefore I do not see how it is possible . . . for any revival of true religion to continue long. For religion must necessarily produce both industry and frugality, and these cannot but produce riches. But as riches increase, so will pride, anger, and love of the world in all its branches.[14]

2. Destiny. Tibi again finds language in the Qur'an that he interprets as supporting the progressive view of destiny: "Whatever good befalls you . . . it is from Allah; and whatever ill from yourself."[15] However, I find those words ambivalent:

if good can only come from Allah, then the idea that humans are largely responsible for their destiny is undermined, even if the Qur'an assigns the avoidance of ill to humans. In any event, Tibi concludes, "the fatalist worldview can be observed at work in reality, even though belied by . . . Islamic revelation."

3. Time orientation. "Punctuality is not a Latin American comparative advantage," as stated in *The Economist* in an article about a national punctuality campaign inaugurated by Ecuadoran president Lucio Gutiérrrez, who appeared at the launching ceremony, "but at the last minute."[16] Participación Ciudadana (Citizen Participation), the civic organization that initiated the campaign, estimates that tardiness costs Ecuador upward of $700 million per year—more than 4 percent of gross domestic product.

The punctuality campaign in Ecuador was the subject of a subsequent article in the New Yorker in which the author, James Surowiecki, writes, "[A]ttitudes toward time tend to pervade nearly every aspect of a culture. In hyperpunctual countries like Japan, pedestrians walk fast, business transactions take place quickly and bank clocks are always accurate. . . . In other words, Ecuadorans . . . are trying to revolutionize the way they live and work."[17]

In this context, Tibi mentions an Egyptian definition of IBM: Inshallah (God willing); **B**ukra (tomorrow); **M**a'lish (it doesn't matter).

4. Wealth. The zero-sum worldview discourages initiative since anyone's gain is someone else's loss. In many traditional societies, a "crabs in a barrel" psychology is operative: people who "get ahead" are pulled back with a variety of sanctions, including redistribution of their wealth to the community. Human nature is affronted when another does better than oneself; this dark recess of human nature is probably also the source of schadenfreude, the satisfaction one derives from another's problems, a satisfaction that is enhanced if the person in trouble is a celebrity (e.g., Martha Stewart). In Protestant/Calvinist societies, where one's state of grace is confirmed by prosperity, culture overrides human nature, and, as Weber stressed, accumulation of wealth is encouraged.

The zero-sum worldview is common to peasant societies around the world in the view of anthropologist George Foster, who perceives a "Universal Peasant Culture" dominated by the "Image of Limited Good," which he defines as follows:

> By "Image of Limited Good," I mean that broad areas of peasant behavior are patterned in such fashion as to suggest that peasants view their social, economic, and natural universes—their total environment—as one in which all of the desired things in life such as land, wealth, health, friendship and love, manliness and honor, respect and status, power and influence, security and safety, exist in finite quantity and are always in short supply. . . . Not only do these and all other "good things" exist in finite and limited quantities, but in addition there is no way directly within peasant power to increase the available quantities.[18]

5. Knowledge. It is evident that a society that doesn't respect facts is at an enormous disadvantage not only in terms of productivity, competitiveness, and economic development but also in building democratic and just institutions. This is particularly true of facts—and their interpretation—that challenge self-esteem and identity, an observation that evokes Bernard Lewis's words: "When people realize that things are going wrong, there are two questions they can ask: One is, 'What did we do wrong?' and the other is 'Who did this to us?' The latter leads to conspiracy theories and paranoia. The first question leads to another line of thinking: 'How do we put it right?'"[19] David Landes notes, "In the second half of the twentieth century, Latin America chose conspiracy theories and paranoia. In the second half of the nineteenth century, Japan asked itself, 'How do we put it right?'"[20]

In his handwritten notes on the draft typology, Michael Novak adds to "Practical, verifiable, facts matter" in the progress-prone column "an evolutionary cosmology in which progress and freedom should flower."

VALUES/VIRTUES

6. Ethical code. The rigor of the ethical code profoundly influences several other factors including rule of law/corruption, radius of identification and trust, and association. Although these latter three factors fall under "social behavior," the ethical code is also highly relevant to economic behavior as well. A rigorous ethical code engenders the behaviors that nurture trust, and trust is central to economic efficiency, as Weber stresses when he speaks of Benjamin Franklin's ethical exhortations.[21] That the Nordic countries do so well on economic indices is almost surely related to the fact that they do comparably well on the World Values Survey data on trust (Table 1.2).

Conversely, Uganda ranks at the bottom of both the competitiveness and trust indices. Uganda is a country, like Haiti, where traditional religions that embrace sorcery persist, often in tandem with Christian religions and, in Uganda, Islam.

Democracy appeared first and most enduringly in countries where the value of fair play, central to the Anglo-Protestant tradition, had taken root. This was a key element of the congeniality between US culture and democracy that Tocqueville perceived. With respect to the much later consolidation of democracy by Catholic countries, I note Weber's observation: "The God of Calvinism demanded of his believers not single good works, but a life of good works combined into a unified system. There was no place for the very human Catholic cycle of sin, repentance, atonement, release, followed by renewed sin."[22]

7. The lesser virtues. A job well done, tidiness, courtesy, and punctuality are lubricants of both the economic and politicosocial systems. The lesser virtues can translate into hard economic data, as the estimate of Ecuador's annual loss to tardiness of upward of $700 million demonstrates. Punctuality is practiced in all of the top ten countries on the World Economic Forum's competitiveness rankings, eight of which are Protestant and two Confucian—Singapore and Japan.

Table 1.2. Nordic Countries Achievement and Trust

	World Economic Forum's Survey Rankings: Competitiveness Index	World Values Survey: Trust
	2008–2009	2000
Denmark	3 (among 134)	1 (among 81)
Sweden	4	2
Finland	6	6
Norway	15	4
Iceland	20	13
Uganda	128	80

8. Education. The value attached to education of both men and women is powerfully linked to modernization. That value is influenced by religion or ethical code: Judaism and Protestantism promoted education to facilitate reading of the Bible by congregants; in Confucianism, learning occupies the highest rung on the prestige ladder; witness the Mandarin scholars who were so powerful in imperial China. I note in passing that more than 90 percent of Japanese elementary school-aged boys and girls were in school in 1905, among the highest percentages in the world at the time.[23]

It is in education that we perceive the powerful connection between human capital and cultural capital. Nobelist economist Gary Becker defines human capital:

> Schooling, a computer training course, expenditures on medical care, and lectures on the virtues of punctuality and honesty are also capital. That is because they raise earnings, improve health, or add to a person's good habits over much of his lifetime. Therefore, economists regard expenditures on education, training, medical care, and so on as investments in human capital. They are called human capital because people cannot be separated from their knowledge, skills, health, or values in the way they can be separated from their financial and physical assets.[24]

ECONOMIC BEHAVIOR

9. Work/achievement. Work as a vehicle to achieve the good life is another value shared by Protestantism and Judaism. In mainstream Catholic doctrine, derivative of classical Greek/Roman philosophy, the good life is found in spiritual matters, contemplation, and artistic achievement. Work, particularly manual work, is below the dignity of the elites and is relegated to the lower classes. Low prestige attaches to economic activity. Particularly when combined with the Catholic doctrinal preference for the poor ("It is easier for a camel to go through the eye of a needle than for a rich man to enter into the kingdom of God," Matthew 19:24), it is easy to understand why Catholic ambivalence about capitalism persists to this day.

The Catholic ordering of values was substantially shared by the Confucian countries until the second half of the nineteenth century in the case of Japan and the second half of the twentieth century in the cases of China and its derivative societies—in Taiwan, Hong Kong, and Singapore—and South Korea. For reasons of national security and prestige, economic activity, which was traditionally the lowest rung on the Confucian prestige ladder—below the scholars, soldiers, and farmers—has been promoted to high prestige. The effect has been to liberate those values that Confucianism shares with the Protestant ethic: education, merit, frugality, achievement, the lesser virtues.

A similar value transformation with respect to economic activity has occurred in the Catholic—now sometimes referred to as "post-Catholic"—societies of Ireland, Italy, Quebec, and Spain, although the incompleteness of the transformation is apparent in the current euro crisis.

World Values Survey data confirm the importance of how work is seen. Inglehart concludes, "Intrinsic motivations for work are positively linked with progress. Societies that emphasize work as a means to live show low levels of progress."[25]

10. Frugality. The economic "miracles" of Japan, South Korea, Taiwan, Hong Kong, Singapore, and now China and Vietnam are in large measure driven by extremely high levels of savings. In 2001, Singapore saved 44.8 percent of gross national income and China 40.1 percent.[26] High savings combined with the Confucian virtues of education, merit, and achievement, and an outward looking set of economic policies, go a long way toward explaining these miracles. Yet frugality is not always an economic virtue—Japan's recent prolonged economic stagnation is in part attributable to low levels of domestic consumption. Nor is frugality a permanent value; witness the low levels of saving in the United States, so contrary to a fundament of the Protestant ethic.

11. Entrepreneurship. The Austrian-born U.S. economist Joseph Schumpeter identified the entrepreneurial function as the engine of development. It was not enough to save and invest, he argued. Human creativity must be injected into the formula:

> [T]he function of entrepreneurs is to reform or revolutionize the pattern of production by exploiting an invention or . . . an untried technological possibility for producing a new commodity or producing an old one in a new way, by opening up a new source of supply of materials or a new outlet for products, by reorganizing industry and so on.[27]

Schumpeter viewed entrepreneurship as requiring "aptitudes that are present in only a small fraction of the population."[28] He was, I think, wrong about this in two senses: (1) the proportion of entrepreneurs in a society varies with culture: Sweden's progress-prone culture produces proportionally many more entrepreneurs than does Argentina's progress-resistant culture, not to mention the world of Islam or Haiti; and (2) in a progress-prone culture, entrepreneurship is much less elitist than Schumpeter supposed: the surge of industrialization and commerce in the United States and Japan was driven by literally millions of entrepreneurs, some creating large businesses, many more creating small ones. Moreover, entrepreneurship is not confined to the private sector—public administration innovators can play a crucial role in the progress of a society through wise policies imaginatively conceived and implemented.

That the proportion of entrepreneurs in Haiti is low challenges the utility of Hernando De Soto's magic wand solution to underdevelopment articulated in *The Mystery of Capital*.[29] He is surely right that there are many potential benefits from regularizing the real property of poor people, which they can then collateralize for loans. But what then happens to the loan monies if the entrepreneurial drive isn't nurtured by the culture (not to mention in the case of Haiti, one of the countries on which De Soto has focused, the absence of a favorable investment climate)? My Haitian son-in-law's reaction is probably on the mark: "Many will use the money to migrate to the United States."

The contrast between the Anglo-Protestant and Ibero-Catholic dispositions to entrepreneurship and the depth of their divergent roots is captured in the diary of the US scholar-diplomat John L. Stephens, who visited Central America in 1839–1840 and noted the following after viewing the Masaya volcano in Nicaragua:

> I could not but reflect, what a waste of the bounties of Providence in this favoured but miserable land! At home this volcano would be a fortune; with a good hotel on top, a railing round to keep children from falling in, a zigzag staircase down the sides, and a glass of iced lemonade at the bottom.[30]

12. Risk propensity. Risk propensity is intimately linked to entrepreneurship. Both are derivative of the worldview, particularly the view of one's possibilities of influencing destiny and one's view of knowledge. In fatalistic cultures, risks are likely to be seen as incalculable since mysterious forces are at work. The incalculability also may encourage adventuresome behavior. In the progress-prone culture, a sense of control over destiny combined with the inclination to confront facts nurtures the capacity to estimate probabilities, to calculate the degree of risk.

13. Competition. Grondona's words in Culture Matters are apt:

> The necessity of competing to achieve wealth and excellence characterizes the societies favorable to development. Competition is central to the success of the enterprise, the politician, the intellectual, the professional. In resistant societies . . . what is supposed to substitute for it is solidarity, loyalty, and cooperation. . . . In resistant societies, negative views of competition reflect the legitimation of envy and utopian equality. Although such societies criticize competition and praise cooperation, the latter is often less common in them than in "competitive" societies. In fact, it can be argued that competition is a form of cooperation in which both

competitors benefit from being forced to do their best, as in sports. Competition nurtures democracy, capitalism, and dissent.[31]

14. Innovation. Innovation is conceptually close to entrepreneurship and risk propensity. Like them, it is powerfully influenced by the worldview, and particularly the degree to which people believe they can control their destiny.

Openness to innovation is a key factor in many of history's success stories. It was, for example, central to the early success of Islam, which revived the wisdom, knowledge, and skills of ancient Greece, and to the transformation of Japan by the Meiji leadership, which widely adopted or adapted the advances of the West in education, technology, organization and administration, military science, and numerous other fields.

With respect to Islam, Tibi sees an unwillingness to learn from others as a huge obstacle to the progress of Islamic countries in general, Arab countries in particular.

15. Advancement. The society that places the most able, best-qualified people into jobs, be they in the public or private sector, is the society that is going to perform the best and progress most rapidly. To be sure, in all human societies, subjective factors enter into personnel decisions. It is a question of degree: in progress-resistant societies, where trust and identification with others is typically low, subjective factors, particularly family connections, are often dominant in personnel decisions—nepotism is common and merit is sacrificed. In progress-prone societies, merit is usually the principal determinant of selection. Merit is one of the central emphases of Confucianism, and it is comparably salient in Protestantism and Judaism.

SOCIAL BEHAVIOR

16. Rule of law/corruption. The degree to which a society is respectful of the rule of law is directly linked to the rigor of the ethical code. With Weber's comparison of the two religions in mind, one would consequently expect that Protestant countries would be less corrupt than Catholic countries, and that is indeed the case according to Transparency International's Corruption Perceptions Index. In the 2010 listing, of the ten least corrupt countries, nine are predominantly Protestant, including four of the five Nordic countries (Iceland is number eleven), New Zealand, the Netherlands, Australia, Switzerland, and Canada,[32] and one—Singapore—is Confucian. In a listing of 178 countries, Catholic Spain is number 30, Italy is number 67, and Argentina is number 105. The United States is tied at number 22 with Belgium; Chile is number 21. Interestingly, Protestant Barbados is tied at number 17 with Japan.

In his analysis of the typology applying the data of the World Values Survey, Inglehart concludes, "The Transparency International measure of corruption . . . shows a remarkably strong . . . correlation with human progress (indicating that human progress goes with low levels of corruption)."[33] He also recognizes that cause and effect move in both directions with respect to corruption:

> It could be argued that governmental corruption is like a cancer that strangles economic development, effective administration of education and human services, and virtually every other element of a healthy society. But it might also be argued that, in a prosperous and effectively run society, corruption is less tempting. Although I think the relationship primarily functions in the former fashion, I would concede that there probably is some truth in the latter claim.[34]

The top ten are strikingly similar in composition to the top ten in the competitiveness index cited above and to another relevant index. In 1998, a group of economists produced a report for the National Bureau of Economic Research on good government around the world, which focused on efficiency, personal freedom, and the degree to which government interferes in the private sector.[35] The top ten are comprised of a by now largely familiar group, in this case all Protestant, except for Japan (Table 1.3). Note that not one predominantly Catholic country appears on any of the three top-ten listings.

17. Radius of identification and trust. Also linked to the rigor of the ethical code is the extent to which people identify with and trust others beyond the family and circle of friends in a society. I have already stressed the key role that trust plays as a lubricant in an efficient economy. It is a comparably important factor for effective democracy. If mistrust is rife, as in Islamic and Latin American societies, people will be reluctant to relinquish political power lest those who accede to power use that new power either to persecute those formerly in power or to deny them access to power in the future.

If one identifies with others in the society, one is more likely to pay taxes willingly; to engage in charitable and philanthropic activity; and to associate with others for common goals of a political, economic, social, or recreational nature. I am reminded of a comment of David Hackett Fischer about New England

Table 1.3.

Good Government	Competitiveness	Corruption
1. New Zealand	1. United States	1. Denmark (3-way tie)
2. Switzerland	2. Switzerland	1. New Zealand
3. Norway	3. Denmark	1. Singapore
4. United Kingdom	4. Sweden	4. Sweden
5. Canada	5. Singapore	4. Finland (tie)
6. Iceland	6. Finland	6. Canada
7. United States	7. Germany	7. Netherlands
8. Finland	8. Netherlands	8. Australia (tie)
9. Sweden	9. Japan	8. Switzerland
10. Australia	10. Canada	10. Norway

Puritanism in his extraordinary book *Albion's Seed*, a comment that may well be relevant to the emergence of the town meeting as an expression of grass-roots democracy in that region:

> [T]he Puritans believed that they were bound to one another in a Godly way. One leader told them that they should "look upon themselves as being bound up in one Bundle of Love; and count themselves obliged, in very close and Strong Bonds, to be serviceable to one another." . . . Long after Puritans had become Yankees, and Yankee Trinitarians had become New England Unitarians (whom Whitehead defined as believers in one God at most) the long shadow of Puritan belief still lingered over the folkways of an American region.[36]

18. Family. In the progress-prone society, the idea of "family"—the radius of identification and trust—extends even to strangers within the society, along the lines of the immediately preceding passage from *Albion's Seed*. In the resistant culture, the radius of identification and trust is confined to the family, which becomes a fortress against the rest of the society. This view of family is prominent in Edward Banfield's classic *The Moral Basis of a Backward Society*, in which Banfield analyzes a village in the south of Italy where identification and trust are confined to the nuclear family, a phenomenon that he views as a major contributor to the relative poverty and institutional weaknesses of the region.[37]

Also highly relevant are the views of the Brazilian anthropologist Roberto DaMatta, who notes in *A Casa e a Rua* (At Home and on the Street), "If I am buying from or selling to a relative, I neither seek profit nor concern myself with money. . . . But if I am dealing with a stranger, then there are no rules, other than the one of exploiting him to the utmost."[38]

Note that Brazil was the world's champion of mistrust: ranked last among eighty-one countries on the World Values Survey in 2000, 3 percent of Brazilians surveyed answered "Yes" to the question "Can most people be trusted?" In the world champion of trust, Denmark, 67 percent of respondents answered "Yes" to the same question.

19. Association (social capital). With Robert Putnam's emphasis on social capital in *Making Democracy Work*[39] and *Bowling Alone*,[40] and Francis Fukuyama's emphasis on it in *Trust*, "social capital" has entered the mainstream lexicon of the social sciences and the development community. James Coleman, who labeled the concept, defined it as "the ability of people to work together for common purposes in groups and organizations."[41] Social capital is intimately linked to Putnam's "civic community" and the "civil society" that one hears referred to frequently in development institutions like the World Bank—sometimes as if civil society were a given and all you have to do is find it and nurture it.

But social capital is not equally distributed among societies, and some societies enjoy the benefits of civic community and civil society more than others. People sometimes forget that Putnam's earlier book was essentially a cultural explanation of the striking contrast between the north and the south of Italy with respect to civic engagement specifically and the level of development generally. Putnam invokes Banfield's *The Moral Basis of a Backward Society* to help explain why the south is so bereft of trust, "an essential component of social capital,"[42] a condition that he traces back to the Norman presence there in the twelfth and thirteenth centuries. Similarly, Francis Fukuyama argues in *Trust* that some societies engender "spontaneous association"—he uses Japan, the United States, and Germany as his principal examples—while others do not.

The key point here is that social capital is essentially a cultural phenomenon. In order to nurture it in a cultural environment of low trust, one must strengthen the cultural factors that build trust, for example, the ethical code, the lesser virtues, and the radius of identification.

Social capital is powerfully influenced—one might even say "shaped"—by cultural capital.

20. The individual/the group. The issue here is a complicated one: individualism is the hallmark of the progressive West, while communitarianism is the hallmark of progressive Confucian Asia. The issue is further complicated by the extreme individualism of Latin America, which has impeded that region—and Spain, at least until the second half of the twentieth century—from consolidating democracy and producing equitably distributed prosperity. An observation of José Ortega y Gasset is relevant:

> The perfect Spaniard needs nothing. More than that, he needs nobody. This is why our race are such haters of novelty and innovation. To accept anything new from the outside world humiliates us. . . . To the true Spaniard, all innovation seems frankly a personal offense.[43]

Moreover, many communitarian societies resist progress, for example in Africa, where, at least in Daniel Etounga-Manguelle's view,[44] emphasis on the group saps initiative and the sense of personal responsibility and does not nurture democratic politics.

Moreover, as Fukuyama points out in *Trust*, strong patterns of association are sometimes found in individualistic societies like the United States and Germany. He argues that the Protestant/individualistic cultures of these two countries have generated substantially more social capital than has the Confucian/communitarian culture of China and Taiwan. But his third model of a high social capital society is Confucian Japan.

Further muddying the waters is the obvious drive for individual achievement, creativity, and entrepreneurship found in the Confucian countries, which has a lot to do with their economic success.

Obviously, the distinction between individualism and communitarianism in terms of their influence on progress is ambiguous and requires a high degree of case-by-case qualification. It is apparent that other cultural factors such as work and achievement, frugality, entrepreneurship, and merit can accentuate either the virtues or vices present in both individualism and communitarianism. Tu Weiming calls for a synthesis of the virtuous aspects of both:

> Surely, [Western] values such as instrumental rationality, liberty, rights-consciousness, due process of law, privacy, and individualism are all universalizable modern values, but, as the Confucian example suggests, "Asian values," such as sympathy, distributive justice, duty-consciousness, ritual, public-spiritedness, and group orientation are also universalizable modern values.[45]

It could be convincingly argued that the synthesis has been substantially achieved in, for example, the Nordic countries and Japan.

21. Authority. A society's view of authority is fundamental to cultural variation. It is substantially rooted in religion and ethical code and obviously has a profound influence on the way societies organize their politics. I have already cited Tocqueville's observation about the strong egalitarian link between Protestantism and democracy in America. That Catholic societies have been generally slower to consolidate democracy than Protestant societies can be interpreted as a reflection of the more authoritarian, hierarchical nature of Catholicism. Islam's administrative structure is closer to Protestant decentralization than to Catholic centralization, but its doctrines have promoted fatalism, absolutism, and intolerance, which in turn have nurtured authoritarianism. Confucian doctrine emphasizes filial piety above all and extends that deference to the ruler, which has a lot to do with the relatively slow evolution emergence of democratic politics in Confucian societies.

22. Role of elites. The extent to which elites assume a responsibility for the well-being of nonelites—*noblesse oblige* captures the idea—is the central issue here, and it is obviously related to the radius of identification within a society. The Nordic countries and Latin America make an interesting contrast in this respect, a contrast that has been the object of a study sponsored by the Inter-American Development Bank.[46] Dag Blanck and Thorleif Pettersson note the following in their Culture Matters Research Project (CMRP) paper on Sweden:

> During the mid-1600s, iron foundries were established throughout central Sweden. . . . The iron was produced in small communities called *bruk* where particular social and cultural relations developed, characterized by a paternalistic relationship between the foundry owners and the workers, but also by a sense of social and economic responsibility on the part of the owners.[47]

It is not difficult to see how this paternalism and sense of responsibility, driven in part by Lutheran doctrine, might have evolved into Sweden's advanced welfare state of today. Contrast this with the enslavement of Indians and blacks throughout Latin America during the same period and the self-centered, self-aggrandizing conduct of many Latin American elites in subsequent centuries.

23. Church–state relations. In none of the advanced democracies does religion play a significant role in the civic sphere. This is above all true of Western Europe, where the link between church and state was broken long ago in most countries and where religiosity has declined notably. But it is also substantially true of the much more religious United States. To be sure, religion can exert influence through the religion-based values and views of politicians and media people, for example, the antiabortion, anti–stem cell research positions pursued by George W. Bush. But the wall of separation substantially prevents intrusion of religious institutions into the political process.

I mentioned earlier that Michael Novak has provided me with comments on the typology, and I want to record here his notes on the church–state relationship, seen through the eyes of a prominent lay Catholic. In the progress-prone column, in lieu of "Secularized: Wall between Church and State," he would say "[d]ivision of powers between religion and state; protection of individual conscience." And in the progress-resistant column, he would prefer "[r]eligious leaders perform political roles, and the state imposes religious mandates."

Robert Hefner adds, "[I]t is the separation of authorities—and not the 'secularist' elimination or even privatization of religion—that is the key to social progress. As the U.S. shows, and as the Protestant reformation in Latin America may be showing, a certain type of religious ethos can be very good for social progress."[48]

Alfred Stepan presents a helpful formulation of "twin tolerations" in the church–state relationship in a democratic society:

> [F]reedom for democratically elected governments, and freedom for religious organizations in civil and political society . . . individuals and religious communities . . . must have complete freedom to worship privately, More: as individuals and groups, they should also be able to publicly advance their values in civil society, and to sponsor organizations and movements in political society, as long as their public advancement of these beliefs does not impinge negatively on the liberties of other citizens, or violate democracy and the law, by violence.[49]

In this context, it is relevant that the "miracles" of Ireland, Italy, Quebec, and Spain have all been accompanied by a significant reduction in the role and influence of the Catholic Church. Also relevant is Turkey, in many respects the most modernized Islamic country in the world—and the most secularized, even under the current Islamic government led by Recep Tayyip Erdogan. As Yilmaz Esmer, author of the CMRP paper on Turkey, observes, Erdogan and those around him "emphasized the fact that they were not 'political Islamists' and were in peace with secularism as well as other founding principles of the Republic."[50] More recently, Esmer's optimistic interpretation has become debatable, with, for example, the Erdogan's government's movement away from Israel.

Finally, events in Iran since the 1979 revolution remind us that theocracy and democracy are incompatible.

24. Gender relationships. For several decades, development experts have recognized the important multifaceted role women play in development: as professionals, workers, teachers, politicians, businesswomen, of course; but also as mothers, with the responsibility for rearing children. Child rearing is a key instrument of cultural transmission, and an educated mother is likely to do a better job of it than an uneducated mother. More than 90 percent of Japanese girls were in school in 1905, and atypically large, for Latin America, numbers of women were literate in Chile in the second half of the nineteenth century.

In contrast, the rates of female literacy in some Islamic countries are astonishingly low: in 2001, 29 percent of women were literate in Pakistan, 37 percent in Morocco, and 45 percent in Egypt.[51]

Alicia Hammond, a Jamaican student at the Fletcher School, wrote an extraordinary term paper[52] for my Cultural Capital and Development Seminar in which she addresses homophobia—she prefers the term "heterosexism"—in her native country. She makes a compelling case for promoting tolerance of sexual preference.

25. Fertility. In peasant societies, children are both a labor force and old-age social security, and these two practical considerations added to religious injunctions to "go forth and multiply," not to mention the universal sexual urge, have generally led to high fertility rates in poor countries.

But large, poor families are a recipe for the persistence of poverty and social pathologies, including high crime rates, common to Latin America and Africa. Pitifully small family budgets are stretched just to keep children fed, not to mention clothed, drinking pure water, and attending school. Harried parents, often single mothers, do not have the time necessary for adequate nurturing.

The reduction of population growth through expanded contraceptive use is a reality in much of the world today. But fertility rates are also declining in most prosperous countries, particularly in Western Europe and Japan. In his notes on the typology, Michael Novak points out that Europe's population is certain to decline by 2050 and goes on to say, "Low fertility is also a problem." I might note, in this connection, that the US Census Bureau projects a population of 439 million in the United States in 2050, a 50 percent increase over the population of 281 million in 2000 (see Chapter 9) . The population growth is largely driven by immigration—about 1 million legal immigrants and 500,000 illegal immigrants annually—and by the higher fertility rates of many immigrants.

Four fundamental questions occur, which I list here without further comment because the issue is clearly outside the scope of this book:

1. Is an ever-increasing population desirable? Is there a limit imposed by environmental carrying capacity?
2. Is prosperity sustainable, not to mention increasable, with a stable or declining population?

3. Can "aging" societies, where the 65-and-over component is proportionally much larger than it is today and the youth component much smaller, sustain or increase prosperity?
4. What is the relationship between national power and population size?

The Essence of the Typology

At the heart of the typology are two fundamental questions: (1) does the culture encourage the belief that people can influence their destinies and (2) does the culture promote the Golden Rule? If people believe that they can influence their destinies, they are likely to focus on the future, see the world in positive-sum terms, attach a high priority to education, believe in the work ethic, save, become entrepreneurial, and so forth. If the Golden Rule has real meaning for them, they are likely to live by a reasonably rigorous ethical code, honor the lesser virtues, abide by the laws, identify with the broader society, form social capital, and so forth.

Universal Progress Culture and Social Capital

Progress-prone culture comprises a set of values that are substantially shared by the most successful societies—the West and East Asia—and, I might add, by high-achieving ethnic or religious minorities like the Jains and Sikhs in India, the Basques, the Mormons, and the Jews wherever they migrate. I speak of a Universal Progress Culture that contrasts with the Universal Peasant Culture perceived by George Foster and others. Clearly, the East–West overlap is most apparent in economic as well as social development (e.g., high levels of income, education, and health, and relatively equitable income distribution). There is an obvious divergence with respect to democracy: Confucian-style authoritarianism persists in China, Singapore, and Vietnam. But the democratic evolution of Japan, South Korea, and Taiwan and the nurturing of democracy by sustained high economic growth suggest that the East–West synthesis of virtues that Tu Weiming calls for may be realizable throughout East Asia. It is already a substantial reality in the West, above all in the Nordic and English-speaking countries.

If Tocqueville and Weber, and a long line of subsequent writers who believe that culture matters, are right, promotion of Universal Progress Culture values will increase a society's cultural capital—and, inevitably, its human and social capital as well. Increased cultural capital translates into swifter progress toward the goals of democratic governance, social justice, and prosperity.

CHAPTER 2

~

Why Jews, Confucians, and Protestants?

There exists today a widespread presumption that all religions must be regarded as of equal worth, or at any rate are not to be the object of comparative value judgments. This presumption—let's label it religious relativism—is arguably dominant in the West and surely in our universities. However, when it comes to the relation between religion and human progress, I find compelling evidence that some religions do better than others in promoting the goals of democratic politics, social justice, and prosperity.

As an example of a religion that is highly resistant to progress, consider again Voodoo, the dominant religion of Haiti and a surrogate for the many animist religions of Africa, the birthplace of Voodoo. Not only does Voodoo nurture irrationality, it also discourages the entrepreneurial vocation. It focuses on the present, not the future. It is also essentially without ethical content. I believe that Voodoo has made a major contribution to the sociopolitical pathology, including poverty and extremely low levels of trust, that has plagued Haiti's history. I also believe that, as Daniel Etounga-Manguelle argues in *Culture Matters*,[1] animist religions have similarly impeded progress in many African countries.

I want to stress that religion is not the only influence on a country's performance, nor on its culture. Geography, including climate, topography, and resource endowment, clearly plays a key role, as do the vagaries of history—for example, wars, colonial experiences, geopolitical forces, and economic models chosen or imposed. The level of prosperity powerfully influences performance. Leadership matters: that Singapore is among the most affluent and least corrupt countries in the world surely reflects the vision and influence of Lee Kuan Yew.

Thus, cultural determinism—the idea that an enduring culture overwhelms all other factors and dictates the trajectory a country or society inevitably must follow—is unviable, in theory and in practice: in theory, because it is obvious that values, beliefs, and attitudes change over time; in practice, because facts demonstrate that culture is not always a decisive factor. Who in 1958 would have believed that fifty years later, an African American would be elected president of the United States? And if culture were determinant, how would one explain the vast gap that separates North and South Korea?

This reminds me of the recent book *Why Nations Fail* by Daron Acemoglu and James A. Robinson.[2] The authors address "the culture hypothesis" in a chapter titled "Theories That Don't Work":

> Is the culture hypothesis useful for understanding world inequality? Yes and no. Yes, in the sense that social norms, which are related to culture, matter and can be hard to change, and they also sometimes support institutional differences, this book's explanation for world inequality. But mostly no, because those aspects of culture often emphasized—religion, national ethics, African or Latin values—are just not important for understanding how we got here and why the inequalities in the world persist. Other aspects, such as the extent to which people trust each other or are able to cooperate, are important but they are mostly an outcome of institutions, not an independent cause.[3]

Acemoglu and Robinson start their next chapter, "The Making of Prosperity and Poverty," with a section, "The Economics of the 38th Parallel," which examines the striking contrast between North and South Korea. They conclude, "neither culture nor geography nor ignorance can explain the divergent paths of North and South Korea. We have to look at institutions for an answer."[4]

Obviously, I disagree with Acemoglu, whom I don't know, and Robinson, whom I do—we debated the role of culture under the auspices of the website CATO Unbound toward the end of 2006, and I subsequently invited Robinson to address my seminar at the Fletcher School. On the narrow issue of North and South Korea's divergence, I disagree that the North's failure has been, fundamentally, a failure of institutions. Rather, I see it as another failure of Marxist ideology, combined with Confucianism's inclination to authoritarianism.

With respect to my fundamental difference with Acemoglu and Robinson, based on a perusal of the index of *Why Nations Fail*, I note the omission of any reference, except in the bibliography in some cases, to Edward Banfield,

Samuel Huntington, David Landes, Robert Putnam, Lucian Pye, and, above all, Alexis de Tocqueville, all of whom believed that culture matters—often decisively. And, while there are four bibliography entries for Douglass North, who won the Nobel Prize for economics because of his work on institutions, according to the *Why Nations Fail* index, there is no mention of North.

We "culturalists" focus on institutions as a manifestation of culture. And so does Douglass North:

> In all societies . . . people impose [formal and informal] constraints upon themselves to give a structure to their relations with others. . . . That the informal constraints are important in themselves (and not simply as appendage to formal rules) can be observed from the evidence that the same formal rules and/ or constitutions imposed on different societies produce different outcomes. . . . Where do informal constraints come from? They come from socially transmitted information and are a part of the heritage that we call *culture*.[5]

Culture and Behavior

Some readers may have difficulty perceiving the link between culture and behavior. In his August 13, 2006, *New York Times* column titled "The Culture of Nations," David Brooks used parking violations by diplomats of various countries in New York City to demonstrate the reality of the link:

> Between 1997 and 2002, the UN mission of Kuwait picked up 246 parking violations per diplomat. Diplomats from Egypt, Chad, Sudan, Mozambique, Pakistan, Ethiopia, and Syria also committed huge numbers of violations. Meanwhile, not a single parking violation by a Swedish diplomat was recorded. Nor were there any by diplomats from Denmark, Japan, Israel, Norway or Canada.
>
> The reason there are such wide variations in ticket rates is that human beings are not merely products of economics. The diplomats paid no cost for parking illegally, thanks to diplomatic immunity. But human beings are also shaped by cultural and moral norms. If you're Swedish and you have a chance to pull up in front of a fire hydrant, you still don't do it. You're Swedish. That's who you are.

Religions and Progress

Culture matters, and culture is profoundly, although not exclusively, influenced by religion or an ethical code like Confucianism.

I have located the position of each of 117 countries with respect to ten indicators or indices and have then grouped these data by predominant religion. The ten indicators are as follows:

1. The UN Human Development Report 2007 Index, which combines health, education, and income data.
2. Literacy data from the UN Human Development Report 2007.
3. Female literacy data from the UN Human Development Report 2007.
4. Fertility data from the UN Human Development Report 2007.
5. Freedom House 2007 survey, which rates countries on political rights and civil liberties (scale 1 for freest to 7 for least free for each: total 2 is best, total 14 is worst).
6. Date of start of democratic continuity (my estimate).
7. Per capita gross domestic product from the World Bank's World Development Report 2007.
8. Income distribution (Gini coefficient) from the World Bank's World Development Report 2007 (lower numbers indicate greater equitability).
9. Trust, from the World Values Survey 2000 (percentage of respondents who believe that people in general can be trusted).
10. Transparency International's Corruption Perceptions Index 2007.

The data are summarized in Table 2.1.

I acknowledge the considerable scientific limits to the analysis. The data were derived from respectable sources, but some distortions are inevitable. For example, while I have generally held to the operating assumption that a majority of a country's people subscribe to the religion in which that country is grouped, there are obviously wide variations in the religious composition of many countries. Although India is predominantly Hindu, it has one of the largest Muslim populations in the world. Indonesia, by contrast, is overwhelmingly Muslim, but its small Chinese, mostly Christian, minority has made a vastly disproportionate contribution to the country's economic development. Although South Korea is treated as a Confucian country, many Koreans practice another religion, Christianity prominent among them. And the label "Confucian" is itself oversimplified: it would be more accurately described as Chinese culture, also embracing aspects of Buddhism, Taoism, and ancestor worship, among other sources.

Finally, I have classified Germany, the Netherlands, and Switzerland as Protestant, although there may today be more practicing Catholics than Protestants in each country. I have done this on the same grounds as the World Values Survey because, to quote Ronald Inglehart, "Historically, Protestantism has shaped them."[6]

I want to reiterate an important point made earlier: within a given religion, there are divisions, cross-currents, and national variations that are

Table 2.1. Performance of World's Chief Religions

Indicator	(Judaism Israel)	Confucianism	Protestantism	Catholicism	Orthodox Christianity	Hinduism	Buddhism	Islam
Total population (millions)	7*	1.514	547	965	254	1.123	158	1.221
UN Index: 1 to 177	23	71	14	66	67	128	105	121
Literacy (%)	97	90	99	90	99	61	89	67
Female Literacy (%)	98	87	99	89	99	48	86	62
Fertility (#kids/woman)	2.9	1.6	1.8	2.7	1.3	3.1	2.2	3.5
Freedom: 1 best, 7 worst	1.5	6	1	2.4	4.3	2.6	3.5	4.4
Democracy Continuity	1948	1976	1826	1940	1985	1950	none	none
Per Capita GDP	$25,280	$9,276	$36,840	$11,939	$9,814	$3,422	$4,330	$3,936
Income Distribution**	39.2	43.9	36.6	43.3	35.8	37	27.7	38.7***
Trust (%)****	23	52	38	16	24	41	not available	26
Corruption: 10 is best	6.1	3.9	7.7	4	2.7	3.5	2.5	2.6

Performance of First World Countries Only (UN DEV. Report 2007 Numbers 1-30)

Indicator	(Judaism Israel)	Confucianism	Protestantism	Catholicism	Orthodox Christianity	Hinduism	Buddhism	Islam
Number of Countries	1	4	14	9	Greece, Cyprus	None: India #128 highest	None: Thailand (#78) highest	None: Kuwait (#33) highest
UN Index: 1 to 30 (average)	23	13	13	16	27			
Literacy (%)	97	95	99	99	96			
Female Literacy (%)	98	99	99	99	94			
Fertility (#kids/woman)	2.9	1.3	1.8	1.5	1.3			
Freedom: 1 best, 7 worst	1.5	1.5	1	1	1.5			
Democracy Continuity	1948	1976	1826	1927	1974			
Per Capita GDP	$25,280	$31,527	$37,148	$28,211	$23,620			
Income Distribution**	39.2	26.3	36.6	33.87	34.3			
Trust (%)****	23	38	38	29	24			
Corruption: 10 is best	6.1	7.6	7.8	6.5	4.6			

*76% Jews, 19% Arabs.
**Lower is more equitable.
***Unweighted by population.
****Percentage who believe that most people can be trusted.

not reflected in Table 2.1. For example, several of the generalizations that follow about Catholicism do not apply to the Basques, who have a centuries-old tradition of entrepreneurship, creativity, and cooperation, and who are nonetheless Catholic (the Society of Jesus—the Jesuits—was founded by a Basque, Ignatius of Loyola; see Chapter 6). Islam is quite different in Indonesia and Saudi Arabia. And our analysis does not disaggregate Sunni, Shia, and Kurdish Muslims, not to mention the progress-prone Ismailis (see Chapter 7).

I also had to make some judgment calls. For example, I had to address the question, "When did democratic continuity start in Great Britain?" Some might argue that the appropriate year was 1215. Partly in recognition of the mathematical distortions that would have resulted had I chosen the year of the signing of the Magna Carta, I chose instead 1832, a year of sweeping political reforms.

I want to stress again that religion is not the only influence on a country's performance with respect to the indicators, nor on its culture. But culture matters, and culture is profoundly, although not exclusively, influenced by religion or an ethical code like Confucianism. Although I am unable to quantify "profoundly" with any precision, the patterns that will appear as we examine the data tend to confirm the conclusion that some religions are more conducive to human development than others. But these patterns must be considered approximations. Narrow differences could too easily be explained away by shortcomings in the data or by the intrusion of noncultural factors. So we have to be looking for patterns that involve significant contrasts.

Seven broad conclusions emerge from the data and are discussed in the sections that follow.

1. Protestantism has been far more conducive to modernization than Catholicism, above all in the Western Hemisphere.

Predominantly Protestant countries do substantially better than predominantly Catholic countries on the UN's Human Development Index. The index is the most comprehensive of the ten, combining life expectancy, adult literacy, school enrollment, and gross domestic product (GDP) per capita. On a scale on which 1 is the best and 177 is worst, the weighted (by population) average of Protestant countries is 14 and that of Catholic countries 66. To be sure, the majority of Protestant countries are in the First World, while the majority of Catholic countries are not. A small difference is also found when comparing First World countries: the weighted average for Protestant countries is 13 and for Catholic countries it is 16.

Differences in literacy rates between the two are distorted by the contrasting First World–Third World composition and don't merit elaboration. I note in passing that substantial adult illiteracy still exists in Latin America—10 percent or more in nine countries.

The Freedom House rankings on democracy do show a significant difference: weighted averages of 1 for Protestant countries and 2.4 for Catholic countries on a scale where 1 is best and 7 is worst. This difference primarily reflects the fragile condition of democracy in Catholic Latin America.

With democratic continuity being at best relatively recent in Latin America as well as in some African and former Soviet-bloc Catholic countries, it is the First World countries that offer the most meaningful grouping for testing Tocqueville's contention that Protestantism is more congenial to democracy than Catholicism. There is a sharp contrast, not in the Freedom House rankings but in the longevity of democracy. The average date for the commencement of democratic continuity in the Protestant countries of the First World is 1852 and of the Catholic countries, 1934. When one weights the countries by population, the discrepancy becomes even wider: 1826 versus 1927, a full century.

Reflecting the difference in First World–Third World composition between the Protestant and Catholic countries, the former enjoy a 3-to-1 advantage over the latter in per capita GDP. This narrows substantially when only First World countries are considered, but there is still a substantial gap—about $9,000 in the weighted average. I might add that Angus Maddison's data for the year 1900 show a substantial advantage for the Protestant countries over the Catholic countries in what is today the First World.[7] The GDP data of course tend to confirm Max Weber's thesis about the economic creativity of Protestantism.

Latin America may be the most inequitable region of the world in terms of income distribution, and that fact skews the income distribution substantially in favor of the Protestant countries overall. But when you focus on the First World, the Catholic countries do better than the Protestant countries, in large measure because among the advanced democracies, income distribution in the populous and predominantly Protestant United States is the least equitable.[8]

Trust, as measured by answers to the World Values Survey question "Can people in general be trusted?," is much higher in Protestant countries (38 percent) than in Catholic countries (16 percent) generally, and while the gap narrows when one considers only First World countries, it is still substantial: a weighted average of 38 percent of trust in others in the First World Protestant countries and a weighted average of 29 percent in the Catholic countries. This may be related to a comparably large gap in corruption. On a scale where the cleanest is ranked 10 and the most corrupt 1, the weighted average for the Protestant countries is 7.7 and for the Catholic countries 4. With respect to First World countries, the Protestant advantage is 7.8 compared to 6.5, respectively.

Of the ten least corrupt countries in the 2010 Corruption Perceptions Index, nine are Protestant and one, Singapore, is Confucian. The data on trust and corruption once again evoke Weber's contrast of the relative rigor of the Protestant "life of good works" with Catholic ethics, in which the cycle of sin, confession, absolution, and renewed sin plays so prominent a role.

An article in *The Economist* highlights the disproportionate contribution of French Protestants to the progress of that country in which Catholicism has predominated:

> [T]he French tend to think that a Protestant background spells honesty, respect for one's word, hard work, a sense of responsibility, a modest way of life, tolerance, freedom of conscience—and a dour inflexibility. Protestants have been in the van of most of the great liberalizing ideas and reforms in French history: the Declaration of Human Rights, the abolition of slavery, the market economy, the devolution of power from the center, the spread of state education, the separation of church and state, advocacy of contraception and divorce.[9]

To be sure, the influence of the two religions on culture was a good deal greater prior to the twentieth century. In most First World countries, a substantial homogenization has occurred in which the dominant ethical code is generally adopted by people of all religions—and agnostics and atheists as well. In this sense, we assimilated Americans, whether Protestant, Catholic, Jewish, Muslim, or nonbelievers, are all Anglo-Protestants, as Samuel Huntington argues in *Who Are We?*

2. The Nordic countries are the champions of progress.

The Nordic countries—Denmark, Finland, Iceland, Norway, and Sweden—all of whose evolution was profoundly influenced by Lutheranism and all of which are relatively homogeneous, get high marks across the board. They are all rated 1—the top—in political rights and civil liberties by Freedom House. Iceland is number 1, Norway 2, Sweden 6, Finland 11, and Denmark 14 on the UN's Human Development Index 2007. All five are among the top-ten countries with the most equitable distribution of income. Denmark, Sweden, and Norway are at the top of the trust listing. All five are among the eleven least corrupt countries in the world.

The same pattern of Nordic achievement appears in four other listings:

- In the National Bureau of Economic Research study of good govern-ment around the world . Norway was number 3 (New Zealand was 1, Switzerland 2), Iceland 6, Finland 8, Sweden 9. All of the top-ten countries were predominantly Protestant.[10]
- The World Economic Forum 2008 listing of countries according to competitiveness ranked Denmark 3, Sweden 4, and Finland 6. (The United States was 1, Switzerland 2.) Nine of the top-ten countries were Protestant; Japan was ranked 9.[11]
- A ranking of countries by scientific article input per million citizens showed Sweden ranked as 2, Denmark as 3, and Iceland as 5. (Switzer-land was ranked as 1, Israel as 4).[12]
- A 2004 listing of rich countries according to their contribution to the progress of poor countries shows Denmark ranked as 2 (the Nether-lands is ranked as 1), Sweden as 3, and Norway as 9. Nine of the top-ten countries are Protestant; France is ranked as 10.[13]

Interestingly, a recent assessment of social capital in the United States (where social capital is defined as "a high level of trust and tolerance, an egalitarian spirit, volunteerism, an interest in keeping informed, and par-ticipation in public affairs") finds Americans of Scandinavian and British descent at the top.[14]

3. Confucianism has been far more conducive to modernization than Is-lam, Buddhism, or Hinduism.

The data for the Confucian countries are, of course, dominated by China, which drives all of the indicators down, particularly when we weight for population. The averages for the Confucian First World societies—Japan, South Korea, Taiwan, Hong Kong, and Singapore—are similar to the Catholic First World country averages in (1) the UN Human Development Index; (2) literacy, including female literacy; (3) per capita GDP; and (4) income distribution. The First World Catholic countries consolidated demo-cratic institutions about a half century before the Confucian First World countries, reflecting in part the authoritarian current of Confucianism; and the First World Catholic countries do slightly better than their Confucian counterparts in the Freedom House Index. Trust is substantially greater in the Confucian countries than in the Catholic countries, while corruption is about the same—with one noteworthy exception: in the Transparency (it's

Transparency International) listing, Singapore is tied for first place with Denmark and New Zealand.

4. **The most advanced Orthodox country, Greece, was the poorest of the European Union members prior to the 2004 accessions. There are some parallels between the Orthodox Christian and Catholic countries. But there are also some apparent residues in Orthodox countries from the communist experience.**

The Orthodox Christian and Catholic countries come out in the same position on the UN's Human Development Index with weighted averages of 67 and 66, respectively, in the rankings, and they are fairly close in per capita GDP and trust. Greece and Cyprus are the only First World countries that are Orthodox, but they are among the least affluent. Reflecting the communist emphasis on education, the Orthodox countries enjoy First World literacy levels. And their worse showing on the Corruption Perceptions Index than the Catholic countries might be explained in part as a result of the widespread corruption nurtured by the communist system.

Greece's economic meltdown in 2011, accompanied by similar problems in Catholic Italy, Spain, Portugal, and Ireland, tends to confirm the foregoing. Russia's performance since the collapse of communism also raises the question of Orthodoxy's influence.

Eastern Europe expert Nikolas Gvosdev perceives a church that in its mainstream doctrine is supportive neither of democratic institutions nor of market economics.[15] The circumstances of Orthodoxy are roughly comparable to the circumstances of Catholicism before the latter opted for full support of democracy in the second half of the twentieth century.

In his Culture Matters Research Project paper on the Republic of Georgia, Irakli Chkonia lists the following characteristics of Orthodoxy, strongly evoking the low cultural capital column of the typology and often contrasted with Western Christianity, and especially Protestantism:

> [S]ubmission to authority, discouragement of dissent and initiative, discouragement of innovation and social change, submissive collectivism rather than individualism, emphasis on ethnic cohesion rather than supranational relationships, isolationism and particularism, spiritual determinism and fatalism. Also embraced in the pattern is the aversion of Orthodoxy to the non-Orthodox Christian West and the Islamic World, political rivals of the past and the present.[16]

With respect to the possibilities of change, in Gvosdev's judgment,

[m]uch depends . . . on two separate but interrelated processes. The first is whether the guardians of the Orthodox tradition—not simply the clergy but also its intellectuals and activists—are prepared to actively "re-imagine" the Orthodox tradition in ways that are more conducive to supporting democracy and free market institutions. The second is whether the bulk of the populations of the Orthodox world—especially the "unchurched"—will accept this re-imagination as a legitimate expression of their traditional culture. Again, the answer is unclear.[17]

With a few modifications, I here restate my concluding comments from Chapter 8 on Catholic Latin America. To be sure, the Orthodox Church's influence is not what it once was. But the Church retains substantial influence, and through reform of its political and economic doctrines and a more aggressive stance on issues of morality and ethics, it could make a critical contribution to modifications in traditional values that would enhance the chances for greater progress in Orthodox countries. Reform could also arrest and possibly even reverse the drift away from Orthodoxy.

5. Islam has fallen far behind the Western religions and Confucianism in virtually all respects. There are some significant differences between Arab and non-Arab Islamic countries.

The data for the Islamic countries reveal a strong resistance to modernization, in striking contrast to the vanguard role of Islam during its first several centuries. The Islamic countries are far behind the Confucian countries and even farther behind the Christian First World countries on the UN Human Development Index; in literacy, particularly female literacy; in per capita GDP; in the World Values Survey data on trust (except the Catholic countries); and in the Corruption Perceptions Index.

Particularly noteworthy are the low levels of female literacy: below 50 percent in Egypt, Morocco, Pakistan, and Bangladesh, among others, reflecting the subordinated position of women in the Islamic religion.

Also noteworthy are the data on fertility. The Islamic countries had the highest fertility rates in the world, according to the UN 1995–2000 estimates. Although they continue to present the highest rates among the various religious groups in the UN estimates for 2000–2005,[18] there is a recent across-the-board decline, as shown in Table 2.2.

The Islamic countries are less free according to Freedom House than any other group except the Confucian countries, where the numbers are overwhelmed by China's authoritarianism. Only one predominantly Muslim country, Mali, was considered free by Freedom House—until soldiers

Table 2.2. Total Fertility Rate (births per woman)

	1995–2000	2010–2015
Algeria	3.2	2.3
Indonesia	2.6	2.0
Iran	3.2	1.7
Morocco	3.4	2.3
Pakistan	5.5	3.6
Yemen	7.6	4.7

Source: UN data.

overthrew the elected government in March 2012. Trust is low in the Islamic countries[19] and corruption is high.

I have disaggregated the Arab and non-Arab Islamic countries to see if there are any significant divergences. The Arab countries do substantially better in per capita GDP, where their oil wealth is reflected, and with respect to corruption. They do marginally better with respect to income distribution. But the Arab countries do measurably worse than non-Arab Islamic countries on the Freedom House political rights and civil liberties scale.

6. **Hindu India's democratic institutions have held up well, and it has experienced rapid economic growth during the past two decades. But it has been very slow to educate its people, particularly its women, and it does poorly in the Corruption Perceptions Index.**

Hindu India scores better than any other religious grouping except the Protestant countries in the Freedom House rankings. British political institutions have taken root.

According to World Bank data, the Indian economy averaged 5.3 percent growth in the 1980s and 6 percent growth in the 1990s, the latter in the wake of the opening up of the economy. India's continuing economic surge is one of the most encouraging development trends of the early years of the twenty-first century, although the Indian economy lost steam in 2011, paralleling the experience of China.

But the literacy data for India are surprisingly low—more than 40 percent of Indian women are illiterate—reflecting the subordination of women in Hinduism and Islam. And India does not do well on Transparency International's 2010 Corruption Perceptions Index, tied with Albania ranked at 87 of 178,[20] behind Morocco, Malawi, and Peru.

7. It is difficult to generalize about Buddhism, but the data suggest that it is not a powerful force for modernization.

The seven countries where Buddhism has predominated are Thailand, Myanmar, Sri Lanka, Cambodia, Laos, Mongolia, and Bhutan. Mongolia is among the freest countries in the Third World; Myanmar is among the least free. The Gini data on Mongolia, Cambodia, and Thailand are typical for Third World countries, but Sri Lanka does much better, in fact better than the United Kingdom and the United States (once again, income distribution in the United States is the most inequitable among the advanced democracies). The only Buddhist country to have experienced sustained high rates of economic development is Thailand, but, as in Indonesia, Malaysia, and the Philippines, the Chinese minority has made a vastly disproportionate contribution to that growth.

The problem of generalizing is further complicated by the diversity of Buddhism, with its major divisions, numerous sects, and sectarian variations over time.

What is clear, however, is that no predominantly Buddhist country has made it into the First World ranking, which up until now includes only Protestant, Catholic, Confucian, Orthodox Christian, and Jewish members.

Why Jews?

The UNDP Human Development Report 2010 data for Israel stand out for the Middle East: in the First World (the "Very High Human Development" UNDP group) it ranks 15, ahead of Finland, Iceland, and Denmark. But Israel contains only about a third of the world's Jewish population[21]—more Jews may live in the United States than in Israel. What in any event warrants the first word in the title of this book (chronology aside) is the extraordinary Jewish contribution to human progress, which we examine in the next chapter.

CHAPTER 3

~

Jews

While it can be argued that phenomenal rates of Jewish achievement arose from genes, second-generation immigrant status, or any number of other factors, in the end those arguments, while interesting, are not compelling. It was their culture, born of religion and circumstance, that spurred exceptional rates of Jewish achievement.

That is the good news and a major reason for this book. The message is not that we should all become Jews. My heritage is Gentile, my upbringing Presbyterian. I am proud of my background and if I can rarely be found in church on Sunday mornings, I'm not about to relegate Christ to the role of an interesting prophet.

The point is that culture matters, and all cultures are not equal no matter how much we might wish it otherwise. Better understanding of the cultural values that induce positive behavior, outstanding rates of achievement, and undeniable contributions that benefit us all, means Jewish success need not be unique. We need not have Jewish genes or convert to appreciate and learn from their performance.

—Steven Pease, from the introduction of his book,
The Golden Age of Jewish Achievement[1]

Wendy Carter Smith, and Alexandra Sullivan Epstein are to be married Sunday at the Harrington Farm and event space in Princeton, Massachusetts. Rabbi Dawn Rose is to lead the ceremony . . .

Ms. Smith, who is taking Ms. Epstein's name . . .

—*New York Times*, May 16, 2010, p. ST12

A personal note: In the interest of full disclosure, I am Jewish. My grand-parents, all from either what is today Lithuania, Belarus, or Ukraine—all part of Russia in the last decades of the nineteenth century—fled the pogroms, arriving in Boston in the 1890s. How did I acquire the WASPy (white Anglo-Saxon Protestant) surname Harrison? My paternal grandfather, Albert, whose surname was Hirschon or Hirschorn, told us that he was peddling on the streets of Boston without a license and was arrested by a Boston policeman of Irish descent. The officer was asked the name of the defendant by the presiding judge. And "Hirschon" or "Hirschorn," pronounced with an Irish brogue, became "Harrison."

None of the people I knew in my grandparents' generation in Boston were "tailors and dressmakers, hat and cap makers, and furriers and tanners"—the characterization of immigrant Jews in New York that appears in Malcolm Gladwell's bestseller *The Outliers*.[2] Yet most of their children attended universities—one of my mother's brothers was a Harvard graduate—and all of their grandchildren were, at the least, university graduates.

My grandparents all spoke Yiddish and Russian. As with so many immigrants, at least those who arrived prior to the restrictive immigration legislation of 1924, my native-born parents—the second generation—spoke the language of their immigrant parents, Yiddish in the case of my parents, fluently. (They were, of course, native speakers of American English.) As with so many second-generation Americans, they spoke their parents' language when they didn't want their third-generation children to understand what they were saying. So, sadly, I know only a few Yiddish words and expressions. But that is how the melting pot works—except for Latino immigrants—an issue to be taken up in Chapter 9.

Jewish Achievement

Early in 2009, I received an email from my friend Lawrence Lederman, a retired Canadian foreign service officer, formerly chief of protocol and Canada's ambassador in Chile, and one of many prominent Canadian Jews.[3] Larry's email forwarded the following article, written by the Pakistani columnist Dr. Farrukh Saleem, who had lived in Canada for many years.

WHY ARE JEWS SO POWERFUL?

There are only 14 million Jews in the world; seven million in the Americas, five million in Asia, two million in Europe and 100,000 in Africa. For every single Jew in the world there are 100 Muslims. Yet, Jews are more than a hundred times more powerful than all the Muslims put together.

Ever wondered why? Jesus of Nazareth was Jewish. Albert Einstein, the most influential scientist of all time and TIME magazine's "Person of the Century," was a Jew. Sigmund Freud—id, ego, superego—the father of psychoanalysis was a Jew. So were Paul Samuelson and Milton Friedman.

Here are a few other Jews whose intellectual output has enriched the whole of humanity:

- Benjamin Rubin gave humanity the vaccinating needle.
- Jonas Salk developed the first polio vaccine.
- Albert Sabin developed the improved live polio vaccine.
- Gertrude Elion gave us a leukemia fighting drug.
- Baruch Blumberg developed the vaccination for Hepatitis B.
- Paul Ehrlich discovered a treatment for syphilis.
- Elie Metchnikoff won a Nobel Prize in infectious diseases.
- Bernard Katz won a Nobel Prize in neuromuscular transmission.
- Andrew Schally won a Nobel in endocrinology
- Aaron Beck founded Cognitive Therapy (psychotherapy to treat mental disorders, depression, and phobias).
- Gregory Pincus developed the first oral contraceptive pill.
- George Wald won a Nobel for furthering our understanding of the human eye.
- Stanley Cohen won a Nobel in embryology.
- Willem Kolff came up with the kidney dialysis machine.

Over the past 105 years, 14 million Jews have won some 180 Nobel Prizes while only three Nobel Prizes have been won by 1.4 billion Muslims (other than Peace Prizes).

Stanley Mezor invented the first micro-processing chip. Leo Szilard developed the first nuclear chain reactor; Peter Schultz, optical fibre cable; Charles Adler, traffic lights; Benno Strauss, stainless steel; Isador Kisee, sound movies; Emile Berliner, gramophone; and Charles Ginsburg, videotape recorder.

Famous people in the business world who belong to the Jewish faith include Ralph Lauren (Polo), Levi Strauss (Levi's Jeans), Howard Schultz (Starbuck's), Sergey Brin (Google), Michael Dell (Dell Computers), Larry Ellison (Oracle), Donna Karan (DKNY clothes), Irv Robbins (Baskins & Robbins), and Bill Rosenberg (Dunkin Donuts).

Richard Levin, president of Yale University, is a Jew. So are/were government luminaries Henry Kissinger, Alan Greenspan, Joseph Lieberman, Maxim Litvinov (USSR foreign Minister), David Marshal (Singapore's first chief minister), Isaac Isaacs (governor-general of Australia), Benjamin Disraeli (British statesman and author), Yevgeny Primakov (Russian PM), Barry Goldwater, Jorge Sampaio (president of Portugal), John Deutsch (CIA director), Herb Gray (Canadian deputy PM), Pierre Mendes-France (French PM), Michael Howard (British home secretary), and Robert Rubin (American secretary of treasury).

In the media, famous Jews include Wolf Blitzer (CNN), Barbara Walters (ABC News), Eugene Meyer (*The Washington Post*), Henry Grunwald (editor in chief, *Time*), Katherine Graham (publisher, *The Washington Post*), Joseph Lelyveld (executive editor, *The New York Times*), and Max Frankel (*The New York Times*).

At the Olympics, Mark Spitz set a record by winning seven gold medals. Lenny Krayzelburg is a three-time Olympic gold medalist. Spitz, Krayzelburg, and Boris Becker are all Jewish.

Did you know that Harrison Ford, George Burns, Tony Curtis, Charles Bronson, Sandra Bullock, Billy Crystal, Paul Newman, Peter Sellers, Dustin Hoffman, Michael Douglas, Ben Kingsley, Kirk Douglas, Cary Grant, William Shatner, Jerry Lewis, and Peter Falk are all Jewish? As a matter of fact, Hollywood itself was founded by a Jew. Among directors and producers, Steven Spielberg, Mel Brooks, Oliver Stone, Aaron Spelling (*Beverly Hills 90210*), Neil Simon (*The Odd Couple*), Andrew Vaina (*Rambo 1/2/3*), Michael Mann (*Starsky and Hutch*), Milos Forman (*One Flew over the Cuckoo's Nest*), Douglas Fairbanks (*The Thief of Baghdad*), and Ivan Reitman (*Ghostbusters*) are all Jewish.

To be certain, Washington is the capital that matters and in Washington the lobby that matters is the American Israel Public Affairs Committee, or AIPAC. Washington knows that if PM Ehud Olmert were to discover that the earth is flat, AIPAC will make the 109th Congress pass a resolution congratulating Olmert on his discovery.

William James Sidis, with an IQ of 250–300, was arguably the brightest human who ever existed. Guess what faith he belonged to? So, why are Jews so powerful? Answer: Education.[4]

Dr. Saleem may be given to some exaggeration. Some of the people he mentions (e.g., Cary Grant and Boris Becker) have questionable Jewish antecedents (although Nobelist economist Gary Becker is Jewish); several have one Jewish parent but may or may not have identified themselves as Jewish (e.g., Barry Goldwater, Harrison Ford, and Paul Newman; and gentile Lee De Forest, not Isidor Kisee, invented sound pictures).

On the other hand, Dr. Saleem omits several prominent Jews:

- Supreme Court Justices Louis Brandeis, Benjamin Cardozo, Felix Frankfurter, Arthur Goldberg, Abe Fortas, Ruth Bader Ginsburg, Stephen Breyer, and Elena Kagan
- Financiers George Soros, Michael Bloomberg, and Walter Annenberg
- Composers Felix Mendelssohn, Gustav Mahler, Arnold Schoenberg, George Gershwin, Aaron Copland, and Leonard Bernstein; and

conductors Serge Koussevitzky, Bruno Walter, Otto Klemperer, Pierre Monteux, Eugene Ormandy, and James Levine

Finally, eighteen of the *Forbes* forty richest Americans in 2000 were Jews.[5]

Jews and *Guide to the Perfect Latin American Idiot*

Carlos Alberto Montaner, a Cuban exile who resides in Madrid, is the coauthor of *Guide to the Perfect Latin American Idiot*,[6] the original Spanish edition of which was a bestseller in Latin America. His coauthors were Alvaro Vargas Llosa, son of Nobelist author Mario, and Colombian journalist Plinio Apuleyo Mendoza. In 2007, the three collaborated again in *El Regreso del Idiota (The Return of the Idiot)*[7]—prompted chiefly by Venezuelan caudillo Hugo Chávez.

El Regreso del Idiota lists ten books that can help to cure Latin America of its "idiocy." Eight of the ten were written by Jews, or people with Jewish antecedence: Ludwig von Mises, Arthur Koestler, Karl Popper, Kenneth Arrow, Gary Becker, Seymour Martin Lipset, Milton and Rose Friedman, and Ayn Rand.

I brought this to Montaner's attention in 2008 and received the following response: "Of course, Larry, Jewish culture has given us the best minds in the West. It's because of that fact that Hitler's crime is even more abominable: he not only murdered 6 million Jews; he was guilty of a terrible and irreparable crime against all humanity."[8]

The Jewish Ethic and the Spirit of Capitalism

In *The Protestant Ethic and the Spirit of Capitalism*, Max Weber explains that his coming across data for the Baden region of Germany in 1895 in part prompted his decision to write the book. The data, which appear in a table within a footnote, present taxable capital for Protestants (954,000 marks per 1,000 people) and Catholics (589,000 marks per 1,000 people). Weber adds, "It is true that the Jews, with over 4,000,000 [marks] per 1,000 [people], were far ahead of the rest."[9]

Weber's footnote goes on to present some data on educational achievement for the three religious groups, as measured by attendance in institutions of higher learning: Catholics, with 61.3 percent of the total population of Baden, accounted for 42 percent of the student population; Protestants, with 37 percent of the total population, accounted for 48 percent of the school population; and Jews, with 1.5 percent of the total population, accounted for 10 percent of the student population. Those ratios work out to Catholics 0.69; Protestants 1.3; and Jews 6.7.

The data on wealth and education are a compelling reminder of the dark current of envy and resentment in human nature that led to the Holocaust. The scale of the Holocaust may trivialize similarly tragic lesser bloodbaths, for example, periodic attacks on the highly successful Chinese minority in Indonesia. But both link back to that dark current, which also springs *schadenfreude*—the perverse satisfaction that humans may experience from the misfortunes of others—above all, of the more successful.

Stingy Jews?

"The basis for the anti-Semitic perception of Jewish miserliness stems from the fact that Jews have had extraordinary success in accumulating wealth in their professional pursuits, and that for many people the 'hateful miser' theory is easier to accept than the fact that hard work, a better education and successful commerce have made them wealthy."[10] This observation by Steven Silbiger rang true for me, in part because in recent years, two gentiles, one a European, the other a Latin American—both with PhDs from prestigious universities—referred to Jewish "miserliness" in conversations with me.

The facts demonstrate just the contrary. Charitable contributions by American Jews are twice the percentage of disposable income contributed to charities by the average American, as Silbiger documents. Moreover, Jews are the only group in the United States who do not become more politically conservative as they accumulate wealth. Striking evidence of Jewish liberalism is the party affiliation of Jewish members of Congress. In the wake of the 2010 elections, 25 Jews—6 percent of the total of 435 members (Jews account for 2 percent of the total population)—were members of the House of Representatives. Of those 25, 24 were Democrats. The lone Republican is Eric Cantor of Virginia, recently named majority leader.

Arizona Democrat Gabrielle Giffords, who was shot in the head by a deranged constituent in January 2011 and resigned from the House of Representatives in January 2012, is Jewish.

Twelve senators (12 percent of the total of 100) are Jewish. Ten are Democrats; two Jewish senators, Joe Lieberman of Connecticut and Bernie Sanders of Vermont, are Independents who caucus with the Democrats.

Jews in Latin America

Because I am familiar with the region, I focus my attention on the Jewish experience in Latin America as being more or less representative of the Jewish experience around the world.

The trajectory of Jews who have migrated to Latin America is similar, albeit on much smaller scale, to that of Jewish immigrants in the United States. According to the Jewish Virtual Library, in 2006 there were about 400,000 Jews in the region.[11] The five largest populations are Argentina: 184,500; Brazil: 96,500; Mexico: 39,800; Chile: 20,700; and Uruguay: 18,000.[12]

Many Jews expelled from Spain in 1492 found their way to the New World, where many converted to Catholicism, often under the pressure of the Inquisition. Early Jewish influence has been cited to explain the relative success of Costa Rica; Monterrey, Mexico; and Medellín, Colombia.

A second wave of Jews arrived in Latin America, above all Argentina, in the last decades of the nineteenth century and early decades of the twentieth, chiefly from eastern Europe, many fleeing pogroms, as my grandparents had done. (Argentine Jews, who at one time may have numbered as many as 500,000, were often referred to as *rusos*—meaning Russians.)

A third wave arrived from Europe in the 1930s and 1940s, fleeing nazism.

Costa Rica

Conversos (sometimes referred to as "New Christians")—Jews who converted to Catholicism under the pressure of the Inquisition, but many of whom continued to practice Judaism clandestinely (those who did are often referred to as "crypto-Jews")—were almost surely among the early settlers of Costa Rica. By one account,[13] 336 of the first settlers were, predominantly, *conversos*, or, as they were commonly called, *marranos*—pigs.

University of Costa Rica political scientist Samuel Zemurrray Stone notes one potentially significant corroboration of early *marrano* presence:

> A Costa Rican historian [Carlos Monge Alfaro] makes a curious comment. . . .
> For a long time the colonists gave such a bad example of Christian life that at the outset of the eighteenth century, the Bishop of Nicaragua excommunicated all the inhabitants of Costa Rica, observing that they made a point of staying away from towns where there was a church.[14]

Stone was, by the way, the grandson of the US Jewish immigrant Samuel Zemurray who wrested control of the United Fruit Company from the Boston Brahmins in the early 1930s and ran the company until the mid-1950s. Contrary to the popular image of United Fruit, Zemurray was a liberal, an advisor to Franklin Roosevelt, and highly regarded by the liberal economist John Kenneth Galbraith, with whom I spoke about him. Zemurray's daughter (and Samuel Stone's mother) Doris Stone told me that her father had dedicated half of his wealth to philanthropy, including support of the liberal magazine *The Nation*.[15]

The current Jewish population of Costa Rica is about 2,000 people, the large majority being descendants of Jews who immigrated from Poland in the 1930s. They are widely referred to as *polacos*. The successful experience of Jews around the world has been repeated in Costa Rica, an atypically democratic Latin American country whose progress has been attributed by some observers as the consequence of the disproportionately large number of *conversos* among the early settlers.[16]

Several Jews have served as cabinet ministers in Costa Rican governments, and three have been vice presidents.

Monterrey, Mexico

The history of Monterrey, the capital of the State of León, is unique in Mexico because the first governor of Nuevo León, Luis de Carabajal y Cueva, was a *converso*. As a consequence, during the last decades of the sixteenth century, Nuevo León became a magnet for *conversos*, who were discriminated against in most other parts of Spain's empire in the New World.

Much of Carabajal's family was wiped out by the Inquisition, but "Monterrey still bears the customs of his Jewish heritage, particularly the cuisine (*cabrito, semitas*), popular Sephardic family names (like *Garza*), and some local festivities. His nephew, Luis de Carabajal the younger, left a memoir, letters and account of the Inquisition proceedings against the extended Carabajal family."[17]

The Instituto Tecnológico y de Estudios Superiores de Monterrey, arguably Mexico's best university, was founded in 1943 by Eugenio Garza Sada, of *converso* antecedence, who had graduated from the Massachusetts Institute of Technology (MIT).

Among other prominent Mexicans with Jewish ancestors was the painter Diego Rivera who wrote in 1935, "Jewishness is the dominant element in my life. From this has come my sympathy with the downtrodden masses that motivates all my work."[18] Other prominent Mexicans who took pride in their *converso* antecedence include presidents Porfirio Diaz, Francisco Madero, and José López Portillo.

Medellín, Colombia

Medellín, capital of the State of Antióquia and Colombia's second largest city, had been regarded as Colombia's most entrepreneurial, creative, and socially conscious city—comparable to Monterrey's special status in Mexico—at least until recent decades marked by drug trafficking and insurgency. In the mid-1950s, MIT economist Everett Hagen examined the oft-heard explanation that the success of, and evidence of high social capital in, Medellín was the result of disproportionate numbers of Sephardim/Marranos in the early colonial period.

> Antioqueños are said to be Jews or Basques, both groups having reputations for hard work and business skill. I have checked into these stories, and research has been done in Colombia to test their validity. I am sure there is nothing to the idea that the Antioqueños have more Jewish blood than other groups. They may have less.[19]

Hagen argued that at the root of Medellín's relative success was the reaction of the Antioqueños to being labeled "second class" by comparison with Bogotá, the bigger capital city of Colombia. But Hagen was, I believe, wrong in his assertion of minimal Jewish influence on Medellín's development. For one thing, over 500 *conversos*/crypto-Jews were executed in Cartagena, Colombia, during the seventeenth and eighteenth centuries, many of whom were rounded up in Medellín.[20] The people who founded Medellín in 1675 are said to have been made up in part of converted Jews. Many Hebrew customs and traits can be observed even today among the extraordinary people of this region.[21]

I received serendipitous confirmation of this observation during a trip to Colombia some ten years ago. At a lunch arranged by the former foreign minister of Colombia, Augusto Ramírez Ocampo, I was seated beside a Sra. Londoño y Londoño, a prominent Antioqueña who dedicated her time to improving Colombia's orphanages. She was quick to identify her Sephardic roots and had visited Seville in Spain to check the colonial records for her surname, Londoño. Failing to find the name, she inferred further proof of her Jewish antecedence. As she said, "It's obvious that my forbears had changed their original surname to one less likely to be taken for Jewish." This practice was widespread during the time of the Inquisition. Sra. Londoño y Londoño then told me that to this day, her family lighted candles on Friday nights, and that her daughter was about to marry a Jew, about which Sra. Londoño y Londoño couldn't be more pleased nor proud.

Jewish Success in Historic Perspective

With the possible exception of a brief period toward the end of the eighteenth century, Jews were the vanguard of intellectual, technological, and economic progress in the West.

The Bible's story of Joseph in Egypt is prophetic of a long, unending line of Jewish leaders: "Joseph was the great minister-statesman of an alien ruler, the pattern of many Jews over the next three thousand years. He was clever, quick, perceptive, imaginative, a dreamer, but more than a dreamer, a man with the creative ability to interpret complex phenomena, to forecast and to foresee, to plan and administer."[22]

Until I did the research for this chapter, I did not appreciate the geographic scope of early Judaism. At the time of the Maccabees, about 100 BC, Jewish colonies were scattered around the Mediterranean. During the early Roman Empire, Jewish communities were established in Lyons, Bonn, and Cologne, in the north; Cádiz and Toledo in the west; and Cochin, in what is today the State of Kerala in India, to the east. They were all predominantly urban communities—Jews were the object of discrimination, in the form of heavy taxation, confiscation, or even prohibition, when it came to land ownership. They were "glassworkers in Aleppo, silkweavers in Thebes, tanners in Constantinople, dyers in Brindisi, merchants and dealers everywhere."[23]

Spain: From Persecution to Favor to Persecution

The Jews in Spain were persecuted by Christian leaders until the Muslims invaded in 711, so the Jews helped the Muslims take control of the Iberian Peninsula. The Ummayid dynasty established its capital in Córdoba "and treated the Jews with extraordinary favour and tolerance. Here, as in Baghdad and Kairouan [in today's Tunisia], the Jews were not only craftsmen and traders but doctors. . . . There were substantial and well-to-do Jewish communities in no fewer than forty-four towns in Ummayid Spain."[24]

Unfortunately, the success and wealth of Ummayid Spain attracted "the envy and fanaticism of a fundamentalist sect," and the Ummayids were ousted in 1013 by "primitive" Berbers from North Africa, who discriminated against the Jews, often with violence.[25] The Berbers were succeeded by the comparably fundamentalist and anti-Semitic Almohads, also from North Africa. It was during the Almohad invasion that the great Jewish scholar, philosopher, and physician Moses Maimonides was born in 1135 in Córdoba. His family soon left Spain and ended up in Egypt, where he was the physician of the Grand Vizier and Sultan.

The *Reconquista* (Reconquest) of Spain by Christians began in AD 790 in the north. By 1150, more than half of the Iberian Peninsula was in their hands. By 1300, a sliver around Granada was all that remained under Almohad control. In 1492, Spain was reunified under the "Catholic Kings," Fernando and Isabel, setting the stage for the banishment, or forced conversion, of the Jews; the Inquisition; and their migration, as *conversos*, *marranos*, or "crypto-Jews," to Latin America.

European Jews: Finance and Conversion

Barred from landholding and the security that it offered, yet profiting from urban trades—and the traditional heavy emphasis on education, saving, and intracommunity trust—Jews often became rich. Paul Johnson notes, "It was the collective instinct of the Jews both to depersonalize finance and to rationalize the general economic process. Any property known to be Jewish . . . was always at risk in medieval and early modern times."[26]

Credit, a foundation of capitalism, was largely a Jewish creation, as were paper securities and stock markets. Traditional values and attitudes combined with the force of circumstances to create a prominent and enduring Jewish role in finance and economics, symbolized by the fact that more than one-third of the winners of the Nobel Prize for economics, awarded for the first time in 1969, have Jewish antecedents.

Also symbolic of the prominent role of Jews in finance is the house of Rothschild, which has played not only a key role in international finance—and politics—since the early nineteenth century but has also engaged in extensive philanthropic activities, particularly for Jewish causes, around the world. The Rothschilds have largely succeeded in maintaining their Jewish identity in the face of pressures to convert to Christianity that other Jews couldn't resist.

In the late eighteenth century and throughout the nineteenth, the pressures on European Jews to convert were enormous, involving not only respectability but also access to social acceptability, wealth, and prestige. Among the Jews who converted was Benjamin Disraeli's father in 1817, when Benjamin was twelve years old. If the father hadn't converted, the son would not have become prime minister, since Jews were barred from Parliament until 1858.

Karl Marx's father, whose father and brother were rabbis in Trier, Germany, converted in 1824. Heinrich Heine, the great German writer/poet whose writings have been memorialized in the music of Felix Mendelssohn, Johannes Brahms, Richard Wagner, and Richard Strauss, among others, converted to Lutheranism in 1825 at the age of twenty-seven. "As Heine said in self-justification, his conversion was 'the ticket of admission into European culture. . . . As Henry IV said, 'Paris is worth a mass'; I say, 'Berlin is worth the sermon.' For much of the rest of his life Heine wrestled over the incompatible elements of his German and his Jewish identities."[27]

Mendelssohn's grandfather was the great Jewish Enlightenment philosopher Moses Mendelssohn. Felix's father converted to Lutheranism and adopted the non-Semitic surname Bartholdy when Felix was seven.

Interestingly, Felix avoided use of the adopted name. There is evidence—for example, in his choice of an Old Testament subject (Elijah) and a New Testament subject (Christ) for his two oratories—that Mendelssohn also wrestled with his two identities. The nazis had no such problem: Mendelssohn was identified as a Jew, and his music was banned.

The Jewish Experience in America— A Personal Reflection

As I reflect on my life at the age of eighty years, I see it as a surrogate for the experience of Jews in America—at the least for the large majority of Jews whose ancestors migrated from Eastern Europe to the United States in the last decades of the nineteenth century and the first decades of the twentieth.

If I were not intensely conscious of my Jewishness before the first grade, I was surely conscious of it thereafter. I attended the Runkle School in Brookline, Massachusetts, a town notable for its substantial Jewish population[28] and its celebrities, including Mike Wallace, Barbara Walters, Conan O'Brien, and Michael Dukakis.

As I was walking home from school in the first weeks of first grade, I was repeatedly the target of acorns thrown by an Irish-Catholic classmate, Richard O'Hearn, who screamed "Dirty Christ-killer!" at me. I soon learned that there were parts of Brookline, particularly Brookline Village, where it was not safe for a Jewish kid to walk.

As an aside, I am astonished at how little parental supervision of our activities occurred in those days by contrast with today. My walk to and from school was about a half mile, which I negotiated alone at age six. At age eight, when I started working at my father's small plant in Waltham, I often took a streetcar (trolley) to North Station and then the train to Waltham, by myself. At age thirteen, I flew from Boston to New York and then took public transportation to Weehawken, New Jersey, to pick up an important package for my father. Of course, in those days we usually left our doors unlocked when we left the house, even for a vacation.

In the 1930s and 1940s, many hotels and resorts in New England were "restricted," that is, Jews were not welcome. The West Chop area of Tisbury, Martha's Vineyard, the town in which I live, was "restricted" until about twenty-five years ago. My family finally found a place in Conway, New Hampshire, the Presidential Inn, where we were welcome. (Conway is near the Presidential Range of the White Mountains of which Mount Washington is the highest—and the highest point in New England.)

I started playing tennis at ten, and five years later, I was the second-ranked tennis player in New England for boys aged fifteen and under—and eighteenth in the nation. That was in 1947. I played in several tournaments at the Longwood Cricket Club in Brookline, the facilities of which included two indoor courts. At that time, indoor courts were extremely rare—tennis was nowhere near as popular as it is today. (Had it been, I'm sure that there would have been many boys in New England better than I was.) That meant that I had to stop playing in October and wait until April to start playing again. So I applied for junior membership at Longwood—and was rejected because I was Jewish, notwithstanding the vigorous support of my application by the *grande dame* of New England tennis, Hazel Hotchkiss Wightman, after whom the Wightman Cup matches between British and US women were named.

I did manage to play a couple of times on the indoor courts of the Country Club in Brookline, famed as one of the golf courses where the US Open golf tournament and Ryder Cup competition are periodically played. I snuck in after 11 p.m. with a Country Club maintenance worker, Tommy Taylor, who was a particularly good golfer but who also played tennis. It never entered my mind to seek membership there, so solid was its reputation as a restricted WASP bastion.

Let's now fast forward to today. Both the Longwood Cricket Club and the Country Club have a number of Jewish—and African American—members. Restricting access to facilities open to the public was outlawed long ago. And, of course, two of the best women tennis players in the world, the Williams sisters—not to mention the best (at least until recently) golfer in the world, Tiger Woods—are black. As is the current president of the United States.

Jews have substantially displaced the WASP establishment, a process for which Samuel Zemurray was a forerunner when he took over the United Fruit Company from the Boston Brahmins in 1933. In the 1930s, there were no Jewish senators, although six Jews had served as senators going back to pre–Civil War days.[29] There are now twelve. In the 1930s, a total of eleven US representatives were Jews; today there are twenty-five.

When I applied to college, quotas for Jews were probably still in force at many of our best universities. At that time, and for the decades of the 1950s and 1960s as well, the presidents of all the Ivy League schools were WASP males. Since then, the WASPs have been substantially displaced by Jews:

Table 3.1 is further evidence that the Jews have replaced the WASPs as the chief conveyers of the Anglo-Protestant culture that Samuel Huntington argues, correctly in my view, is the principal source of our success: "the rule

Table 3.1. Jewish Presidents of Ivy League Schools

School	Wasps	Jews	Other
Brown	1764–2000	none	Ruth Simmons 2001– African American
Columbia	1754–1980 1993–2002	Michael Sovern 1980–1993 Lee Bollinger 2002–	
Cornell	1865–2003	Jeffery Lehman 2003–2005 David Skorton 2006–	
Dartmouth	1769–1970	John Kemeny 1970–1981 James Freedman, 1987–1998	Jim Yong Kim 2009– Korean American
Harvard	1636–1991	Neil Rudenstine 1991–2001 Lawrence Summers 2001–2006	Drew Gilpin Faust 2007–
U. of Penn.	1740–1970 1981–1993	Martin Meyerson 1970–1981 Claire Fagin 1993–1994 Judith Rodin 1994–2004 Amy Gutmann 2004–	
Princeton	1746–1988	Harold Shapiro 1988–2001	Shirley Tilghmann 2001–
Yale	1701–1993	Richard Levin 1993–	

of law, the responsibility of rulers, and the rights of individuals; and dissenting Protestant values of individualism, the work ethic, and the belief that humans have the ability and the duty to create a heaven on earth, a 'city on a hill.'"[30] This is why I am comfortable with the label Anglo-Protestant Jew. The shared set of values and beliefs was also a foundation of my friendship with Sam Huntington—and his Anglo-Protestant Armenian wife, Nancy.

Harvard Law School professor Noah Feldman made a similar point in a *New York Times* op-ed article published on June 27, 2010, titled "The Triumphant Decline of the WASP." In it, Feldman mentions that the US Supreme Court in 2005 had a plurality of white Protestants. He then points out that, with the confirmation of Elena Kagan, the number of Protestants "will be reduced to zero, and the court will consist of six Catholics and three Jews." He goes on:

> It is cause for celebration that no one much cares about the nominee's religion. . . . But satisfaction with our national progress should not make us forget its authors: the very Protestant elite that founded and long dominated our nation's institutions of higher education and government, including the Supreme Court. Unlike almost every other dominant ethnic, racial or religious group in world history, white Protestants have ceded their socioeconomic power by

hewing voluntarily to the values of merit and inclusion, values now shared broadly by Americans of different backgrounds. The decline of the Protestant elite is actually its greatest triumph.

The Jewish "Hall of Shame"

I am sure that some readers will have concluded by now that I am a Jewish chauvinist. They are probably right. Having suppressed my Jewishness in my early years to become an *American*, it was not until I began my second career, in the pursuit of an understanding of the religious roots of culture and of how culture influences the behavior of individuals and societies, that I developed a deep respect for Jewish culture.

But my chauvinism doesn't blind me to the criminal behavior of some Jews, and in the interest of preserving at least some objectivity, I am devoting this section to Jews who have done anything but enhance the reputation of the Jews.

Topping my list are Julius and Ethel Rosenberg, US communists, who, out of misguided idealism, passed information to the Soviet Union crucial to its development of the atomic bomb. They were executed on June 19, 1953. I regret that they were not given life sentences without parole so that they could have witnessed the events leading to the collapse of communism, including, early in 1956, Nikita Khrushchev's lashing out at Stalin's abuse of power; the subsequent 1956 Hungarian revolution, suppressed by Soviet military force; the defection of ballet star Nureyev (1961) and Stalin's daughter (1967) to the West; the forceful suppression of the "Prague Spring" in 1968; the Chernobyl nuclear accident of 1986; and the collapse of the Soviet empire during the period 1989–1991, including the end of communism in Russia itself.

Other prominent members of the Jewish "hall of shame" include the Jewish gangsters of the early and mid-twentieth century, among them, Jacob "Greasy-Thumb" Guzik, Al Capone's financial advisor; Arnold Rothstein, "the pioneer of big business crime"; Meyer Lansky, most memorable for his appearance in *The Godfather Part II* as "Hyman Roth"; Dutch Schultz, né Arthur Flegenheimer, Prohibition bootlegger and numbers racketeer; Louis Lepke Buchalter, a founder of Murder Incorporated; and "Bugsy" Siegel, flamboyant Hollywood figure and a founder of modern Las Vegas—and the title character in the film *Bugsy*, played by Warren Beatty.

Jews have been prominent in white-collar crime: Michael Milken spent two years in prison for securities fraud in the early 1990s (he has since spent much of his time and money on good works—in 2004, *Fortune* magazine devoted a cover story to him, with the title "The Man Who Changed

Medicine"); Andy Fastow, chief financial office of Enron, currently serving time in a federal prison in Louisiana; and now, the person who has done more to give Jews a bad name than anyone since the Rosenbergs, Bernard Madoff, architect of the biggest Ponzi scheme in financial history: $50 billion of phony investments, resulting in bankruptcy for many of his clients, Jews and Jewish charities prominently among them.

Closing the Nostalgia Loop

On January 14, 1990, my beloved Patricia Crane Harrison and I were married in her house in Vineyard Haven, Massachusetts. My best man was Richard O'Hearn—the same Richard O'Hearn who assaulted me with acorns and "Christ-killer!" a half century earlier. What better metaphor for the Jewish-American experience during those fifty years?

Let me explain. Dick O'Hearn was the third child—second son—of an Irish Catholic family that was famous for its football players. His uncle Charlie O'Hearn had been an All-American at Yale, and since Dick had just the right equipment for a running back—solid, powerful legs, fast, and shifty—his family was confident they had bred another star. The only problem was that Dick didn't like football. He liked tennis.

The O'Hearns lived in an apartment on Beacon Street in Brookline that abutted the Dean Road playground tennis courts, where I learned to play. By the time we entered Brookline High School as freshmen, Dick had firmly decided against football and in favor of tennis. And so we became doubles partners, and friends. He spent a lot of time in my house, and my mother responded to him more than to my Jewish friends, with whom Dick also became friendly. Dick and I ignored the ethnic line at Brookline High School that separated the Jews and the gentiles.

In our senior year, the Brookline High School tennis team, which I captained, won the state championship. (Michael Dukakis was a member of that team. So was Robert S. Rubin, who would become the president of Lehman Brothers at the time of its first crisis, in 1984.) Dick beat me in the semifinals and went on to captain the Brown University tennis team.

We remained in touch over the years. Dick was commissioned as a Marine Corps officer and was stationed at the Atsugi Naval Air Station in Japan. I was commissioned as a naval officer, and when my destroyer arrived in Japan, I visited him. He finished his military service and went to work for the Gillette Company. I went to work for the US government and soon was spending most of my time in Latin America. But we stayed in touch and played golf together whenever the opportunity presented itself. (We had both concluded that we could get better at golf and that our best tennis days were behind us.) He was the obvious choice for best man when Pat and I decided to get married.

Some ten years later, Dick was diagnosed with pancreatic cancer. He passed away soon after the diagnosis. I was asked to do the eulogy in a Catholic church in Brookline Village—where Jewish kids dared not go fifty years earlier.

Explaining the Jewish Phenomenon: Genes?

Several explanations for the extraordinary achievements of Jews come to mind. The first, and one that I have avoided, is genetic. Charles Murray, gentile coauthor with Richard Herrnstein, a Jew, of *The Bell Curve*,[31] believes that Ashkenazi Jews, after centuries of inbreeding, have evolved into a disproportionately high-IQ group.[32] After having fought a quarter-century battle to provoke awareness of the role of culture as a key factor in explaining why some countries and ethno-religious groups do better than others—a quarter century during the reign of multiculturalism and political correctness, I might add—I am loath to take on genetic explanations.

One anecdote will capture the essence of the environment in which I have tried to promote the idea that culture matters. During the fall of 1993, I accompanied my wife, Pat, to Ottawa, Ontario, where she started her Cordon Bleu cooking studies. I arranged an association with the Norman Paterson School of International Affairs at Carleton University, where, at a lunch, I presented my views to a group of professors. One of them, a Jewess, was enraged by what I had to say. Her comment: "It's ideas like that that led to the murder of six million Jews!"

But aside from the even more intense emotional problems presented by genetic explanations of achievement, too many other issues arise to bolster my reluctance. For starters, why only Ashkenazim? Why not the Sephardim, too? After all, the Jewish influence that, arguably, lies behind the relative success of Monterrey and Costa Rica was Sephardic. Maimonides was Sephardic; so was Spinoza. The first Jews to settle in the United States were Sephardim. And if inbreeding has resulted in a superior Ashkenazim, why hasn't the same inbreeding resulted in a superior Sephardim?

And how about the comparable achievements of Confucian Asians and Nordics? How would one use a genetic argument to explain their success?

I cannot categorically dismiss the genetic argument. But what I can say is that if there is validity to it, the influence on outcomes must be small by comparison with cultural influences, as the contrast between Haiti and Barbados strongly suggests.

Paul Johnson's Conclusions

In his epilogue to A *History of the Jews*, Paul Johnson sums up as follows:

> All the great conceptual discoveries of the intellect seem obvious and inescapable once they have been revealed, but it requires a special gift to formulate them for the first time. The Jews had this gift. To them we owe the idea of equality before the law, both divine and human; of the sanctity of life and the dignity of the human person; of the individual conscience and so of personal redemption; of the collective conscience and so of social responsibility; of peace as an ideal and love as the foundation of justice. . . . Above all, the Jews taught us how to rationalize the unknown. The result was monotheism and the three great religions that profess it. . . .
>
> In antiquity they were the great innovators in religion and morals. In the Dark Ages and early medieval Europe, they were still an advanced people transmitting scarce knowledge and technology. Gradually they were pushed from the van and fell behind. . . . But then came an astonishing second burst of creativity. Breaking out of their ghettoes, they once again transformed human thinking, this time in the secular sphere. . . .
>
> If the earliest Jews were to survey . . . the history of their progeny, they would find nothing surprising in it. They always knew that Jewish society was appointed to be a pilot project for the entire human race. . . . The historian may say: there is no such thing as providence. Possibly not. But human confidence in such an historical dynamic . . . is a force in itself, which pushes on the hinge of events and moves them. The Jews believed they were a special people with such unanimity and passion, and over such a long span, that they became one. They did indeed have a role because they wrote it for themselves. Therein, perhaps, lies the key to their story.[33]

A Group High in Cultural Capital

Jewish culture clearly falls in the "High Cultural Capital" column of the Chapter 1 typology for the areas listed below. Judaism seems uniquely hand tailored to several of the factors:

1. **Religion: Nurtures rationality, achievement; promotes material pursuits; focus on this world; pragmatism**

Comment: Johnson's epilogue powerfully captures this feature of Judaism, which puts it in stark contrast with other religions, for example Islam and Catholicism, which focus on the afterlife and are more utopian and rigid in their doctrines.

2. Destiny: I can influence my destiny for the better

Comment: This is a central concept in Jewish doctrine, one that contrasts sharply with the Islamic and Ibero-Catholic fatalism explicit in the expressions *Inshallah* and *Si dios quiere* (meaning "God willing" in Arabic and Spanish, respectively).

3. Time orientation: Future focus promotes planning, punctuality, deferred gratification

Comment: In the words of a former chief rabbi of Great Britain, "Judaism clings to the idea of Progress. The golden Age of Humanity is not in the past, but in the future."[34]

4. Wealth: Product of human creativity, expandable (positive sum)

Comment: It could be argued that the Jews created this high cultural capital definition of wealth. In any event, they have come to symbolize it.

5. Knowledge: Practical, verifiable; facts matter

Comment: The Jews have clearly made a disproportionate contribution to science and the evolution of the scientific method, witness their Nobel Prizes in the sciences and economics. Pursuit of the truth has characterized Jewish culture beginning with Abraham in the Bible.

8. Education: Indispensable; promotes autonomy, heterodoxy, dissent, creativity

Comment: The Jewish commitment to education is legendary and best captured in the story about the Jewish mother who was out walking with her two toddlers when a stranger stopped to ask the age of the kids. The mother responded, "The doctor is four, the lawyer two." It is also apparent from an observation by Joan Moore, in her 1970 book *Mexican Americans*: "Jewish and Japanese children . . . march off to school with enthusiasm. Mexican and Negro children are much less interested. Some sort of cultural factor works here."[35]

9. Work/achievement: Live to work: work leads to wealth
Comment: The Jews' commitment to work is comparable to their commitment to education. "There's no free lunch" must have been first articulated

by Jews. Work is a good thing not only because it profits the individual, but also because it profits the society and is central to the mission of *Tikkun olam*—"Repair the world" (see comment of Jim Lederman, below).

11. Entrepreneurship: Investment and creativity
Comment: Jewish entrepreneurship explains, in part, the extraordinary success of Jews not only in the private sector, apparent from their disproportionate presence—eighteen among the *Forbes* top forty richest Americans in 2000. But the Jewish entrepreneurial/creative experience extends beyond the private sector to the universities and government as well.

16. Rule of law/corruption: Reasonably law abiding; corruption is prosecuted
Comment: The rule of law is a concept originated by the Jews, as Paul Johnson points out. Although Israel does not do all that well on the Corruption Perceptions Index—it is ranked 36 of 180 in the 2011 rankings—it surely must be among the world's leaders with respect to the independence and incorruptibility of its judicial branch. Three Israeli lawyers I met at Stanford University in 2009, Yonatan Arbel, Tal Lieber, and Ayelet Sela, all agree that the Israeli judiciary is the backbone of Israel's democracy, witness the legal proceedings against prominent politicians, such as former Prime Minister Ehud Olmert, and the defense of Israeli Arab interests.

24. Gender relationships: If not a reality, equality at least not inconsistent with value system

Comment: In striking contrast to other religions, for example Islam and Catholicism, women have played significant leadership roles since the early Old Testament years. Miriam was a prophetess and leader of comparable rank to Aaron, Moses' brother. Deborah was a judge, military leader, and the highest-ranking person of her time in Israel. Esther, beautiful, principled, and committed to her people, became queen of the Persians. In recent times, Golda Meir was the Israeli prime minister from 1969 to 1974, the third woman in modern history to lead a country. (Sirimavo Bandaranaike was Sri Lanka's prime minister for the first of three terms from 1960 to 1966; Indira Gandhi led India from 1966 to 1977 and from 1980 to 1984.)

Steven Silbiger's and George Soros's Insights
Steven Silbiger concludes his book *The Jewish Phenomenon* with seven lessons that can be learned from the Jewish experience. Note the close parallels with the twenty-five-factor typology:

1. Make long-range goals.
2. Work harder at tasks that require mental manipulation.
3. Take prudent risks.
4. Work for tangible and intangible rewards.
5. Take responsibility for decisions, and create results.
6. Accept other entrepreneurs as role models.
7. Believe in your own self-determination.[36]

Silbiger believes that the roots of Jewish success are found in their condition as a persecuted minority. He cites George Soros:

> I identify being a Jew with being a minority. I believe that there is such a thing as Jewish genius; one need only look at the Jewish achievements in science, in economic life or in the arts. These were the results of Jews' efforts to transcend their minority status, and to achieve something universal. Jews have learned to consider every question from many different viewpoints, even the most contradictory ones. Being in the minority, they are practically forced into critical thinking. . . . I am also aware that there is a certain amount of Jewish utopianism in my thinking.[37]

Soros's emphasis on minority status as the chief motivator of Jewish success evokes the superb British movie *Chariots of Fire* in which the sprinters Eric Liddell, a Scottish Presbyterian missionary, and Harold Abrahams, a Jew, each win gold medals in the 1924 Olympic Games. Liddell, running for his God, wins at 400 meters after refusing to run a preliminary 200-meter heat on a Sunday because it was the Sabbath. Abrahams wins at 100 meters, running to prove himself as good as—if not better than—anyone else.

Although I agree that being a persecuted minority is a factor in the motivation of Jewish achievement, it cannot be the only, nor necessarily even the principal, factor, because other persecuted minorities, for example African Americans, Roma (Gypsies), and indigenous peoples in Canada, the United States, Latin America, Australia, and New Zealand, have not experienced anything approaching Jewish success.

The Views of Jim Lederman

In his chapter on Judaism in *Developing Cultures: Essays on Cultural Change*, summarized in *The Central Liberal Truth*, Canadian journalist Jim Lederman, who resides in Israel, provides us with the following insights into what in Jewish culture drives achievement. Many of his comments evoke the High Cultural Capital column of the typology as well as similar aspects of Protestant and Confucian doctrine:

Jewish tradition holds that life, and living in the world, is essentially an incomplete, individual and group, "work-in-progress." Death is not sought. . . . Final judgment is based on the sum of a life as it was lived.

All human activities and policies must, therefore, be directed towards the living and the living-to-be—and thus must also be future and long-term oriented. This, in turn, demands continuous social entrepreneurship and social engineering that can only be halted with the coming of the Messiah. . . . Participatory activism by everyone to improve the world is, therefore, a human obligation.[38] The guide to what should be done, and the ways in which it should be done, are embodied in a code of laws to which everyone must adhere—especially the Jews themselves.

The basic rules of ethical behavior are believed to be immutable. However, implementation is subject to conflicting views and interpretations, debate and change. Thus, among Jews, uniqueness or novelty is not automatically disdained—and appreciation for the potential value of invention is carried over into almost all aspects of human activity.

Among Jews, there is a . . . tension between innovation based on rationalism, and protective orthodoxy; between the desires for group survival, and individual expression; and between regulation, and creative freedom and personal responsibility.

Leadership is self-selected and devolves to those who exhibit continuing merit in belief and practice. Merit is assigned based on proof over time. It is an award that can be withdrawn. While Jewish law requires obedience and obeisance to the sovereign (in the case of democracies this includes the will of the majority), this does not preclude the idea that one can be a member of a loyal opposition without being treasonous.

Central to Jewish beliefs is the concept of *Tikkun Olam*, "repairing the world" . . . [and central to *Tikkun Olam*] is . . . the need to establish a level playing field for all. Utopian egalitarianism is, in general, rejected as denying the God-given uniqueness and creativity present in each individual. Instead, the purpose of almost all Jewish Law that does not deal directly with behavior towards the Divine is to encourage fairness in human relations.

Social status and social mobility [are] predicated on an individual's personal accomplishments and his pursuit of excellence. Scholarship remains . . . the highest social value. However, skilled, knowledge-based employment [comes] a close second.

Activism to "repair" human-created law where it is faulty or inadequate is deemed to be an obligation. For the most part, behaviors are viewed as means that can be altered, not objectives in themselves.

Individual and group self-criticism, self-assistance, and a willingness to battle corruption are perceived to be required traits and assets.

Notably, among Jews, in almost all matters, immediate responsibility for creativity and action lies with the individual; but long-term success belongs to the group that sets the norms that foster accomplishment.[39]

I believe that it is in a combination of the interpretations of Steven Pease, Paul Johnson, Steven Silbiger and George Soros, and Jim Lederman that the roots of Jewish success can best be understood. "Above all, the Jews taught us how to rationalize the unknown," an observation echoed by Soros: "Being in the minority, they are practically forced into critical thinking."[40] Johnson goes on to cite the doctrine of "the Chosen People" as being a self-fulfilling force in Jewish achievement. Soros goes on to mention Jewish utopianism—not always a constructive force, as the tragic case of the Rosenbergs demonstrates. Lederman adds further support for placing the Jews in the high cultural capital column of the typology, adding substance to Soros's idea of Jewish utopianism.

I am sure that there are other valid explanations for Jewish success. But for our purposes, the views cited in this chapter should suffice. And they should add credibility to the last paragraph of the Pease quote that appears as the epigraph to this chapter.

CHAPTER 4

~

Confucians

In 1853, Japan's Tokugawa dynasty had been in power—and self-imposed isolation, above all from the West—for 250 years, having been founded by Tokugawa Ieyasu in 1603. (Tokugawa was the "Toronaga" of James Clavell's bestselling novel *Shogun*.) On July 8, 1853, Commodore Matthew Perry led a flotilla of US warships into Iedo (now Tokyo) Bay, sending a shudder through the *Bakufu*, the Shogunate bureaucracy. Perry's mission was to open up Japan to trade, but the advanced technology of his warships made it apparent to the Japanese that he had the capability of bringing the capital city to its knees, since much of its food arrived by sea.

Fifteen years later, in 1868, the Tokugawa Shogunate was overthrown by a group of *daimyo* (feudal chieftains) led by two enlightened young Samurai: Kido Koin and Okubo Toshimichi. The Meiji Restoration—really a revolution not entirely unlike the American and French revolutions—was under way. Three years later, Kido and Okubo led a delegation of Japanese officials in consecutive eight-month visits to the United States and Western Europe. They were astonished at the progress they saw, and they initiated a process of broad-scale adoption of Western technology, public and business administration, and education.

In 1871, 40 percent of Japanese school-age boys and 15 percent of girls were enrolled in school. By 1905, 98 percent of boys and 93 percent of girls were enrolled. By 1895, Japan's industrial base had expanded so rapidly that it was able to defeat China in a war, acquiring Taiwan as a colony. In 1905, it defeated Russia, leading to the acquisition of Korea as a colony in 1910.

Increasingly under the influence of its military, particularly as its civilian officials grappled with the Great Depression, Japan invaded Manchuria in 1931 and then China in 1937, leading to the attack on Pearl Harbor in 1941.

At the time of Japan's unconditional surrender in 1945, a good part of its industrial base and its infrastructure had been destroyed by US bombing. Yet by 1953, the Japanese economy was poised to perform another miracle: from 1954 to 1973, the Japanese economy grew at an average rate of 9 percent per year. It had experienced a sixfold increase during those two decades, which vaulted it into third place among the world's economic powers, behind the United States and the Soviet Union.

In 1945, Taiwan and Korea were liberated from the crumbling Japanese empire. Both were extremely poor in terms of human well-being as well as natural resource endowment. Both soon confronted major threats to their security: Taiwan, from a newly communist mainland China; Korea, from a Soviet- and Chinese-supported assault by the North Koreans on the South. Both Taiwan and South Korea received substantial economic and military support from the United States.

Sixty-five years later, Taiwan and Korea are established members of the ranks of the advanced democracies. For much of the period since 1960, they sustained growth rates in the vicinity of 9 percent annually, as have their fellow "dragons," Hong Kong and Singapore. Their exports, which were inconsequential in the 1950s, have grown explosively, to the point where they, along with Hong Kong and Singapore, are among the twenty most important exporting countries in the world. Moreover, their astonishing economic growth has been accompanied by a substantial degree of social justice and consolidation of democratic institutions.

Sound long-range economic policies emphasizing the world market have had a lot to do with the success of Taiwan and Korea. But those policies would not have gone as far had it not been for the blossoming of entrepreneurship in both countries. That entrepreneurial drive is, I believe, rooted in some of the key tenets of Confucianism, as are the two countries' effective policies.

As an extension of Chinese civilization, Taiwan is by definition a Confucian society. Korea and Japan have both been powerfully influenced by Confucianism. Korea has been referred to as more Confucian than China.[1] The powerful influence of Confucianism on Japan is underscored by, among others, Ruth Benedict in her classic *The Chrysanthemum and the Sword*.[2]

There is another society in East Asia that can be labeled "Confucian": Vietnam.[3] Chinese influence on Vietnam started about 100 BC when Vietnam became a province of China, a condition that lasted until 939

AD. But even after gaining its independence, Vietnam continued as a Confucian society until the French took control of "Indo-China" following the war between China and France of 1884–1885. "Under French rule, Confucianism declined. It encountered new ideas and forces, and long before the end of the colonial period it had lost its dominant position. . . . Its basic precepts, however, remained deeply imbedded in the morals and values of the people."[4]

Since free-market reforms were introduced in 1986, the Vietnamese economy has grown at an average rate of more than 7 percent annually. William Ratliff concludes his essay on Vietnam, "Confucianism and Development in Vietnam," in the collection *Culture Matters, Culture Changes*[5] with the following:

> Thus in recent years Vietnam's government has opened the national economy up in many respects and the improvement of living conditions for the majority of the people is beyond question. Still, some aspects of governance deriving from the tradition of "Imperial Confucianism" and communism that inhibit national economic development must be effectively addressed.
>
> Pham Duy Nghai concludes that "by consolidating traditional institutions to promote a market-oriented economy, Confucianism offers a rich source of norms and institutions that could underpin economic and social development in Asia in general, and Vietnam in particular."[6] Some aspects of this have already happened in other Asian countries, but Vietnam has yet to decide how to most effectively coordinate traditional devotion to community needs and the individual and family entrepreneurial surge that has highlighted development in recent years. Mao Zedong in China frequently spoke of the need to deal with contradictions, a challenge that should finally be faced forthrightly and objectively by Vietnam's leaders and people. Perhaps Vietnam's main inspirations today should be Singapore, Taiwan, and South Korea, where the balance has been more effective overall than in China, although often deriving from similar Confucian practices.

The Confucian Value System

Confucianism is not the only source of values and attitudes of Chinese civilization, including those neighboring countries influenced by it, but it is certainly the main one.[7] Confucius (the name is the Latinized version of K'ung-fu-tzu), who lived about 500 years before Christ, was a secular thinker and educator whose philosophical concerns were similar to Plato's. Confucius dedicated himself to the building of the good society in this life, and, as the Asian experts Edwin Reischauer and John Fairbank note, "[t]his lack of concern with the otherworldly . . . led in time to a strong agnostic strain in the Confucian tradition."[8] Confucianism assumes that human nature is basically good, and that the good, ethical life can be ensured by order, harmony, moderation, good manners, and his formulation of the Golden Rule: "Do not do unto others what you would not have others do unto you."

The Confucian system is built on five relationships: father/teacher and son (filial piety is the most important of all virtues), ruler and subject, husband and wife, older brother and younger brother, and friend and friend. Three of the five concern the family, which is the building block of society and is organized on authoritarian principles. Reischauer and Fairbank observe, "This authoritarian family pattern was applied to the whole of society. . . . The role of the emperor and his officials was merely that of the father writ large."[9]

Although the first four relationships are those of superior to subordinate, responsibilities run in both directions for all five. If both participants in the relationship respected their responsibilities, peace and harmony would be ensured. If the ruler were wise, virtuous, and responsible, the society would follow his lead. If the ruler strayed from righteousness, he relinquished his entitlement to lead.

The traditional Confucian society was aristocratic, authoritarian, and static. Hierarchy was a dominant feature, and the five basic relationships tended to keep people in their places. But Confucius also placed heavy emphasis on education as an engine of progress. The goal was the achievement of a level of knowledge—principally knowledge of classical Chinese literature—that would qualify a person for the most important human activity: governing. Merit thus formed the basis for selecting those who governed, and merit was determined by testing the scholarly achievements of those who would aspire to govern.

Thus, social mobility was possible, and there are many examples in Chinese history of talented people rising from the lower strata to leadership. Merit and testing, of course, continue to be emphasized in the selection of future leaders in Taiwan, Korea, and Japan. And in all three countries today, the public administration and teaching professions have substantially higher prestige than in the United States.

Confucius ranked agriculture as the second highest calling, after government/education. Crafts followed agriculture, and at the bottom of the scale was commerce, which, because of its association with profit, was viewed as somewhat illicit.

Confucius's focus on the family reinforced China's tradition of extended familialism and ancestor worship. Reischauer and Fairbank note,

The Chinese kinship group was extensive in scope and was conceived as reaching out in each direction to the fifth generation. This meant that an individual's ancestors back to his great-great-grandparents, his descendents down to his great-great-grandchildren, and his contemporaries to his third cousins (descendants of his great-great-grandparents) were all acknowledged members of his family nexus.[10]

This tradition is the root of the clan, which has played such an important role in Chinese history.

The desire to please ancestors has been a very practical concern for the Chinese: if the ancestors were displeased, they might return as spirits to wreak their displeasure on their living relatives. Ancestor worship was thus a spur to achievement and accumulation of wealth, and a reinforcement of the Confucian emphasis on education. During a 1990 trip to East Asia, my wife observed that, for the Chinese, today's child is tomorrow's ancestor. The orientation of the Chinese is very much toward the future, as well as the past. "In this sense, East Asia has always been 'otherworldly,' if 'the other world' is taken to mean the world of the future for one's associates and descendants."[11]

Confucian values ebbed and flowed in China and elsewhere in East Asia in the centuries that followed. But the other popular systems of thought, Taoism and Buddhism foremost among them, were of the other world—the world of gods, spirits, and life after death—and it was possible to adhere to them and Confucianism at the same time. Taoism was, in part, an individualistic protest against the hierarchical communitarianism and snobbery of Confucianism. Taoism consequently held special appeal for the common people. It has left its imprint on East Asian culture as the source of the philosophical/religious emphasis on frugality but also in its emphasis on restraint and inaction: "Do nothing and nothing will not be done," which Reischauer and Fairbank translate as "Everything will be achieved spontaneously."[12] But it was also mystical and spiritualist, and these dimensions of Taoism were tolerated by the Confucian Mandarins.

Buddhism reached China a hundred or so years before Christ. Its focus on salvation filled a void in Chinese thought that led to its dominance from the fourth to the eighth centuries. It reinforced the asceticism of Taoism and co-existed comfortably with Confucianism. Buddhism also reached Japan during this period and was a dominant element of Japanese religion and philosophy until it was supplanted by the Confucianist emphasis of the Tokugawas in the seventeenth century.

But against the sweep of Chinese—and Korean and Japanese—history, it is clear that Confucianism has most profoundly influenced the value system. Reischauer and Fairbank conclude, "Moderation and balance are perhaps the major reasons for the eventual triumph of Confucianism in China."[13]

Moderation and balance surely characterize the recent economic and political history of Japan, South Korea, and Taiwan.

Confucianism, Pluralism, and Social Equity

In the political sphere, Confucianism is principally a force for authoritarianism, hierarchy, and orthodoxy, and East Asian political history is similar in many respects to that of Iberian and Ibero-American countries. There are, for example, analogies to be made between the political evolution of Taiwan and Korea since the1950s and that of Mexico.

Some years ago, I attended a lecture in Seoul by Gari Ledyard, a historian at Columbia University and an expert on Korea, who argued persuasively that the difficulties Korea had experienced in constructing a modern pluralistic political system were largely the consequence of Confucian values and practices. He stressed that, in the Confucian system, power is unitary, flowing from the leader, whose unitary power is reinforced by the legal and administrative system; people have their place, and harmony depends on people knowing their place; the individual is subordinated to the group; peace and harmony depend on consensus (correspondingly, dissent and voting are disruptive of consensus, peace, and harmony).

Ledyard also noted that, in both China and Korea, cities were formed not on the basis of economic/marketing activity, as in the West and Japan, but as bureaucratic centers. Thus, economic pluralism, whose early emergence played so prominent a role in the subsequent evolution of political pluralism in the West, is but a few decades old in Korea. Ledyard concluded, "Most Koreans think that Confucianism is old-fashioned but inside their psyche there is a heavy residue of Confucianism that they are not conscious of." In the discussion period following the lecture, I observed that almost everything he said about Korea applied with equal force to Taiwan; he agreed.

The conservative, even reactionary, nature of Confucian politics is underscored by Lucian Pye in a paper analyzing the cultural currents behind the 1989 Tiananmen massacre:

> [Of Chinese political culture] Any conflict arouses hate, and it becomes almost impossible to disagree without becoming disagreeable . . . in Chinese political culture the ultimate sin is selfishness, and hence the Chinese abhorrence of individualism. . . . Every issue has to be dressed up as being in the collective interest. There is no room for respecting individual rights . . . there are few political cultures in which there is greater sensitivity to matters of status and gradations of hierarchy.[14]

With respect to social justice, Confucianism cuts both ways, as it does in economic development. In theory, its rigid hierarchical structure operates in the context of the Golden Rule, and superiors are bound to treat inferiors with respect and decency. Pye observes, "The most basic principle of Confucianism . . . holds that a ruler should always be benevolent and kind to the people."[15] Compensating somewhat for the importance of people knowing their place is the emphasis on merit (in contrast to "connections") as the basis for advancement. High respect for education also implies social mobility.

Japan, Taiwan, and South Korea have achieved patterns of income distribution that are substantially more equitable than those of the United States: the UN Development Program's *Human Development Report 2006* shows the poorest 20 percent of the US population accounts for 5.4 percent of national income, the richest 20 percent for 45.8 percent. The figures for Japan were 10.6 percent and 35.7 percent, respectively, and for South Korea 7.9 percent and 37.5 percent. Although UN data for Taiwan are not available, there is strong evidence that Taiwan's income distribution is comparable to South Korea's, and far more equitable than that of the United States.[16]

Traditional familialism and clanism notwithstanding, the radius of identification and trust in Taiwan and South Korea substantially exceeds what one finds in most Ibero-Catholic societies. In the 2000 World Values Survey data, eleven Latin American countries average 17 percent of those polled who believe that most people can be trusted; the figure for Japan is 42 percent, for Taiwan 38 percent, and for South Korea 27 percent. The world champion of *mistrust* is Brazil, where but 3 percent of those polled believed that most people can be trusted. Interestingly, the European champion of *mistrust* is Portugal, where but 10 percent of those polled are trusting of others.

The racial, ethnic, and linguistic homogeneity of the East Asian societies obviously contributes to national identity. Although the ruler-subject relationship comes after filial piety in the Confucian scheme of things, it is in many respects similar—the ruler is a father figure. Respect for the ruler, the symbol of community as well as nationhood, is something that all East Asians learn along with their ABCs (or ideographs). But they also learn some respect for their fellow citizens through the fifth—and only nonauthoritarian—Confucian relationship: friend to friend.

Max Weber on Chinese Culture

Max Weber's *Confucianism and Taoism* was published in German (*Konfuzianismus und Taoismus*) in 1920. It was first published in English in 1951 as *The Religion of China*. In it, Weber analyzes the impact of Confucianism and Taoism on the capacity of the Chinese to achieve dynamic capitalism, particularly in contrast to the Protestant ethic and, especially, Calvinism. The subsequent success of the Chinese (and the Koreans) has been cited as evidence of a fundamental flaw in Weber's analysis.[17]

In noting the absence of modern capitalist development in China between the middle of the seventeenth century and the end of the nineteenth, Weber points to the power of the literati elite—the Mandarins—as a force against innovation: "each and every innovation could endanger the interests of the individual official with regard to the perquisites of his office." Yet he gives full recognition to "the quite extraordinary degree of development and intensity of the money-making urge of the Chinese," and adds, "Material well-being has never in any civilized land been so emphatically represented as the ultimate goal as it has been in China."[18]

In stressing the absence of capitalist accumulation and investment, he notes that, whereas the rural population of Western Europe declined as capitalism spread and farm size there increased through consolidation, in China, the rural population expanded rapidly while farm size shrank. The resulting predominance of small farms reinforced both traditional rice agriculture and the traditional peasant worldview.[19] The failure to modernize the rural sector was an important consequence of the Mandarins' resistance to tax and administrative reforms that threatened their interests.

Weber also cites the absence of an effective legal system: "The best known of [the imperial] edicts constituted codifications of ethical, not legal, norms, and were distinguished by their literary scholarship." Subjective and often irrational decisions by the emperor or the Mandarins discouraged investment. Weber further observes that, in contrast with Protestant ethic Puritanism, which "impersonalized everything . . . in China, all communal activity remained enclosed in and conditioned by purely personal relations." He concludes,

> The limitation of viewing things in an objective manner imposed by the ascendancy of personal relations has . . . had considerable significance for economic attitudes as an obstacle to objective rationalization . . . it had a tendency to bind the individual over and over again in his inmost feelings to the members of his kinship group and those with whom he had kinship-like relations. . . . The great achievement of the ethical religions, and in particular of the ethical, ascetic sects of Protestantism, was to break down kinship bonds and confirm the superiority of community based on faith and an ethical way of life over community based on blood ties. . . . In economic terms this meant confidence

in business matters *being founded on ethical attributes of each* individual as proved in his objective work at his calling [emphasis added].[20]

But it is in another dimension of the Confucian value system that Weber encounters the principal obstacle to the development of rational enterprise capitalism. The Confucian values riches but sees them as the natural consequence and perquisite of the Mandarin's role—or of luck or corrupt behavior. The other way of making money—producing, buying, and selling—is, in the Confucian view, infra dig. (This looking down the Confucian nose at artisans and tradespeople has its analog in the traditional attitudes of landed gentry toward the "working classes" in other cultures, including traditional Iberia and Latin America.) Weber put it this way:

> For Confucius all real economic vocational work was the Philistine task of professionals. The specialist . . . could, for the Confucian, never be elevated to a position of really positive honour, whatever his value in terms of social utility. The reason for this—and this was crucial—was that "the superior man" (the Confucian gentleman) was not a "tool," i.e. he was in the self-perfection of his adaptation to the world an ultimate goal in himself; he was not . . . a means to impersonal goals of any kind whatsoever. *This central statement of the Confucian ethic was a rejection of specialization of profession, of a modern professional bureaucracy and of vocational education; above all . . . it constituted a rejection of economic training in the pursuit of profit* [emphasis added].[21]

The Mandarins were not only snobbish but also intrusive. Historian John K. Fairbank observes, "Merchants were dominated by officials, on whom they depended for protection, or else they became semi-officials themselves, showing the spirit of monopolistic tax-gatherers rather than of risk-takers in productive enterprise. The classical doctrines of the state gave little thought to economic growth and stressed the frugal use of agrarian taxes rather than the creation of new wealth."[22]

The Mandarin administration created a two-tiered society: the literati and the others. The Mandarin structure extended down to the district (but not village) level. Aloofness of local administrators was ensured not only by virtue of their self-assessed intellectual and moral "superiority" but also by such standing policies as moving administrators every three years and prohibiting their assignment to their hometowns. Those people governed by the literati generally had no use for them and ignored them as much as possible in pursuing their own interests.

For this second tier, the masses, frugality was "a form of hoarding, ultimately to be compared with the peasant accumulating his savings in his stocking. Saving was undertaken in order to guarantee funeral expenses and the good name of the family, and in addition for the sake of the honour and delight of possession as such, as is the case everywhere where the attitude towards wealth has not yet been broken down by asceticism."[23] That translates into accumulation of wealth without investment. (Iberian—and Latin American—mercantilism could be similarly characterized.)

Weber believed that Confucianism propagated passive attitudes about accumulation of wealth. Since accumulation of wealth was, in the Calvinist doctrine, the evidence of God's grace, a key difference between Confucianism and Calvinism is the latter's stress on striving for success (what Pye refers to as "psychic anxiety" leading to "desire for achievement").[24]

The Cross-Currents of Confucianism

Weber's analysis highlights the powerful cross-currents that characterize the traditional Chinese value system. The dualism is apparent from a shift one often hears mentioned: in the 1950s, US professionals cited Confucianism as a major impediment to progress; nowadays, many see Confucianism as the principal engine of progress.

With respect to economic development, the Confucian emphasis on education, merit, hard work, and discipline, combined with the achievement-motivating tradition of ancestor worship and Tao emphasis on frugality, constitute a potent, albeit largely latent, formula for growth comparable in its potential to Weber's view of Calvinism. This potentially explosive mixture was suppressed by the low prestige the Confucianists attached to economic activity; by the limits placed on such activity by the Confucian emphasis on the family or clan above the broader society; by the relative rigidity of Confucian hierarchy and authoritarianism (the merit system serving as the principal path for social mobility); by the burden of filial piety (Lucian Pye observes, "For the Chinese the rules of Confucian filial piety make loyalty the supreme value, even to the point of hobbling merit and effectiveness"[25]); and above all, by the extraordinary influence of the literati bureaucrats in the shaping of national policies, which almost always reflected their interest in preserving their privileged position as well as their disdain for economic activity.

But the latent positive forces as well as the stultifying forces have been perpetuated. When the Chinese have emigrated, a process of self-selection of achievers, as John Kenneth Galbraith has pointed out in *The Nature of Mass Poverty*, they have almost always found themselves in circumstances where the stultifying forces have been diluted: economic activity has been more prestigious in most of the societies to which they have migrated (as indeed it has become in Taiwan and Korea, and now Vietnam and China itself). In an alien setting, the family or clan became a particularly valuable institution for self-help, especially since most emigrants were natives of southern China, where the clan structure was most highly developed; the weight of filial piety was often removed by geographic separation; and the Confucian (and Marxist/Maoist) unification of politics and economics, which underlay the disproportionate and suffocating influence on economic matters by the Mandarins, did not confront the Chinese overseas, as it ceased to do when Deng Xiaoping announced "To get rich is glorious."

With the suppressing forces of traditional Chinese culture diminished, the explosive potential of the positive forces has been substantially realized not only in Taiwan, Korea, and now China itself, but also by the Chinese in Hong Kong, Singapore, Thailand, Indonesia, Malaysia, the Philippines, and elsewhere, including the United States. And Japan's spectacular performance has been driven in part by some of the same Confucian ideas, although they operate in a distinctive setting.

Edward Mason and his colleagues pose "the perplexing question why the Confucian culture, which assigns so low a value to business activity, has accommodated itself to the rise of so many successful entrepreneurs."[26] The answer, it seems to me, lies in the conflicting currents of Confucianism itself. Neutralize the forces that suppress entrepreneurship, above all bureaucratic suffocation, but also promote entrepreneurship's prestige, and you have a critical mass of achievement motivation that approximates that of Weber's Calvinists. As Ambrose Y. C. King observes in explaining the extraordinary levels of entrepreneurial activity in Hong Kong, "Unlike Imperial China, the most promising road to social eminence in Hong Kong is not by becoming officials and scholars, but through gaining wealth in the business world."[27]

If there is any doubt about what happens to Chinese entrepreneurship in the absence of an overbearing bureaucracy, it should be dispelled by the performance of the Chinese economy after Deng Xiaoping's economic liberalization of 1978: growth had averaged 10 percent annually until the 2008–2009 crisis. Deng's reforms, by the way, also document the crosscutting nature of Confucian values: one of his objectives in 1977 in reinstituting the examination system (an eminently Confucian concept) that was discontinued (as elitist) by Mao early in the Cultural Revolution was to combat the familialism/clanism (eminently Confucian) that had evolved as the basis for personnel decisions,

To be sure, as I have already noted, other, noncultural factors also contributed to the Taiwan and Korea miracles, for example, the security threat from a neighbor, substantial aid and generally good advice from the United

States, sound policies, and continuity of policy. But I believe that culture may be more important than any other single factor. For one thing, sound policies do not appear from out of the blue, and good policies in part reflect the Confucian tradition. But particularly compelling is the performance of overseas Chinese in countries where policies have not always been sound or purposefully executed, for example, the Philippines, as well as their superior performance in good policy settings like the United States.

Weber's analysis of the impact of Chinese culture on economic growth identifies both positive and negative forces. Where both forces have been preserved—as in China itself, at least until Deng's reforms—the result has been entirely consistent with his observations about the suffocating effects of Mandarinism. That Chinese have migrated to settings where the negative forces have been suppressed or diluted, often under Western influence, and done very well, as have the Koreans and Vietnamese with pro-growth leadership (and also with some Western influence), would not, I think, have come as a surprise to Weber.

Contrasts: East Asia and Latin America

There are both parallels and divergences between the cultures of Confucian East Asia and Ibero-Catholic Latin America. With respect to the radius of identification and trust, the Chinese (and Taiwanese) and Koreans are family or clan focused, as in Iberian culture, but that focus extends to nonfamily members through the fifth Confucian relationship (friend to friend) and to the broader community and nation through the first Confucian relationship (ruler to subject).

These broader identifications are substantially stronger than those of traditional Iberian culture, which is reflected in the income distribution patterns of Japan, Taiwan, and Korea, which are so much more equitable than the typical Latin American pattern (and Spain's, until recent decades). The radius of trust in Taiwan and Korea is probably not as far-reaching as it is in the Protestant (and perhaps secularized Catholic) countries of the West, where a universal ethical code tends to override familialism. One indicator of this difference is that most enterprises in Taiwan are family owned. The same is true in Korea, where the *chaebol* conglomerates, similar in structure to the Japanese *keiretsu*, are usually run by the founding family, unlike the Japanese model, where professional managers are in charge.

The five Confucian relationships largely circumscribe the East Asian ethical code, while Catholicism is the principal source of the Iberian ethical system. The former is more exigent than the latter, although the familialism, common to both cultures (and enshrined in three of the five Confucian relationships), is a force for a double ethical standard: rigorous within the family, flexible and self-serving outside.

Authoritarianism is deeply rooted in four of the five Confucian relationships, and it has been the hallmark of the political history of China and Vietnam, and until recent decades, Japan and Korea. The authoritarian traditions of East Asia and Latin America are both strong, and both regions have had difficulties in constructing democratic/pluralist institutions.

But unlike Iberian culture, East Asian culture also stresses values—education, work, discipline, merit, frugality—that, if not squelched by bureaucracy, are powerful engines of economic growth and economic pluralism. Progress toward political pluralism in Japan, Taiwan, and Korea has been driven by the attitudes and educational levels engendered by dynamic economic pluralism, and by the achievement of relatively equitable patterns of land and income distribution.

Moreover, all three countries have been profoundly influenced by the United States and its value system, principally, in the cases of Korea and Taiwan, through large aid programs related to security concerns; a US military presence (still substantial in Japan and Korea); the many East Asians who have either migrated to or studied in the United States; and extensive business relationships.

Another Group High in Cultural Capital
Like Jewish culture, Confucian/East Asian culture clearly falls in the High Cultural Capital" column of the Chapter 1 typology for the following areas:

1. Religion: Nurtures rationality, achievement; promotes material pursuits; focus on this world; pragmatism

Comment: Because it is not a religion but an ethical code, Confucianism focuses on what happens in this world, not the afterlife. Its heavy emphasis on education is reflected in the highly disproportionate numbers of students of East Asian antecedence who attend the best US universities and their subsequent achievements.

2. Destiny: I can influence my destiny for the better

Comment: The importance that Confucianism attaches to education plus the responsibility one has to ancestors and successive generations underscore the cultural inoculation against fatalism.

3. Time orientation: Future focus promotes planning, punctuality, deferred gratification

and

10. Frugality: The mother of investment and prosperity

Comment: Like Judaism, Confucianism focuses on the future. Its core beliefs include the idea that the future should be better. Ancestor worship imparts a responsibility of each individual to five generations of relatives back and *five generations forward*—a powerful force for future orientation.

5. Knowledge: Practical, verifiable; facts matter

and

8. Education: Indispensable; promotes autonomy, heterodoxy, dissent, creativity

Comment: Once again, the Confucian emphasis on education, reflected in the disproportionate number of East Asian students in the best US universities, clearly places the East Asian countries in the high cultural capital column.

9. Work/achievement: Live to work: work leads to wealth

and

11. Entrepreneurship: Investment and creativity

and

12. Risk propensity: Moderate

and

14. Innovation: Open, rapid adaptation

Comment: Confucian emphasis on achievement, reinforced by ancestor worship, is highly relevant. The success of the Japanese and now Korean (Hyundai and Kia) automobile industry is an appropriate symbol.

15. Advancement: Merit, achievement

Comment: The ubiquitous national examination, so central to Confucianism, is the symbol of the high value that merit plays in personnel decisions, at least in the early stages of a career. Thereafter, at least in Japan, seniority often displaces merit. But that it still a far cry from the *amiguismo* and "connections" that are commonly encountered in low cultural capital societies like Latin America.

17. Radius of identification and trust: Stronger identification with the broader society

and

18. Family: The idea of "family" extends to the broader society

and

19. Association (social capital): Trust, identification breed cooperation/ affiliation/participation

Comment: Although three of the five Confucian relationships relate to the family, the idea of "family" tends to extend beyond blood relatives to others in the society, although not as powerfully as in the Lutheran Nordic countries. One favorable consequence for development: relatively high levels of interpersonal trust—and of social capital, the latter underscored by the emphasis on the group.

Confucianism and Democracy

Universal Progress Culture embraces three goals: (1) democratic governance, (2) social justice, and (3) an end to poverty. In four Confucian societies— Japan, South Korea, Taiwan, and Hong Kong—the four goals have been substantially attained. In Singapore, the latter two goals have been, one might say, overachieved, while the country remains in the beneficent Confucian thrall of Lee Kwan Yu, who celebrated his eighty-eighth birthday in September 2011. In China (and in Vietnam), the latter two goals are increasingly within reach—but under clearly authoritarian governance.

The Confucian scholar Tu Weiming, former director of the Yenching Institute at Harvard, has contributed an essay to *Culture Matters, Culture Changes* that sees the seeds of conversion to democracy in China and Vietnam in the branches of Confucianism:

[What is] noteworthy is that an increasingly vocal group of China scholars, both domestic and abroad, apparently without government sponsorship or encouragement, has been publishing articles and books arguing that Western, specifically American, democratic institutions and practices are incompatible with Chinese governance. This stance implies that either a different form of democracy or even a nondemocratic system is better suited to the Chinese. Academicians such as Henry Rosemont, Roger Ames, and particularly Daniel Bell go so far as to question the validity of "human rights" for social well-being in China (or for that matter, in the United States). Of course, the focus of their attack is not human rights per se but the liberal concept of individualism as the precondition for human rights. A conspicuous example is Daniel Bell's argument in favor of "illiberal democracy."

My own position is substantially different. I consider myself a transmitter of the Confucian Way as embodied in the first- and second-generation thinkers and practitioners of the Confucian revival. Carson Zhang's Confucian Constitutionalism and Xu Fuguan's Confucian Liberalism do not passively accept the Western model. Indeed, they creatively transform it in the best tradition of Western Enlightenment: liberty, rationality, rule of law, human rights, and the dignity of the individual. What they advocate is a new Confucian polity that opposes authoritarianism, conformism, and collectivism. They never doubt that, under the influence of the West and in light of the Enlightenment mentality, the modern Confucian personality ought to be liberal minded, rational, law abiding, respecting and promoting human rights, and powerfully defending the dignity of the individual. After all, Confucian learning "for the sake of the self," "body and mind," "human nature and the Mandate of Heaven," to become a profound person," or "to emulate the worthy and the sage" cannot afford to undermine the values that have been the basis of human flourishing in modern times.

In other words, there is no justification for a Confucian democracy that is in principle non-democratic or anti-democratic. Furthermore, although we may question the universality of the individual-based liberal thinking, we must recognize that the liberal concern for distributive justice, equality of opportunity, and freedom of speech, press, assembly, and religion, are now world ethics, if not abstract universal ethics. Indeed, it was in the great Confucian tradition of the critical spirit that Xu Fuguan defined himself as a Confucian liberal.

I would like to conclude by noting that the communal critical self-consciousness among the New Confucians is thoroughly democratic. The politics mainland China manifests are far from democratic. By definition they are also un-Confucian and anti-Confucian. The claim that Chinese polity is an alternative form of "modern democracy" cannot be substantiated by simple empirical observations. To advocate a "Chinese model" is not only ignorant but also arrogant. Confucian revival is a double-edged sword. The danger of a pretext for authoritarianism and of a blind support for aggressive nationalism is real. Yet Confucian democracy is not a figment of the mind. It is a vision of China's transformation into a new form of liberal democracy, which is not only an authentic possibility but also a moral imperative.[28]

Malcolm Gladwell's Outliers and East Asia's Success

In his bestselling *Outliers*, Malcolm Gladwell runs the risk of oversimplifying and looking gimmicky. For the most part, he successfully avoids this pitfall and is generally respectful of the importance of cultural values, beliefs, and attitudes. However, in looking for an explanation for the success of Jewish immigrants, at least those who migrated to New York, he shortchanged culture and ended up with a superficial and misleading emphasis on skills related to clothing production that Eastern European Jews brought with them.

With respect to the success of the East Asians, Gladwell focuses on the rigors and disciplines of paddy rice production as the key. His chapter in this book *Outliers* makes no reference whatever to Confucianism or to Chinese, Japanese, or Korean culture more broadly. Yet, remember Weber's observation (page 78): "In stressing the absence of capitalist accumulation and investment," he notes that, "whereas the rural population of Western Europe declined as capi-talism spread and farm size there increased through consolidation, in China, the rural population expanded rapidly while farm size shrank. The resulting predominance of small farms reinforced both traditional rice agriculture and the traditional peasant worldview."

The fundamental flaw in Gladwell's argument is also apparent from the UN's Food and Agriculture Organization's data on paddy rice production.[29] The second most important producer of paddy rice after China is India, followed by Indonesia, Bangladesh, Vietnam, Thailand, Myanmar, and the Philippines. Of these countries, only India and to a lesser extent Vietnam have achieved high, sustained rates of economic growth. But the Indian "miracle" has little to do with agriculture and a lot to do with high-tech industries and India's rich English language resources, while Vietnam is a country powerfully influenced by Confucianism.

None of the others have experienced economic miracles, nor have their immigrants performed anywhere near as brilliantly in the United States as have the East Asians.

CHAPTER 5

~

Protestants

I think that a good case can be made that the Reformation was the single most important event in the history of human progress. If this sounds rash, just contemplate what the world might look like today if the Catholic Church had maintained its monopoly in the West:

- The Industrial Revolution would not have happened.
- Democratic governance would be largely unknown. Authoritarian, hierarchical societies would be the norm.
- Scientific discovery would have been proceeding at a snail's pace: we might still be living without automobiles, airplanes, penicillin, and the telephone, not to mention televisions, computers, and the Internet.
- The United States and Canada would be former Spanish colonies, confronting continuing problems of political instability, social injustice, and poverty.
- Japan would have continued on the feudal course set during the Tokugawa dynasty, substantially isolated from the rest of the world.
- China would be well off, relative to the West and the rest of the world, complacent in its "Middle Kingdom," but isolated and backward relative to its current condition.
- India would still be an authoritarian, caste-dominated, poor country.
- The Ottoman Empire would still exist.

Obviously, the foregoing is conjectural. But an argument can be made for each of the assertions. It was not until Pope John XXIII's 1963 encyclical *Pacem in Terris* that the Catholic Church unreservedly endorsed democratic governance, a shift that almost surely would *not* have occurred, at least not for some considerable time thereafter, had the Catholic monopoly continued. (We should remember that Pope Pius XII congratulated Spanish dictator Francisco Franco on his victory in the 1936–1939 Civil War.)

To this day, the Church remains ambivalent on capitalist economics—and that includes the US Council of Bishops. Leading lay Catholic writer Michael Novak's campaign to liberalize Catholic economics, symbolized by his 1993 book *The Catholic Ethic and the Spirit of Capitalism*,[1] has not succeeded in persuading many Church leaders.

Scotland and Ireland Compared

Neighboring Scotland and Ireland provide a good laboratory for comparing the long-term effects of the divide of the two religions. Scotland's and Ireland's roots are in the same Celtic culture that also embraces Wales, Cornwall, and France's Brittany. Ireland's resource endowment, particularly in terms of arable land, is far more favorable than Scotland's.[2] Catholicism was established in Scotland at the end of the fourth century and continued to hold the allegiance of most Scots until it was banned in the wake of the Scottish Reformation in 1560.

Catholicism dates from about the same time in Ireland. Saint Patrick was born in Scotland in about 372. He was sold as a slave in Ireland, escaped, and became a priest and then a bishop in Rome. He was sent back to Ireland in 432 and started a process of mass conversion from paganism to Catholicism. Thus, the two countries, which sprang from the same ethnolinguistic Celtic roots, both experienced more than a millennium as Roman Catholic societies.

It was the Calvinist branch of Protestantism in the form of the Presbyterian Church that John Knox brought to Scotland in 1560, displacing Catholicism. It was Calvinism, of course, that Max Weber had most in mind when he wrote *The Protestant Ethic and the Spirit of Capitalism*. Weber argued that the Calvinist concept of *predestination* coupled with the concept of *calling* set up an "ascetic" tension of self-denial and self-discipline that was the engine of capitalist development. God had decided which persons were to be in a state of grace even before they were born, and the only way an individual could know whether he[3] was of *the Elect* was through successful pursuit of his calling, often measureable in financial terms.

The principal doctrinal differences between the Calvinist Presbyterianism of Scotland and Ireland's Catholicism were threefold:

1. The Presbyterians emphasized the importance of universal literacy, so that every member of the church could read the Bible. In *How the Scots Invented the Modern World*, Arthur Herman notes that "[John] Knox's original 1560 Book of Discipline had called for a national system of education. . . . Scotland's literacy rate would be higher than that of any other country by the end of the eighteenth century . . . despite its relative poverty and small population, Scottish culture had a built-in bias toward reading, learning, and education in general."[4]

2. Like other Protestant sects, the Presbyterians did away with the superstructure of authority that was synonymous with Catholic administration. In *Democracy in America*, Alexis de Tocqueville notes: "[The British settlers] brought with them into the New World a form of Christianity which I cannot better describe than by styling it a democratic and republican religion. This contributed powerfully to the establishment of a republic and a democracy in public affairs; and from the beginning, politics and religion contracted an alliance which has never been dissolved."[5] Tocqueville goes on to make the point that Catholicism would be better suited to democratic practice if it could rid itself of the Church's superstructure—since the Catholic faithful were all on the same footing.

3. The Golden Rule came alive in the Presbyterian Church, much as it did in other Protestant sects. Democracy appeared first and most enduringly in countries where the value of fair play—the Golden Rule in action, and central to the Anglo-Protestant tradition—had taken root. This was a key element of the congeniality between US culture and democracy that Tocqueville perceived. With respect to the much later consolidation of democracy in Catholic countries, I note Weber's observation: "The God of Calvinism demanded of his believers not single good works, but a life of good works combined into a unified system. There was no place for the very human Catholic cycle of sin, repentance, atonement, release, followed by renewed sin."[6]

The French Protestant Napoléon Roussel presented data on Scotland and Ireland in his 1854 book *Catholic and Protestant Nations Compared*[7] that support Weber's contrast of the two religions, as shown in Table 5.1.

The French Enlightenment thinkers appeared on the scene in the sixteenth century, starting with Michel de Montaigne; running into the seventeenth

Table 5.1. Nineteenth-Century Crime Rates: Scotland and Ireland

Accusations of crimes and offenses (annual average 1831–35)	
Scotland	1 in 880 inhabitants
Ireland	1 in 460 inhabitants
Thefts (1834–36)	
Scotland	1 in 13,000 inhabitants
Ireland	1 in 2,700 inhabitants
Homicides(annual average 1830-35)	
Scotland	1 in 400,000 inhabitants
Ireland	1 in 107,000 inhabitants
Condemnations to death (1804–1811)	
Scotland	1 in 257,000
Ireland	1 in 32,900
Executions (annual average 1831–35)	
Scotland	1 in 610,000 inhabitants
Ireland	1 in 221,000 inhabitants

Source: Napoléon Roussel, *Catholic and Protestant Nations Compared* (Lenox, MA: Hard Press, 2007), pp. 90–91.

century with René Descartes and Blaise Pascal; and concluding in the eighteenth century with Baron de Montesquieu, Voltaire (François-Marie Arouet), and Jean-Jacques Rousseau. "They believed that human reason could be used to combat ignorance, superstition, and tyranny and to build a better world. Their principal targets were religion (embodied in France in the Catholic Church) and the domination of society by a hereditary aristocracy."[8] They were all influenced by the Reformation. Their ideas, based on liberal theory, contributed a philosophical foundation for the French Revolution.

The Scottish Enlightenment was an eighteenth-century phenomenon. Prominent among the Scottish Enlightenment thinkers were David Hume, Francis Hutcheson, and Adam Smith. "The efforts of the Scottish school led Voltaire to note that 'we look to Scotland for all our ideas of civilization.'"[9] Based on reason and pragmatism, the Scottish Enlightenment contributed much to the American Revolution.

Americans of Scottish antecedence played a crucial role in the early years of American independence, among them Thomas Jefferson, Alexander Hamilton, Henry Knox, and John Paul Jones. Of the thirteen governors of the original states, nine were of Scottish ancestry. In addition to Jefferson, presidents of Scottish antecedence included James Polk, James Monroe, James Buchanan, Andrew Jackson, William McKinley, and Woodrow Wilson.

In the middle of the nineteenth century, the population of Scotland totaled 3 million.[10] At that time, Ireland's population approximated 8 million.[11]

Scotland was riding the wave of the Industrial Revolution to which it had contributed so much. Its wage rates were five to six times those of Ireland, where the "potato famine" had killed about a million people and forced another million to emigrate between 1845 and 1852, most of them to the United States. "Altogether, almost 3.5 million Irishmen entered the U.S. between 1820 and 1880."[12]

The Irish Miracle of the Past Half Century

In 1960, Ireland was among Europe's poorest, least educated countries. In 2010, it was among the most affluent and best educated. What explains the "Irish miracle"?

Dick Spring was Ireland's deputy prime minister during the periods 1982–1987, 1993–1994, and 1994–1997. He has also held several ministerial posts in Irish governments. In his contribution to *Developing Cultures: Case Studies*,[13] he explains the Irish socioeconomic miracle as a consequence of the following:

- The liberalization of economic policy in the late 1950s—at about the same time that Spain opened up its economy.
- Creation of the Industrial Development Authority, which was charged with attracting foreign investment; the subsequent reduction of the corporate tax rate to 10 percent enhanced Ireland's attractiveness to foreign investors.
- Ireland's joining the European Economic Community in 1973, which enhanced Ireland's foreign investment promotion and brought substantial flows of development assistance from Europe.
- An English-speaking labor pool.
- Budgetary discipline.
- High priority for education (Ireland now dedicates more of its budget to education than any other European country), including the introduction of free public secondary schools in 1968. Up until that time, the Catholic Church had a virtual monopoly on secondary education and charged fees that deterred many Irish parents from enrolling their children.

As in Portugal, Spain, and Quebec, the Irish transformation was accompanied by a diminution of the Catholic Church's influence to the point where today one hears references to "post-Catholic" Ireland, Portugal, Spain, and Quebec.

Writing in 2005, Spring stressed that Ireland is not Eden. Its economy is heavily dependent on foreign, above all US, investment, and it has suffered in the current worldwide recession. Should the investors choose to move their operations to lower cost countries like China and India, the consequences for Ireland could be grave. Spring also notes social problems that were far less acute before the miracle: soaring crime rates, homelessness, marriage breakdown, and alcohol-related violence. But for all that, Ireland, for so long a country of massive emigration, now attracts immigrants—or at least did until the current prolonged recession.

The PIIGS Threaten the Euro

The European financial crisis that dominates the global economy, with palpable repercussions on the United States and Canada; Australia and New Zealand; Confucian East Asia; India; and indeed all the countries of the world, is loaded with cultural forces. Achievement of the goal of a united Europe, at least in part motivated by concern about the region's ability to compete with the United States, ultimately depends on sufficient similarity of value and attitude systems among the European countries to ensure the effectiveness of regional institutions and policies. If Alexis de Tocqueville were alive today, he would almost surely have counseled against creation of the single currency early in the integration process because it places such strains—above all at a moment of economic crisis—on the cultural foundation on which the entire structure rests.

The dominant role of culture in the European project can be readily appreciated from the cultural commonality of the five countries that, at least at the time of writing this (early June of 2012), most threaten the viability of the euro. The five countries have acquired the unfortunate acronym PIIGS: Portugal, Ireland, Italy, Greece, and Spain. Portugal, Ireland, Italy, and Spain may all be "post-Catholic" in terms of the reduced influence of the Church; but their economic performance during the prolonged recession starting in 2008 looks much more like Latin America than like the United States and Canada—and Germany.

As I noted in Chapter 2, the overall performance of the Orthodox Christian countries, of which Greece is one, is very similar to that of the Catholic countries. Orthodoxy of course broke away from Roman Catholicism in AD 1054. In his Culture Matters Research Project paper on Orthodox Christianity, Nikolas Gvosdev concluded that it was on balance a force against progress, although the influence of the United States in Greece had mitigated the adverse influence somewhat. "Protestantism has been far more conducive to modernization than Catholicism, above all in the Western Hemisphere."[14]

I shall refer back to the lead paragraph in Chapter 2 of the first finding of our study of 117 countries grouped by predominant religion. I will elaborate on these finding by examining one representative—Sweden—of the "champions of progress," the Nordic countries, and one representative of the runner-up group, the United Kingdom and its offspring: the United States. The runners-up also include other advanced Anglo-Protestant societies: Canada, Australia, New Zealand, and now "Afro-Saxon" Barbados, which, ranked at forty-two, finds itself in the top category—the First World—of the UNDP listing.

Sweden

In the middle of the nineteenth century, Sweden was among the poorest of the European countries. That was, of course, a time when large numbers of Swedes (and Norwegians and Finns) immigrated to the United States, particularly, in the case of the Swedes and Norwegians, to Wisconsin and Minnesota, two of the most progressive states.[15] Today, the Nordic countries attract immigrants.

The economic boom that started in the 1860s was accompanied by advances in democratic governance that culminated in 1921 with full and equal suffrage. But the roots of Sweden's advanced welfare system go deeper, at least back to the seventeenth century when iron production took place in small communities in which the foundry owners, while paternalistic in their dealings with their employees, also felt responsible for their well-being. Over the centuries, this social responsibility has been transferred to a strong state and a strong, independent civil service, the roots of which go back even farther, to the sixteenth century.

But one must ask why this kind of socially responsible management, atypical for the times, occurred in Sweden? And why were the peasants given a political voice as far back as the sixteenth century? Historian Dag Blanck and political scientist Thorleif Pettersson, both from Uppsala University, note the consolidation of Lutheranism in Sweden during the sixteenth century.[16] They quote Nils Ekedahl: "Through the true, Lutheran faith and through obedience to the theocratic monarchy, the Swedish people were bound together into one community which united the subjects of the realm into one soul."[17] We are reminded of David Hackett Fischer's observation (see Chapter 1) that "the Puritans [of Massachusetts] believed that they were bound to one another in a Godly way. One leader told them that they should 'look upon themselves as being bound up in one *Bundle of Love*; and count themselves obliged, in very close and Strong Bonds, to be serviceable to one another.'"

Blanck and Pettersson also note the profound influence of Lutheranism on education. Fewer than 10 percent of all Swedes were illiterate in the 1850s, perhaps the lowest rate in the world at that time along with Scotland's. But they also note that most Swedes no longer attend church.

The idea of social justice was translated into a metaphor for "the home" by Per Albin Hansson, Sweden's prime minister from 1932 to 1946. I quote it here for its relevance and eloquence:

> The basis of the home is togetherness and common feeling. The good home does not consider anyone as either privileged or unappreciated; it knows no special favorites and no stepchildren. There no one looks down on anyone else, there no one tries to gain advantage at another's expense, and the stronger do not plunder or suppress the weaker. In the good home, equality, consideration, co-operation, and helpfulness prevail. Applied to a home for all the citizens, this would mean the breaking down of all the social and economic barriers that now divide citizens into the privileged and the unfortunate, into rulers and subjects, into rich and poor, the glutted and the destitute, the plunderers and the plundered.[18]

Blanck and Pettersson conclude by stressing two key civic virtues of the Swedes: willingness to follow the society's rules and regulations, and readiness to participate in creating them.

Anglo-Protestant Culture in the United States

In his final book, *Who Are We? The Challenges to America's National Identity*, Samuel Huntington devotes a chapter to Anglo-Protestant culture, of which he writes, "For almost four centuries this culture of the founding settlers has been the central and lasting component of American identity."[19] What is the essence of Anglo-Protestant culture? What are the principal features of this product of "the dissenting, evangelical nature of American Protestantism"?[20] Huntington points to the American Creed, a term popularized by Gunnar Myrdal (appropriately a Swedish Nobel Prize winner) in his 1944 book *An American Dilemma*: "Myrdal spoke of 'the essential dignity of the individual human being, of the fundamental equality of all men, and of certain inalienable rights to freedom, justice, and a fair opportunity.'"[21]

The work ethic and individual responsibility are also central to Anglo-Protestant culture, as is opposition to hierarchy. Huntington observes,

The work ethic is a central feature of Protestant culture, and from the beginning America's religion has been the religion of work. In other societies, heredity, class, social status, ethnicity, and family are the principal sources of status and legitimacy. In America, work is. Both aristocratic and socialist societies demean and discourage work. Bourgeois societies promote work. America, the quintessential bourgeois society, glorifies work.[22]

Also central are the "long-standing English ideas of natural and common law, the limits of government authority, and the rights of Englishmen going back to Magna Carta. To these the more radical Puritan sects of the English Revolution added equality and the responsiveness of government to the people."[23]

Anglo-Protestant "dissenting, evangelical" culture has profoundly influenced the course of US history, time and again driving reform initiatives, including the Revolution itself; the movement to abolish slavery; the Progressive movement, beginning in the 1890s; the fight for racial equality, beginning in the late 1950s; and the more general challenging of US institutions in the 1960s.

Anglo-Protestant culture has also influenced foreign policy. "In conducting their foreign policy, most states give overwhelming priority to what are generally termed the 'realist' concerns of power, security, and wealth. When push comes to shove, the United States does this too. Americans also, however, feel the need to promote in their relations with other societies and within those societies the moralistic goals they pursue at home."[24]

"The Missionary Roots of Liberal Democracy"

Just as I was completing the final manuscript of this book, I received an article from the May 2012 *American Political Science Review* by Robert D. Woodberry of the National University of Singapore that states,

[H]istorically and statistically . . . conversionary Protestants (CPs) heavily influenced the rise and spread of stable democracy around the world. It argues that CPs were a crucial catalyst initiating the development and spread of religious liberty, mass education, mass printing, newspapers, voluntary organizations, and colonial reforms, thereby creating the conditions that made stable democracy more likely. Statistically, the historic prevalence of Protestant missionaries explains about half the variation in democracy in Africa, Asia, Latin America and Oceania and removes the impact of most variables that dominate current statistical research about democracy. The Association between Protestant missions and democracy is consistent in different continents and subsamples, and it is robust to more than 50 controls and instrumental variable analyses.[25]

After twenty-six double-columned pages, including six regression tables, Woodberry concludes,

A century ago Max Weber (1958, 1968) argued that Protestantism helped spur the rise of capitalism. Some of his causal mechanisms may be wrong, but his main intuition seems right: Religious beliefs and institutions matter. What we consider modernity was not the inevitable result of economic development, urbanization, industrialization, secularization, or the Enlightenment, but a far more contingent process profoundly shaped by activist religion.

CHAPTER 6

~

Other High Achievers I
Basques and Sikhs

If we consider those peoples who have been influenced by Chinese culture, itself so powerfully influenced by Confucianism, there may be as many as 1.5 billion "Confucians," at least as I define them, including China, Japan, the two Koreas, Vietnam, Singapore, and their diasporas. There are about 600 million Protestants. But there are only about 13 million Jews—we are reminded of the data contained in Steven Pease's book *The Golden Age of Jewish Achievement*[1] and the author's awe at the achievements of such a small group of people.

Several other groups, some more numerous than the Jews, but nonetheless subnational or transnational minorities, also demonstrate high cultural capital with high levels of achievement. I have selected four—the Basques, who are Catholics; India's Sikhs; the Mormons; and the Ismailis, who are Muslims and who are models for reform of Islam.

The Basques

The Basques are an ethnolinguistic group residing principally in the north of Spain but also in the neighboring border regions of France. With a history going back possibly as far as 5,000 years, the Basques may be the oldest extant ethnic group in Europe. The Basque language is virtually unique: the only other language that resembles it at all is that spoken in the Republic of Georgia. The Basques converted to Catholicism in the tenth century AD and produced some prominent clerics, such as, Saint Ignatius Loyola, founder of the Jesuit order, and his student, Saint Francis Xavier, who brought Catholicism to East Asia.

The Basque provinces of Spain, on the Bay of Biscay near the French border, have long been considered, along with Catalunya, the most progressive, prosperous, and democratic regions of Spain. During the Spanish Civil War (1936–1939), most Basques supported the Republican "left" side. The town of Guérnica, made famous by Pablo Picasso's painting of the 1937 attack on it by German and Italian aircraft in support of the Nationalist forces of Francisco Franco, is in the Basque Country.

On consolidating power in 1939, Franco unleashed a campaign to suppress the Basque language and culture that persisted until his death in 1975. The roots of the Basque drive for sovereignty, including the Euskadi Ta Askatasuna (ETA; "Basque Homeland and Liberty") separatist group, can be found in Franco's campaign of suppression.

The Basque entrepreneurial tradition contributed to a degree of industrialization in the nineteenth century that far exceeded that of the rest of Spain. Before industrialization, Basque land-tenure patterns were dominated by small farms, in contrast to the plantation—*latifundio*—patterns in most of Spain. The earliest successful experiments in Spain with the cooperative form of organizing private enterprises occurred in Mondragón, near Bilbao, the capital of the Basque province of Vizcaya. The Basques took advantage of their head start in industrialization to move quickly into finance, a sector where they are highly influential to this day.

I might mention that Sovereign Bank, a prominent bank with a branch in Vineyard Haven, Massachusetts, where I reside, was recently acquired by Banco Santander, a bank created by Basques in 1857 that continues to be managed by Basques to this day.

Industrialization was stimulated by the British, who, in the middle of the nineteenth century, found near Bilbao rich deposits of the red hematite ore needed for Bessemer steel production. But long before that, the Basques had earned a reputation for industriousness and creativity.

François Depons, a Frenchman who lived in Caracas for some two decades at the turn of the nineteenth century, described economic life in Spain's Venezuelan colony in a book published in 1806.[2] Depons noted,

> [P]lantation owners . . . ordinarily live in the cities . . . where expenditures . . . reflect the plantation's production, but are calculated in accordance with the most fertile and abundant year. Consequently, it is only exceptionally that income exceeds spending, and rather than economizing to improve the crops, they load themselves up with debts and attribute those debts to bad weather and defective laws, when they are due only to the lack of order among the

owners. . . . The plantation owner who visits his estates once a year is satisfied that he has taken care of his interests. He has often not even informed himself on the work being done on his plantation. . . . A country which holds agriculture in such contempt does not deserve the favors of nature.[3]

Depons then notes some exceptions to this pattern of extravagance and waste:

As proof of the advantages agriculture would reap if the owners lived on the estates, suffice it to observe the farms which prosper, those which sustain themselves . . . it will be noted that [they] are managed by their owners, who channel all their ambition into increasing their income and take pride in being farmers; in general those who act in this way are Basques.[4]

Depons also notes a parallel pattern in the city, including the success of a large company "due to their effective administrators, who always came from the Basque provinces, which seems to be the refuge for good customs."[5] In breaking down the population of Caracas, he notes,

[A] second class of Europeans resident in Caracas is comprised of those who came here to engage in industry or make their fortune. Almost all are from the Basque provinces or Catalonia. Both are equally industrious, but the Basques, without exhausting themselves as much, manage their businesses better. Willing to take economic risks and perseverant in agriculture, they tend to be more successful than the Catalonians. . . . The Basque is never intimidated by the size or the risk of a business proposition. He trusts even in chance.[6]

The Basques and Chile

There are today about 18 million people of Basque descent worldwide.[7] Interestingly, most Basques are found not in the Basque regions of Spain and France but in Latin America. One estimate puts the numbers of people of Basque origin in Argentina at 3.1 million (8 percent of a total of about 40 million), about the total of Basques living in Spain and France combined. But the Latin American country where the Basque influence has been most profound is Chile—perhaps 4.5 million (27 percent of a total of 16.8 million Chileans).[8]

Chile experienced a remarkable transformation in the nineteenth century. Its evolution toward political pluralism was more rapid than that of any other South American country, including Argentina and Uruguay; Chile was commonly referred to as "the model republic." A disproportionate number, by Latin American standards, of Chilean women were literate. And Chile displayed an uncommon economic dynamism that extended to neighboring Argentina, where many Chilean entrepreneurs were successful.

How can one explain this early transformation? Clearly, several factors are relevant, including rich resource endowment, a favorable climate, and a geographic position at once remote and advantageous. But the principal explanation for Chile's progress, I believe, is Basque immigration:

> Between 1701 and 1810, some 24,000 immigrants arrived in Chile from Spain (about doubling the number of Spaniards), and forty-five percent of these came from the Basque provinces and Navarre (a province just east of the Basque Country, whose people share many Basque traditions). Everyone agrees on the extraordinary impact these . . . groups had, including [the renowned Basque writer] Miguel de Unamuno, who called Chile, along with the Jesuit order, the two great creations of the Basque people. Their road to economic success and social prominence ran from commerce to the countryside to office. . . . Luis Thayer Ojeda, one of the most accomplished of many Chilean genealogists, thought that "three-fourths of the distinguished personages of nineteenth-century Chile were of Basque descent.[9]

Among them were Bernardo O'Higgins Riquelme, one of Chile's founding fathers (his mother was a Basque), and presidents Federico Errázuriz Zañartu (1871–1876), Aníbal Pinto Garmendia (1876–1881), José Manuel Balmeceda (1886–1891), Juan Luis Sanfuentes Andonaegui (1915–1920), Pedro Aguirre Cerda (1938–1941), Salvador Allende (1970–1973), and now Sebastián Pinera Echenique (2010–).

Chile is today widely considered to be the most successful country in Latin America, a judgment underscored by the Chileans' management of a vastly larger earthquake than Haiti's, both in early 2010, with a fraction of the casualties—fewer than 1,000 deaths compared with 300,000 in Haiti. Democracy was restored following the Allende-Pinochet detour (1970–1990). But the Pinochet "neo-liberal" economic policies, much maligned by the Latin American left, were continued by the left-of-center Concertación governments that followed until 2010, when the right-of-center candidate, businessman Sebastián Pinera Echenique (his mother was of Basque descent), won the presidency. Chile sustained high rates of economic growth, almost 4 percent per capita annually, for the thirty-year period of 1975–2005—almost quadrupling during those thirty years.

Chile is not paradise. In 2003, the top 10 percent of income earners accounted for 45 percent of national income. By comparison, the top 10 percent in the United States—the most inequitable society among the advanced democracies—accounted for 29.9 percent in the 2000 census. But Chile is far ahead of most other Latin American countries in the following measures:

- On Transparency International's Corruption Perceptions Index—it was ranked twenty-third in 2008, tied with France and Uruguay, and just behind Barbados
- On the World Competitiveness Forum's 2008 competitiveness rankings, where it is ranked twenty-eighth, ahead of Spain and China
- In the solidity of its democratic institutions, where Freedom House gives Chile, along with Costa Rica and Uruguay, its top grade

A personal reflection: I first visited South America in 1961 as the representative of the Office of the Secretary of Defense on a State Department/USAID/Defense Department team researching the potential contribution of Latin American military institutions to development—what would subsequently be called "civic action."[10] I remember a briefing in which we were told that the only police force in Latin America that was not corrupt was the Chilean national police force, the Carabineros. This judgment was reconfirmed more than forty years later by David Hojman in his essay on Chile for the Culture Matters Research Project:

> In Dakar, Senegal, the standard rate if you wish to bribe a traffic policeman (many, or maybe all of them stop taxi drivers and ask for it) is one pound sterling and ten pence (about $2.00). Some policemen are so cheeky that they will do it even in front of obviously European passengers. Refusal to pay means that you will have to retrieve your documents the next day from the local police station, which will cost several times more in cash, apart from the waste of time. In contrast, in Santiago de Chile, an attempt to bribe a traffic policeman will almost inevitably end up with the driver in jail. As far as I know, this has always been the case. Chile's Carabineros are . . . incorruptible.[11]

I add another comment by Hojman because of its relevance to Chile's unique, Basque-influenced culture. (I am reminded of the success of Basque cooperatives symbolized by the Mondragón co-op.) But the comment is also highly relevant to a point raised later in this book.

> In Spanish, the meaning of *compromiso* is closer to "commitment" or "obligation" in English than the give-and-take mutuality of the English word "compromise.". . . Nowhere in Latin America has the meaning of the word "compromise" become so close to that of the English word as in Chile.[12]

Basques and the Catholic Church
Traditional Basque attachment for the Catholic Church is suggested by the high profile of the two aforementioned Basque saints: Ignatius Loyola,

founder of the Jesuit order, and Francis Xavier, who brought Catholicism to East Asia. But that strong tie to the Church has become seriously frayed, above all by the sympathy of the Basques for the Republican cause during the 1936–1939 Civil War. This led to Franco's policy of suppression of Basque language and culture, and Franco of course was supported by the Vatican.

> [Ramon Echeverría, an American of Basque antecedence] points to the historical tendency of the Basques to be anticlerical and fiercely democratic. They fought any form of institutional hierarchy. The Catholic Church is full of this kind of hierarchy. Even the Basque clergy was historically opposed to the central power in Rome. Added to the mix were the leftovers from the Spanish Civil War and bitterness toward Franco. To this day, Basques are not opposed to the Catholic Church in and of itself, but rather to the hierarchical power structure it sustains. . . .
>
> Young people in the Basque country are leaving the church in droves, rejecting much of what it has to teach. Priests in the Basque country are alarmed that the enrollment in seminaries has dropped sharply over the past years. . . . He makes some predictions for the future of the Catholic Church and the priesthood especially in poor, developing countries. There is a great deal of pressure within the church to do away with as much of the hierarchy as possible, to open the church and democratize it. He sees a turnaround for the church in the future, a decrease in the clerical part of it.[13]

Prominent Basques

Although the Basques cannot compete with the Jews for Nobel Prizes, they have made a disproportionate contribution to human achievement and progress. I've been able to identify only one Nobel Prize winner of Basque extraction, the Chilean poet Gabriela Mistral, pseudonym for Lucila de María del Perpetuo Socorro Godoy Alcayaga, who won the prize for literature in 1945, the first Latin American to do so. Like most of the people on the following list, she had one Basque parent (an asterisk indicates that both parents were Basques):

Jerry Apodaca, former governor of New Mexico
José Joaquín de Arrillaga, former governor of California
Cristóbal Balenciaga,* fashion designer
Simón Bolívar,* hero of South American independence
Juan María Bordaberry, former president of Uruguay
Luis Echeverría, former president of Mexico
Emilio Garrastazu Medici, former president of Brazil
Ernesto "Che" Guevara, Marxist revolutionary
Roberto Goizueta, former chief executive officer of Coca-Cola
Dolores Ibárruri, La Pasionaria, Spanish communist leader

José Iturbi, conductor, composer, pianist
Octaviano Ambrosio Larrazolo, former governor of New Mexico
Paul Laxalt,* governor of Nevada from 1966 to 1970
Robert Laxalt,* American writer
José Carlos Mariátegui, prominent Peruvian Marxist
Eva Perón, Argentine first lady
Paco Rabanne,* fashion designer
Maurice Ravel, composer
Miguel Ángel Rodríguez Echeverría, former president of Costa Rica
Roberto Urdaneta, former president of Colombia
Álvaro Uribe, former president of Colombia

The Cost of Success Revisited: Winnemucca, Nevada
In early June 2009 I was driving back to Massachusetts from Palo Alto, California, with my son-in-law, Francisco "Kiko" Thébaud. Our first overnight stay was at a pet-friendly motel in Winnemucca, Nevada, on Interstate 80. (I was traveling with my two dogs, a thirteen-year-old Maltese and a six-year-old mini-dachshund.)

After settling in, I went to the motel office to ask for the name of a good restaurant. I was startled to hear the response: "Basque or American?" It turns out that Basques settled in Winnemucca at the turn of the twentieth century, bequeathing to this town of 8,000 people more Basque restaurants per capita than any other town or city in the United States. As might be expected, the Basques prospered in Nevada.

We ate family style—big tables with strangers often seated at the same table—at the Martin Hotel, established in 1898. The food was excellent and plentiful, and the conversation—with a recent Smith College graduate, who had recently gone to work for a gold mining company, and her family—enjoyable. As we were about to leave I noticed a couple of men standing at the bar and I asked them about the Basques. Their response echoed the comments about Jews made to me by a Mexican and an Italian, both highly educated and urbane, which my Martin Hotel interlocutors were anything but: "They all got rich—but you know how stingy they are!"

The Sikhs

In March 2010, I enjoyed lunch one day with my Stanford University Hoover Institution colleague and friend Bill Ratliff at the excellent Peking Duck restaurant in Palo Alto when, as we were leaving, I noticed a distinguished looking turbaned man lunching with a younger woman. I paused to ask the man if he were a Sikh. Not only was he a Sikh, but he was one of the most distinguished Sikhs—and indeed one of the most distinguished human beings—in the world: Narinder Singh Kapany, the inventor of fiberoptics. The younger woman was his daughter, Kiki, about whom more later. I had serendipitously run into a goldmine of Sikh lore—the founder of the Sikh Foundation in Palo Alto, an institute dedicated to research and informing the public about the Sikhs.

The Sikhs are an Indian group who live mostly in the Punjab. Sikhism was founded in the fifteenth century. Today there are about 30 million Sikhs, about 20 million residing in India. There are close to 1 million living in the United States. Most Sikh men have Singh (lion) and women Kaur (princess) in their surname. (The golf champion Vijay Singh is a Sikh.)

Narinder Singh Kapany and the Sikh Foundation are the principal source of what follows.

Sikh Scriptures and Values

Sikhs are particularly proud of their religious heritage. Their religious beliefs are memorialized in the book *Sri Guru Granth Sahib* (SGGS), initially prepared by their Prophet Guru Nanak (1469–1539). The first version was completed by the fifth prophet Guru Arjan (1563–1606) and canonized by the tenth (and final) prophet, Guru Gobind Singh (1666–1708). SGGS is a document of 1,430 pages written by the Sikh Gurus and Hindu and Muslim saints. It is written in poetry and set to music and focuses on spiritual and human needs to dwell upon the almighty and formless God. Interspersed between the teachings concerning the relationship between humans and their Creator one finds personal and interpersonal jewels of learning for all.

Of course, there are historical, cultural, economic, and secular influences on the Sikhs. The cumulative effects of all these factors have led the Sikhs to the following key teachings and practices:

- Absolute equality between all humans, in particular the *equality of men and women*, sanctified in its scriptures more than 500 years ago.
- Tolerance: opposes forced conversion, recognizing the greatness of all religions.
- Hard work: progressive, competitive, and entrepreneurial in their endeavors.
- Obligatory charitable contributions.
- A need to fight to preserve what is right and to change what is wrong.
- Belief in creativity and advancement by merit.

Sikh Teachings and the Typology

The following verses from the *SGGS* support the High Cultural Capital column in the twenty-five-factor typology. The verses are followed by the page numbers on which they appear in the *SGGS* (wherever available). Contributors include Dr. Kapany, Prof. Harbans Lal, Mr. J.S. Sethi, Dr. Nirvikar Singh, Prof. Gopal Singh, and Sonia Dhami. Their contribution was compiled by the Sikh Foundation, Palo Alto, California.

I. WORLDVIEW

1. **Religion: Focus on this world**
   a. Laughing and playing, adorning and feasting, salvation is found within Life itself.
   SGGS M5 522
   b. Truth is higher than everything; but higher still is truthful living.
   SGGS 62
2. **Destiny: I can influence my destiny for the better**
   a. Don't blame others, O people; as you plant, so shall you harvest.
   SGGS 888
   b. I shall reap the fruit of my labour. (Guru I, Asa Rag)
   c. Earn your living
   With your own efforts,
   Thus you will obtain happiness. (Guru V, Suhi Rag)
   d. With our own hands, let us resolve our own affairs.
   SGGS 477
3. **Time Orientation**
   a. Look to the future, and cast no glance behind.
   SGGS 1096
   b. Keep moving forward; do not turn your face backward.
   SGGS 109
5. **Knowledge**
   a. Ignorance hinders progress. (Kabirji, Asa Rag)
   b. The ignorant man wastes his valuable life,
   And cuts at his own roots. (Guru V, Gauri Rag)

II. VALUES, VIRTUES

6. **Ethical code: Rigorous within realistic norms; feeds trust**
   a. When trust is ended because of self-willed personality, no one places any reliance on that person.
   SGGS 643

7. **The lesser virtues: A job well done; tidiness, courtesy, punctuality**

   a. Contentment, peace and happiness will fill your mind deep within, when you do your job according to restraint dictated by truth and self-discipline.
   SGGS 591

   b. Should you neglect altruism and cleansing habits, it is as if your head is doomed to dust.
   SGGS 150

   c. Listen, O foolish and ignorant mind, harsh words bring failure and grief.
   SGGS 15

   d. Sweetness and humility, says Nanak, are the essence of all virtues.
   SGGS 470

   e. One who steadily lives with discipline of virtues is neither disappointed nor fails or struck down, and is saved from going round and round like animals.
   SGGS 76

   f. When you live in consistency with the laws of nature, and vow in purity and self-discipline, you will harvest the fruits of your life's desires.
   SGGS 1423

8. **Education: heterodoxy, dissent**

   a. In order to enlighten one's mind one must study and acquire knowledge.
   SGGS 340

   b. Cultivate knowledge through discourses with spiritually elevated co-seekers.
   SGGS 180

   c. You can be an effective servant of society and help the civil society if you imbibe education.
   SGGS 356

   d. The Eternal Creator has staged a play of His creation. He has created no one like anyone else. He made them different, and he gazes upon them with pleasure; he placed all the potential in everybody.
   SGGS 105

   e. We return home by different routes.
   SGGS 74

III. ECONOMIC BEHAVIOR

9. **Work/achievement**

   a. With your hands and feet, do all your work, but let your consciousness remain with the Immaculate Lord.
   SGGS 213

   b. Instead of wearing these beggar's robes, it is better to be a householder, and share with others.
   SGGS 587

15. **Advancement**
   a. They are few and far between who accomplish; everything else is but a pompous show and wrangling in this world.
   SGGS 1411

IV. SOCIAL BEHAVIOR

17. **Radius of identification and trust**
   a. Seek the almighty in everyone.
   SGGS 274
   b. I have no enemies, no adversaries. I walk arm in arm, like kin, with all.
   SGGS 887
19. **Association**
   a. First, God created His Light; and from were all men made: Yea from God's Light came the whole Universe: so, whom shall we call good, whom bad?
   SGGS 1349–1350
22. **Role of elites**
   a. He alone, O' Nanak, knows the way, who earns an honest living and then shares it with others.
   SGGS 496
24. **Gender relationships**
   a. From woman, man is born; within woman, man is conceived; to woman he is engaged and married. Woman becomes his friend; through woman, the future generations come. When his woman dies, he seeks another woman; to woman he is bound. So why call her bad? From her, rulers are born. From woman, woman is born; without woman, there would be no one at all.
   SGGS 473

Distinguished Sikhs

As the father of fiberoptics, a prominent educator, and world-class philanthropist, Narinder Kapany alone could document Sikh distinction. However, there are several other prominent Sikhs, including the following:

- Ujjal Dosanjh, premier of British Columbia, Canada (2000–2001) and minister of health for Canada (2004–2006);
- Giani Zail Singh, president of India (1982–1987);
- Dr. Manmohan Singh, Indian prime minister (2004–), the only non-Hindu to occupy the office;
- Harvinder "Harry" Anand, currently the mayor of Laurel Hollow, a prestigious community on the North Shore of Long Island, New York,

and the first elected mayor of South Asian descent in the State of New York;

- Sukhinder "Sukhi" Turner, first female and the youngest candidate elected (for three terms—1995–2004) as mayor of Dunedin, the second largest city in the South Island of New Zealand;
- Sir Rabinder Singh, an English High Court judge of the Queen's Bench Division, formerly a barrister, and the first judge in the United Kingdom to sit in the high court wearing a turban instead of a wig. At thirty-nine, he was appointed a deputy High Court judge in 2003— the youngest person to sit as a judge in the UK high court;
- And as a golfer myself, I must again mention Vijay Singh.

Kiki Kapany, Michael Schwarz, and Kikim Media

At the outset of this section, where I described my serendipitous meeting with Narinder Kapany, I mentioned that he was having lunch with his daughter, Kiki. As might be expected, Kiki Kapany is a high achiever in her chosen field: public interest media journalism. She and her husband, Michael Schwarz, who is Jewish, combined their given names to form Kikim Media in 1996.

> Kikim Media . . . has been honored with some of the most prestigious awards in broadcasting. These include three national Emmy Awards, two George Foster Peabody Awards, the Alfred I. duPont-Columbia University Journalism Award for Investigative Journalism, the Investigative Reporters and Editors Award, Red and Blue Ribbons from the American Film Festival, the Grand Prize in the Robert F. Kennedy Journalism Awards for Coverage of the Disadvantaged, and numerous Ciné Golden Eagles and local Emmys.[14]

CHAPTER 7

~

Other High Achievers II
Mormons and Ismailis

The Mormons

Edward Banfield introduces the Mormon community of St. George, Utah, early in *The Moral Basis of a Backward Society* (1958). Banfield had done a study of St. George shortly before he and his Italian American wife, Laura, visited Chiaromonte in the southern Italian region of Basilicata (Banfield gave Chiaromonte the fictitious name of "Montegrano"). In stark contrast with St. George, Chiaromonte was totally bereft of any organizations. Of St. George, Banfield said,

> For example, a single issue of the weekly newspaper published in St. George, Utah population 4,562, reports a variety of public-spirited undertakings. The Red Cross is conducting a membership drive. The Business and Professional Women's Club is raising funds to build an additional dormitory for the local junior college by putting on a circus in which the members will be both clowns and animals. The Future Farmers of America whose purpose is "to develop agricultural leadership, cooperation, and citizenship through individual and group leadership" are holding a father-son banquet. A local business firm has given an encyclopedia to the school district. The Chamber of Commerce is discussing the feasibility of building an all-weather road between two nearby towns. Skywatch volunteers are being signed up. A local church has collected $393.11 in pennies for a children's hospital 350 miles away. The County Farm Bureau is flying one of its members to Washington, 2,000 miles away, to participate in discussions of farm policy. Meetings of the Parent Teachers Associations are being held in the schools. "As a responsible citizen of our community," the notice says, "you belong in the PTA."[1]

One would conclude that Chiaromonte should lean substantially toward the Low Cultural Capital column and St. George toward the High Cultural Capital column. And indeed, other controversial aspects of Mormonism (e.g., the validity of the Book of Mormon;[2] the religion's former approbation of polygamy; its staunch opposition to gay marriage; its baptism of dead Jews[3]) notwithstanding, the Mormons have to be judged as among the most successful minorities in America in economic and social terms.

Mitt Romney, former governor of Massachusetts and the Republican nominee for the presidency in 2012, has attracted attention to the Mormons, much as did his father, George Romney, former governor of Michigan and 1964 presidential candidate.

I was astonished to discover the prominence—and diversity—of Mormons, although I was well aware of some, for example, the Marriotts, and, as a fan of the television quiz show *Jeopardy*, Ken Jennings, winner of more than $1 million. Among others are Jon Huntsman, former Republican governor of Utah (2005–2009) and President Barack Obama's ambassador to China (2009–2011); Nevada Democratic Senator Harry Reid, majority leader of the senate; David M. Kennedy, secretary of the treasury during the first Richard Nixon administration; Morris "Mo" Udall, for three decades a widely respected Democratic congressman from Arizona, and his brother Congressman Stewart Udall, secretary of the interior throughout the John F. Kennedy and Lyndon B. Johnson administrations; Brent Scowcroft, national security advisor under Gerald Ford and George H. W. Bush; Clayton Christensen, professor of business administration at Harvard Business School; entertainer Donny Osmond; Danny Ainge, president of the Boston Celtics basketball team; golfer and now television golf commentator Johnny Miller; Boston Red Sox All-Star outfielder Jacoby Ellsbury. (I apologize for the evident Boston bias.)

Although males tend to dominate the famous Mormons' listings, several females have also achieved prominence, for example, Paula Hawkins, Republican senator from Florida; entertainer Marie Osmond; and Ivy Baker Priest, US treasurer under President Dwight D. Eisenhower (her signature appeared on US currency from 1953 to 1961). And several prominent Latin Americans are converts, for example, Peruvian general Antonio Ketin Vidal, the youngest general in the Peruvian National Police Force, as of 2002, reflecting the success of Mormon missionaries in that region.[4]

Comments of Jeremi Brewer

Jeremi Brewer is currently conducting his postdoctoral research at Brigham Young University where he is leading the Micro-Enterprise Education Initiative at the Ballard Center for Economic Self-Reliance in the Marriott School of Management. He is also the executive director of the Academy for Creating

Enterprise, a multinational nongovernmental organization operating in the Philippines, Mexico, Brazil, and Zimbabwe. I asked him to consider the relevance of the typology to his religion. His comments follow—LDS refers to "Latter Day Saints," a preferred identifier for many Mormons:

Religion

LDS faith nurtures rationality—explaining that the faithful must do all that they can, all that is within their reach, before laying claim on providential intervention.

- While the LDS religion is somewhat ambiguous about material pursuits, it does not place monetary wealth as the highest priority. The phrase "sufficient for our needs" expresses their perspective on accumulation of wealth.
- LDS members focus heavily on the importance of this life as it directly correlates with the afterlife; LDS religion/doctrine claims that all human beings were spirit entities living in the presence of God prior to being born into this world, and therefore, there is a direct relationship with this life and the afterlife. They hope to return to God's kingdom after this life, and that prospect depends heavily on how they live in mortality.

Destiny

LDS members believe that they are responsible and accountable for what they do in this life. They believe that they are agents unto themselves, to act and not be acted upon, and that they must always be engaged in a good cause. They certainly believe that they can influence their destiny in this life.

Time Orientation

Time is a critical component of the LDS religion. Punctuality is highly emphasized, expected, and usually respected. The past, the present, and the future are often discussed among Mormons—both spiritually and temporally:

- Spiritually: Mormons often discuss the past: the pre-mortal life, the decision they made there to follow Christ, and how that decision directly impacted their mortal existence. As for the present, Mormons discuss the importance of correct decisions and the principles that will permit them to return to the presence of God.
- Temporally: At the age of eight, children are baptized into the church—their names are officially written into the records of the church. Even before baptism, young children are taught their roles as children of God: they are to grow up, get an education, be kind, remember God, get married, have a family, and continue obeying God's commandments.

- Young men are expected to serve a two-year, full-time mission for the church when they turn 19. The young women of the church are invited to serve an 18-month mission at the age of 21, but they are not commanded to do so.

Wealth

The LDS priority is to satisfy the needs of their families (food, shelter, love, education, etc.). They do not believe wealth is a sin, nor do they claim that it should be avoided. They do believe that the priority should first be to build the kingdom of heaven and then search for the riches of the world. Mormons are highly entrepreneurial and creative; they believe that wealth is expandable. Innovation, since the days of the pioneers crossing the plains, has always been an established trademark of the Mormon people.

Knowledge

Mormons are commanded to seek after all good things with the understanding that any intelligence, wisdom, or knowledge they acquire in this life will then be brought with them into the afterlife. Thus, while there is a large emphasis placed on the afterlife, they fully appreciate and exhort their members to obtain as much education (knowledge) as possible. Fact-based decisions, coupled with prayer, are highly emphasized. Mormons do base their decisions on facts, pragmatics, and verifiable data, but they expect the Lord to accompany them with their daily decisions.

Ethical Code

Integrity, trust, and honesty are key factors of the Mormon faith. Obedience to laws of the land is of high importance. Corruption is frowned upon. Mormons anticipate the best from others; but they recognize the importance of verifying and using contracts to help keep people honest. Honesty is a personal responsibility.

The Lesser Virtues

A job well done, tidiness, courtesy, and punctuality are essential components of the LDS faith. They hold these lesser virtues as core concepts that must be taught to children. Parents often hold weekly family meetings emphasizing time, future planning, frugality, respect for all, compassion, and integrity toward all people.

Education

Education is one of the most highlighted areas of the LDS faith. Mormons began their Utah experience by building educational facilities—Brigham Young University dates from 1875. Children and youth are constantly counseled to receive as much education as possible, to attend the best institutions that they can, to learn about other cultures, and to seek to teach, learn from, and appreciate others. Both men and women are told to seek as much education as possible, but there is an underlying understanding that women are expected to be the primary educators in the home.

Work/Achievement

Work is highly valued and expected by the LDS faith. Mormons have always been regarded as hard workers. It is not uncommon for large companies to recruit graduates from LDS schools: they are considered hard working and honest. Balancing spiritual and temporal affairs is also stressed—there must be a balance between spiritual work and temporal work. Having deep roots in nineteenth-century American history, Mormons have a rich legacy of hard workers who value sacrifice and integrity.

Frugality

Frugality and Mormonism are virtually synonymous. Mormons are always on the lookout for the best deals. Businessmen are searching for the most cost-effective way to make the transaction work. Mormons are often heard quoting the phrase "Use it up, wear it out, make it do, or do without," which was passed down from their Mormon pioneer ancestors. Frugality is also stressed in the LDS faith because it helps sustain perspective—we don't *need* to have the most expensive material objects in order to be happy.

Entrepreneurship

Because the LDS pioneers were often discriminated against, they were forced to innovate and create solutions. Entrepreneurship is very much a part of the Mormon way of life. Risks are carefully calculated, and spiritual confirmation is sought through prayer and meditation. Many of the most prominent LDS members (e.g., Mitt Romney, Jet-Blue Airways founder David Neeleman) are creators of large companies. Additionally, Brigham Young University offers degrees in business management with an emphasis on entrepreneurship.

Risk Propensity

The LDS faith promotes the idea that Mormons are able to calculate their own risks, make a decision, and bring that decision to God for any type of providential intervention.

Competition

In a spiritual context, Mormons tend to avoid competition or comparisons with one another. In a temporal setting, however, competition is valued and understood. There is a time and a place for competition, but cooperation is also valued. In a social setting, competition is usually suppressed in the interest of cooperation and the need to focus on each person's well-being. In a business setting, being the best one can be is highly valued.

Innovation

Mormons believe that they can influence their own destiny. Openness to innovation is not only accepted, but it is expected. In the Mormon culture, there are always ways to improve, increase gain, decrease costs, and achieve more.

Advancement

Finding the right person for the job is critical, and since nepotism is a form of corruption, the practice is shunned by Mormons. Merit is one of the central emphases of Mormonism.

Rule of Law/Corruption

Mormons are highly respectful of law and regulation. Children are constantly educated on the importance of obeying God's commandments, which strongly implies that they live by the law of the land. Daily good deeds are expected and respected amongst Mormons.

Radius of Identification and Trust

Family is the central unit of trust. Mormons believe that all human beings are children of God. They also believe that, as Mormons, they are bound together as spiritual brothers and sisters. Mormons tend to be very open to other people outside of the home, accepting of differences, and trusting. Mormons are actively engaged in their communities, schools, and in the public and private sectors. They are also commonly known for being kind and hospitable. Mormons feel a sense of duty to protect the future of their children and therefore are actively engaged in politics.

Family

Parents believe their children to be a gift from God and accept the responsibility to rear children according to the principles of righteousness and godliness. Families of the Mormon faith are expected, by way of commandment from church authorities, to hold weekly meetings (Family Home Evenings) every Monday night. In those meetings, parents assume the responsibility to teach their children the commandments of God, help children understand right from wrong, explain the dangers of drugs, alcohol, pre-marital sex, pornography, and so on, and also teach the importance of education, love, cooperation, and having high standards. Children are expected to prepare lessons for these meetings and share them with their families. The family unit is very highly regarded and treasured amongst LDS members and given the highest priority.

Association

Mormons have an extensive worldwide network. If an individual from one country is going to arrive in another country, arrangements can be made at any time, for any place, and there are rarely issues of worry. Provided that humanitarian aid is given priority, Mormons are easily brought together in large groups, told what is expected of them, and then asked to work. Mormons have a healthy and extremely strong ability to work together and with other organizations. Since Mormons are accustomed to working in large congregations comprised of units of families grouped together based on geographic locations, it is natural for them to convene and accumulate strong social capital at a rapid rate.

The Individual/The Group

Mormons have the ability to be individualistic *and* communitarian. In this sense they are symbolic of the broader US society. At times they are focused on their role as individuals, as entrepreneurs, while at other times they are inclusive. While they understand that the individual unit of family takes precedence over all other groups, there is an understanding within Mormonism that the community and world is also a critical component to the eternal family of God. The balance between the individual and the group has fomented progress.

Authority

Mormons are taught to obey their local, national, and worldwide ecclesiastic leaders—and the law of the land. Mormons respect and honor their ancestors, the Mormon pioneers who journeyed west in the 1800s, for they sacrificed their lives so that their posterity could have what they have today.

Role of Elites

Mormon elites feel it their duty to give back, provide for others, and, in general, be charitable. Mormons are required to pay a tithe of 10 percent of their income. The Church uses the tithe income to fund construction of chapels and temples, missionary work, and humanitarian aid. Undergirding the tithe is the idea that men and women should give back to mankind and help improve the world. One is reminded of the Hebrew incantation *tikkun olam* by which Jews are enjoined to repair or perfect the world.

Church–State Relations

Most Mormons would prefer Michael Novak's modification of the typology statement on church–state relations: in the high cultural capital column, instead of "Secularized: wall between church and state," Novak would say, "Division of powers between religion and state; protection of individual conscience." And in the low cultural capital column, he would prefer, "Religious leaders perform political roles, and the state imposes religious mandates."[5]

Gender Relationships

"The family is ordained of God. Marriage between man and woman is essential to His eternal plan. Children are entitled to birth within the bonds of matrimony, and to be reared by a father and a mother who honor marital vows with complete fidelity. Happiness in family life is most likely to be achieved when founded upon the teachings of the Lord Jesus Christ. Successful marriages and families are established and maintained on principles of faith, prayer, repentance, forgiveness, respect, love, compassion, work, and wholesome recreational activities. By divine design, fathers are to preside over their families in love and righteousness and are responsible to provide the necessities of life and protection for their families. Mothers are primarily responsible for the nurture of their children. In these sacred responsibilities, fathers and mothers are obligated to help one another as equal partners. Disability, death, or other circumstances may necessitate individual adaptation. Extended families should lend support when needed."[6]

Fertility

Historically, the Mormons were instructed that they were to bring as many children of God into this world as possible, and that they were not to avoid having children nor delay their entrance into this world. In recent years, however, Mormons have seen a change in guidelines about childbearing and fertility. Presently, there exists no official declaration on when to have children, but there is still a lingering culture of resistance when young couples delay having children because of other interests. However, the current guidelines have moved toward leaving the responsibility in the hands of the husband and the wife.

A Postscript
Coincidentally, as I was editing this section on the Mormons, Stephen Pease, author of *The Golden Age of Jewish Achievement*, sent me a copy of a June 9, 2011, article in *Bloomberg Businessweek* titled "God's MBAs: Why Mormon Missions Produce Leaders." Steve's comment is apt: "Mormons, like Jews, are roughly 2% of the American population. Yet they are counted in great numbers among CEOs of major corporations and successful entrepreneurs. . . . 'God's MBAs' makes the case for culture as the cause, namely the experience of serving as a missionary [and] living the Mormon life and Mormon culture. . . . And of course we now have two successful Mormons [Mitt Romney and Jon Huntsman] running for president." (personal communication)

The Ismailis

I spent the last few days of 2008 in Ottawa, Ontario, accompanied by my daughter Beth and my two dogs. My wife, Pat, and I had lived in Ottawa with our dogs through the 1993–1994 fall and winter as she started the Cordon Bleu cooking school. And notwithstanding the extreme rigors of the climate—at one point our car's external thermometer registered –26°F—we had loved the experience and the city. It was then that we became friendly with Larry Lederman (see Chapter 3), a career Canadian foreign service officer who was the chief of protocol at the time and subsequently served as Canada's ambassador to Chile.

The visit to Ottawa was my first since Pat's death in November 2005. It was the first leg of my trip to Palo Alto, California, where I would spend the next five months—and four months each of the following two winters—at Stanford University's Hoover Institution as a visiting fellow working on this book, among several other activities. After settling in at the Capital Hill Hotel, where Pat and I had lived during that cold, wonderful winter fifteen years before, I visited Larry Lederman and met his houseguest, Azim Fancy.

Azim is a tall, distinguished-looking, well-dressed man. He is also an Ismaili Muslim. The Ismailis are, as I discovered in conversation with Azim, a Shiite sect that differs from the Shiites as to who was the rightful successor to Mohammed. They believe that the line of succession should have run through the sons of Mohammed, whose descendant is the Aga Khan. The Shiites believe that it was Muhammad's son-in-law Ali, and the Sunnis that it was the elected caliph Abu Bakr, Mohammed's father-in-law and close friend. The Ismailis number about 13 million—about the same as the Jews—and are distributed through the northern tier of South Asia: Pakistan, Afghanistan, Iran. They also have migrated to Europe, Canada, and the United States.

It was clear to me from Azim's comments that the Ismailis are a very different breed of Muslim, if for no other reason than the status of Ismaili women. They are not required to wear veils, burkas, or any other religiously mandated apparel. But Azim also told me that the Aga Khan had recently advised his followers that if, at the margin, they had to choose between boys and girls to receive education, they should give preference to females. This enlightened guideline reverberated loudly for me because it was one of the findings of the Culture Matters Research Project.

A year earlier, I had read an article by Pervez Hoodbhoy, a Pakistani physicist in which the author called for an Islamic Reformation. Hoodbhoy had received his PhD from the Massachusetts Institute of Technology, where he had also done his undergraduate work. I contacted him and invited him to present a paper at the October 2008 conference that produced the *Culture Matters, Culture Changes* collection. The paper was excellent, and when Evgeny Yasin and I decided to organize the May 2010 symposium in Moscow, I invited Pervez to present a paper.

It was at the Moscow symposium that I learned that Pervez had been an Ismaili. I asked him to review the twenty-five-factor cultural capital typology from the viewpoint of an Ismaili. Here are the results:

WORLDVIEW

1. *Religion*: Ismailis believe in a Hazir-Imam (living, appointed by divine order, descended from Prophet Mohammed). He is also known as Aga Khan and is empowered to interpret the Quran in accordance with the times. He has chosen to emphasize the faith as this-worldly rather than other-worldly.
2. *Destiny*: Attitudes are not fatalistic; there is a strong focus on personal initiative and entrepreneurship.
3. *Time orientation*: Various Ismaili organizations are engaged in community planning. Meetings generally start on time, punctuality in schools and offices is considered important, and saving for the future is an essential virtue. This has made Ismailis excellent managers and businessmen.

4. *Wealth*: All Aga Khans have been personally wealthy and have assiduously applied themselves to increasing their wealth—they have encouraged their followers to follow suit. Ismailis tend not to be big risk-takers and generally invest their capital and efforts in the hotel industry, retail and wholesale businesses, medium-tech manufacturing.

5. *Knowledge*: Ismailis tend to take a functional, utilitarian view of knowledge. Business administration programs are very popular, as is acquisition of vocational and technical skills.

VALUES, VIRTUES

6. *Ethical code*: Ismailis quickly adapt to the ethical norms of the diverse societies in which they are embedded. This sometimes leads to shady business practices, but they are relatively more honest in dealing with other Ismailis.

7. *The lesser virtues*: Ismailis are noticeably less aggressive, less inclined to posture, and generally more polite than others in their local environment.

8. *Education*: New generation Ismailis have the highest rate of literacy among Muslims and the highest per capita university degrees. But there is a marked absence of artists and scientists; the emphasis on wealth has caused Ismailis to ignore academics and the fine arts and to target lucrative professions.

ECONOMIC BEHAVIOR

9. *Work/achievement*: Ismailis are hard workers, using the extra work to create extra wealth.

10. *Frugality*: Ostentatious display of wealth is common and is used to advertise success. One display mode is to give large sums of money to the Aga Khan since it improves status.

11. *Entrepreneurship*: Ismailis exhibit considerable originality, but in a limited number of areas only—this is probably because experience within high-tech fields is still quite limited.

12. *Risk propensity*: Moderate.

13. *Competition*: Ismailis appear willing to compete by the rules of the game. Strong-arm tactics are not generally used.

14. *Innovation*: Considerable, but limited to certain areas where there is adequate technical expertise and experience.

15. *Advancement*: Family businesses are the rule rather than the exception. However, serious breakups are making Ismailis more cautious, and there is a trend toward diversification. Non-Ismailis are employed in Ismaili businesses on the basis of strict merit.

SOCIAL BEHAVIOR

16. *Rule of law/corruption*: As long as other Ismailis are not defrauded, shady business practices are probably sanctioned just as much as in other communities.
17. *Radius of identification and trust*: This extends to the Ismaili local community, and possibly the diaspora as well, but not the entire society.
18. *Family*: Extended families tend to keep their identification.
19. *Association (social capital)*: A strong propensity for collective welfare schemes in education, health, and housing.
20. *The individual/group*: The individual is allowed to keep his or her identity and allowed considerable latitude in personal development, but there is also a strong group pressure toward conformity in religious and social matters.
21. *Authority*: Although the Aga Khan is the ultimate reference point, local Ismaili councils are responsible for development and community work. Participation in decision making is welcomed.
22. *Role of elites*: There is hierarchical structuring, and local elites wield considerable power. Accountability to popular opinion is something of which elites are conscious.
23. *Church–state relations*: As a community, Ismailis bend over backward to appear supportive of whichever government is in power. But, as in Idi Amin's Uganda, this could not stop them from being expelled.
24. *Gender relations*: Ismaili women do not cover their faces. Head covering, except at *dua* (supplication) time, has become less common in modern times. This runs counter to the general Muslim trend.
25. *Fertility*: The fertility rate has decreased sharply over the decades. Capacity to feed, educate, and house children is a strong determining factor.

Ismailis in Canada

In Toronto in May 2010, Canadian prime minister Stephen Harper and the Aga Khan celebrated the inauguration of the first Islamic art museum in North America. This event spotlighted the Ismaili presence in Canada:

Ismailis in Canada are among the richest citizens of the country, with famous names including former Conservative MP Rahim Jaffer and current CEO of Rogers [one of Canada's largest communications companies] Nadir Mohamed. In fact, a 2006 British Columbia business profile of the Ismaili community described it as almost "too good to be true," listing BC's richest Ismaili families including luxury hotel owners, mineral resource developers, real-estate moguls and more, many worth hundreds of millions of dollars. Ismailis are required to give 5–12 percent of their annual income to the Aga Khan, who is then said to allocate the funds to various non-profit ventures.[7]

Larry Lederman informs me that the mayor of Calgary, Alberta, is Naheed Nenshi, an Ismaili—and the first Muslim mayor of a Canadian city; he also notes that the celebrated Canadian author Moyez Vassanji is an Ismaili.

Ismailis are not Nordics. But neither are they Jihadist Muslims. In the continuum between Denmark and Somalia, it is clear that the Ismailis lean more toward the former than the latter.

Needed: An Islamic Reformation

Islam is the chief source of values, beliefs, and attitudes for most of its believers. In this respect, Islam is unique: no other religion today so powerfully influences the culture of its faithful. In the West, with the exception of the United States, the influence of religion has given way to secularism—a secularism, to be sure, that has been profoundly influenced by earlier religiosity, as in the Nordic countries. But the cultural power exerted long ago by religion in Scandinavia is very much a reality in the Islamic world today. Whereas Lutheranism was a force for progress (e.g., with respect to universal education and a rigorous ethical code) in the Nordic countries, Islam today, with a few exceptions, is not. Unlike medieval Hellenized Islam and even the nineteenth-century Islam of reform and liberal thought, contemporary Salafist-Wahhabist and Islamist Islam reject learning from others.

Although there are numerous factors that lie behind the slow progress of the Islamic countries, a major contributor has been clerical interpretations of the Qur'an that have transmitted fatalistic dogma; permitted adoption of scientific and technological advances from outside but closed the door to the liberalizing cultural forces that made these advances possible; and perpetuated the subordination and illiteracy of women. This condition is not uniform throughout the Islamic world, as Turkey and Indonesia demonstrate. But it is the predominant condition.

As Islam has steadily slipped from its early leadership in the arts and sciences, and with the subsequent collapse of the once-powerful Ottoman empire, most Muslims today are constantly reminded of how far behind the West and East Asia they have fallen. This insistent insult to self-respect— humiliation—was central to the motivation of Osama bin Laden and his followers. Richard Lamm has brought to my attention the following excerpt from Stephen Pinker's recent book, *The Better Angels of Our Nature: Why Violence Has Declined*:

> Violence is sanctioned in the Islamic world not just by religious superstition but by a hyper-developed culture of honor. The political scientists Khaled Fattah and K.M. Fierke have documented how a "discourse of humiliation" runs

through the ideology of Islamist organizations. A sweeping litany of affronts—the Crusades, the history of Western colonization, the existence of Israel, the presence of American troops on Arabian soil, the underperformance of Islamic countries—are taken as insults to Islam and used to license indiscriminate vengeance against members of the civilization they hold responsible, together with Muslim leaders of insufficient ideological purity. The radical fringe of Islam harbors an ideology that is classically genocidal: history is seen as a violent struggle that will culminate in the glorious subjugation of an irredeemably evil class of people. Spokesmen for Al Qaeda, Hamas, Hezbollah, and the Iranian regime have demonized enemy groups (Zionists, infidels, crusaders, polytheists), spoken of a millennial cataclysm that would usher in a utopia, and justified the killing of entire categories of people such as Jews, Americans, and those felt to insult Islam.[8]

The UNDP Arab Human Development Reports are crystal clear: the reform of Islam is indispensable for accelerated progress toward the goals of democratic governance, social justice, and prosperity. Among the key elements of reform are openness to the values, ideas, and institutions of the non-Islamic world; tolerance of other religions; and a broad commitment to excellence, education, and gender equality.

The Arab Spring from a Latin American Perspective

As I viewed photographs of people in Cairo and elsewhere in the Arab world, mostly young and brimming with enthusiasm, often with fingers raised in a "V" for victory, I was reminded of three similar moments in recent Latin American history, all of which I witnessed firsthand: the Dominican revolution of 1965; the Sandinista revolution of 1979; and the inauguration of Jean-Bertrand Aristide as Haiti's president in 1991.

Decades later, what looked at the time as promising divergences from an authoritarian, unjust, poverty-filled past now is, in essence, more of the same. Will the Arab countries do any better?

The Dominican Case

The Dominican revolution resulted in the ouster of a government installed by the military after they had removed Juan Bosch, the first democratically elected president following three decades of Rafael Leónidas Trujillo's tyranny. President Lyndon Johnson, fearing another Cuban revolution, intervened in force. The president's representative, Ellsworth Bunker, negotiated a provisional government, presided over by the centrist Dominican democrat Hector García Godoy, who brought the country to the elections of 1966, in which Joaquín Balaguer defeated Bosch. Democratic norms, with a few zigs and zags, have been respected since.

When the revolution erupted, on April 24, 1965, I was enjoying my first overseas assignment with USAID as the program officer in Costa Rica. Some days later, I received instructions from Washington to get to a US military airbase in Puerto Rico as quickly as possible for a three-week temporary assignment in the Dominican Republic. Those three weeks turned into three and a half years, during which I became deputy director of the USAID mission.

I gravitated to young Dominican professionals, almost all of whom supported the revolution with the same kind of enthusiasm evinced almost a half-century later by young Arabs. Among them was Bernardo Vega, a Wharton School graduate who would subsequently move from his position as the Central Bank's economic advisor to the leadership of the Central Bank, and then his nation's ambassador in Washington. He now writes articles and columns, including a recent one titled, "We Got Bad Marks in Davos," in which he notes the following, from the 2010–2011 Global Index of Competitiveness:[9]

- The Dominican Republic is number 101 of the 139 countries that participate in the Global Index.
- Corruption is rampant in the public sector.
- The public lacks confidence in the politicians.
- Organized crime, most of it drug-related, reaches into the security forces.

I visited the Dominican Republic two years ago and was struck by two contrasting impressions: (1) the physical changes—buildings, roads, resorts—were dramatic; but (2) the culture—the injustice, generalized abuse of power, the lack of consideration for others, the inefficiency—seemed substantially the same as it had been in the 1960s.

Sandinista Nicaragua

The Sandinista revolution reached its climax on July 19, 1979, with the entry of the Sandinista army into Managua. The *caudillo* Anastasio Somoza Debayle had fled the country two days earlier, ending the forty-two-year-long Somoza family monopoly of power. On that July 19, Managua looked a lot like Cairo in February 2011, with young people cheering and raising their hands in the "V" gesture.

I was named USAID director by President Jimmy Carter, leaving the USAID director job in Haiti so as to arrive in Managua a week after the July 19 celebration. Symbolic of President Carter's commitment to demonstrate the will of the United States to live with revolutionary regimes in Latin America, I flew into Managua in a Flying Tigers stretch jet filled with the first shipment of food, initially to be distributed by the Red Cross but then transferred to the Sandinista government at my recommendation and that of Ambassador Lawrence Pezzullo, an entrepreneurial career Foreign Service Officer and, like myself, a Democrat.

I should mention that, during the first 18 months of the Sandinista regime, the United States was its principal source of financial, food, and technical aid. But this is not the place to review the relations between the two governments. Suffice it to mention my relationship with Jaime Wheelock Román, *jefe* of the farthest left faction—the Proletarios—of the three that formed the Sandinista Front. Wheelock was named minister of agriculture and agrarian reform, and we provided a lot of help to him, including advisors from the University of Wisconsin Land Tenure Center.

Wheelock initiated a sweeping land reform that confiscated the largest farms, many, but not all, belonging to Somoza supporters. The owners were referred to as *terratenientes*, in the revolutionary environment a term of opprobrium.

Today, thirty-three years after the Sandinista revolution, Jaime Wheelock is among Nicaragua's principal *terratenientes*. And Daniel Ortega, first Sandinista president, is again president—but acting anything but democratically. After Fidel Castro, Ortega is Hugo Chávez's closest ally. According to a *Washington Post* report on February 22, 2012, "Ortega has been telephoning Moammar Gadhafi to express his solidarity."

Jean-Bertrand Aristide's Haiti

François ("Papa Doc") Duvalier ruled Haiti—an African American country—with an iron hand, as had most of his predecessors since the country won independence from France in 1804. His reign lasted from 1957 until his death in 1971, at which point his son Jean-Claude ("Baby Doc") became president for life at age nineteen. Fifteen years later, in 1986, he fled into exile in the wake of food riots. A bloody period of unrest followed under military governments until the United Nations, the Organization of American States, and the governments of Canada and the United States joined forces to set up an election on December 16, 1990, that brought Aristide to power.

That election has been described as the first clean election in Haiti's history. It is also eloquent testimony to the relative ease with which elections can be organized in even the most democracy-averse countries. Converting such countries to stable democracies is an altogether different story.

Aristide had been a Catholic priest who had been removed from the Salesian order of priests by the Vatican. He had built his political base on Liberation Theology, the left-wing Catholic doctrine that promotes socialism and the redistribution of wealth, and views imperialism, above all US imperialism, as the root cause of poverty in the Third World. Concerns were registered about Aristide in the US foreign policy establishment. But the United States supported him fully following his election.

As evidence of that support, I was in Haiti at the time of Aristide's inauguration on February 7, 1991, working on a project to strengthen Haiti's democratic institutions. I might add that I undertook a similar mission for USAID in Egypt a few years later—with obviously similar results.

As I described the inauguration in my June 1993 *Atlantic Monthly* article "Voodoo Politics",

> Port-au-Prince . . . experienced a rebirth for Aristide's inaugural. The residents of each block tidied up or even painted their houses and joined the neighborhood cleanup platoons. Streets were swept, and curbs, telephone poles, and trees were painted. The mood of the city was atypically upbeat, almost jubilant.

A scant eight months later, Aristide was ousted in a broadly supported military coup. His relations with the bicameral parliament, chosen in the same elections that brought him to power, were deteriorating, in no small part because his goons had threatened and even roughed up some opposition legislators. What followed was more "Voodoo politics," and then the horrifyingly destructive January 12, 2010, earthquake. A year later, Baby Doc Duvalier has showed up in Haiti, and Jean-Bertrand Aristide soon followed.

The Relevance of Alexis de Tocqueville

In his 1835 book for the ages, *Democracy in America*, Alexis de Tocqueville argues that you can't have democracy without democrats. He explains the successful US experiment as importantly the consequence of "a form of Christianity which I cannot better describe than . . . a democratic and republican religion. This contributed powerfully to the establishment of a republic and a democracy . . . from the beginning, politics and religion contracted an alliance which has never been dissolved."

He goes on to explain the undemocratic route taken by Latin America as essentially a cultural phenomenon, and he concludes,

> I am convinced that the luckiest of geographic circumstances and the best of laws cannot maintain a constitution in despite of mores whereas the latter

can turn even the most unfavorable circumstances and the worst laws to advantage. The importance of mores is a universal truth to which study and experience continually bring us back. I find it occupies a central position in my thoughts: all my ideas come back to it in the end.[10]

Implications for the Arab Countries

There are some obvious cultural differences between the Arab world and Latin America. Particularly as Evangelical and Pentecostal Protestantism make inroads on the former Roman Catholic monopoly in Latin America, receptivity to the democratic–capitalist model of the West is likely to increase.

It is noteworthy that not one Arab country has achieved democratic stability; only two—Indonesia and Mali—of the forty-seven Muslim majority countries are ranked "free" by Freedom House in its 2012 rankings. Mali has recently experienced a military uprising, and Indonesia barely made the "free" category—a total of five points for political rights and civil liberties. The most advanced Muslim country, Turkey, is ranked "partly free," with a total of six points. (Most first world countries have a total of two points.)

Moreover, Turkey may slip in future Freedom House ratings. Thomas Friedman notes in his June 10, 2012, *New York Times* column that, while Turkey has done well economically under the Islamist leadership of its Prime Minister Recep Tayyip Erdogan, Erdogan has been "eliminating any independent judiciary in Turkey and . . . intimidating the Turkish press so that there are no more checks and balances . . . [moreover] Erdogan announced out of the blue last week that he intended to pass a law severely restricting abortions."[11]

Turkey's inevitable influence on the Arab Spring may thus be highly negative; in Friedman's words, "Give your people [economic] growth and you can gradually curb democratic institutions and impose more religion as you like."

In 2012, Freedom House rated Egypt and Iraq "not free" with a total of eleven points. Non-Arab Afghanistan received twelve points. Freedom House's bottom reading is fourteen points.

That culture matters was eloquently restated in the UN Development Program's celebrated study, *Arab Human Development Report 2002*, written by Arab professionals, and evoking Tocqueville:

Culture and values are the soul of development. They provide its impetus, facilitate the means needed to further it, and substantially define people's vision of its purposes and ends. Culture and values are instrumental in the sense that they help to shape people's hopes, fears, ambitions, attitudes and actions, but they are also formative because they mould people's ideals and inspire their dreams for a fulfilling life for themselves and future generations . . . values are not the servants of development; they are its wellspring. . . .

Governments . . . cannot decree their people's values; indeed, governments and their actions are partly formed by national cultures and values. Governments can, however, influence culture through *leadership* and example, and by shaping education and pedagogy, incentive structures in society, and use of the media . . . by influencing values, they can affect the path of development.[12]

Many and perhaps most of the young demonstrators in Tahrir Square were motivated by frustrated job aspirations. But Egypt's gross domestic product of less than $3,000 (Table 7.1), this after decades of big aid programs, above all from the United States, suggests some fundamental problems, rooted in Egyptian–Islamic culture, that are unlikely to be resolved for many years.

One of the most telling antiprogress features of Islamic societies is the inferior position of women, symbolized by the gender discrepancy in literacy. Uneducated women are transmitters of orthodoxy to their children. According to the Human Development Foundation (HDF), a research entity formed by Pakistani expatriates in the United States, the discrepancy is substantial in Arab countries.

Table 7.1 derives chiefly from HDF data for 2007: I am adding a column that places the seven countries in the 2010 Corruption Perceptions Index (CPI) of Transparency International, where Denmark, New Zealand, and Singapore are tied as the cleanest (number 1) and Somalia, at number 178, is the most corrupt. (Interestingly, Afghanistan is tied with Burma at 176; Iraq is 175.)

Table 7.1. Selected Arab Countries: Per Capita GDP, Education by Gender, and Corruption

Country	Per Capita GDP 2010	Adult Male Literacy (5%)	Adult Female Literacy (%)	Transparency CPI
Egypt	$2,771	66	43	98
Libya	$12,062	90	67	146
Tunisia	$4,160	89	59	59
Algeria	$4,477	77	56	105
Morocco	$2,868	61	35	85
Syria	$2,892	88	59	127
Saudi Arabia	$16,641	84	66	50

Source: The Human Development Foundation (HDF), a research entity formed by Pakistani expatriates in the United States.

One must ask what proportion of those people in Tahrir Square were venting their frustration with their lot in life—as was largely the case in Santo Domingo in 1965, Managua in 1979, and Port-au-Prince in 1991—and what proportion were genuinely committed to democratization of their society? And what will happen, even with the emergence of truly democratic political institutions, if the Arab economies continue to grow slowly? Surely the Dominican/Nicaraguan/Haitian scenario is a distinct possibility in the absence of fundamental cultural change.

Hope and enthusiasm are not enough to bring these countries into the modern world.

CHAPTER 8

~

Catholic Latin America

Latin America's history bears witness to the failure of Catholicism, in contradistinction to Protestantism, or, at least, to the defeat of the Catholic ethic by the Protestant ethic, which shaped the development of the United States . . . the North American Protestant society appears more Christian, or perhaps less anti-Christian, than Latin American Catholic society. It demands of its followers a pattern of social behavior that dictates reasonably good faith in daily affairs and interpersonal relations and requires socially constructive action even of those in opposition.

—Carlos Rangel, *The Latin Americans* (1987)[1]

When the people in Anglo-Saxon societies, above all the United States, identify a common infrastructure need, they look to one another; they meet and refine their ideas; they agree on a course of action; and then they volunteer their time and resources to bring the project to fruition.

In Latin America, when the people identify a common need, they raise their eyes to the central government as supplicants; and they lose all hope for commerce, bridges, piers if the government doesn't do it all.

—Juan Bautista Alberdi, Argentine statesman (1880)[2]

> The future prosperity and happiness of [Mexico] now depend on the de-
> velopment of Protestantism. . . . Protestantism would become Mexican
> by conquering the Indians; they need a religion to compel them to read
> and not to spend their savings on candles for their saints.
>
> —Benito Juárez, a full-blooded native Mexican,
> five-time president of Mexico (1858–1872)[3]

The striking contrast in the evolutions of post-Reformation Protestant Scotland and Catholic Ireland, as discussed in Chapter 5, has been repeated, but on a vastly larger scale, in the Western Hemisphere. This is above all true of the contrast between Ibero-Catholic Latin America and the Anglo-Protestant United States (and, we might add, Anglophone Canada). It has also been repeated, on a smaller scale, within Canada itself: between the Anglo-Protestant provinces and Catholic Québec.

Spain's and Portugal's former colonies, which had a century's head start and are half again more populous than the United States and Canada taken together, are today roughly half a century behind the United States and Canada with respect to the maturity and stability of their political institutions, prosperity, and social justice. It is only in recent years that democratically elected governments have predominated in Latin America and several of the democratic experiments have ceased. The standard of living is roughly one-tenth that of the United States and Canada. Distribution of land, income, wealth, and opportunity is highly inequitable by the standards of the advanced democracies.

The Venezuelan writer Carlos Rangel, who in the mid-1970s incurred the wrath of the Latin American intellectual and political establishments with his book that stated that Latin Americans and their Ibero-Catholic cultural inheritance were responsible for Latin America's condition, notes, "As late as 1700, the Spanish American empire still gave the impression of being incomparably richer (which it was!), much more powerful, and more likely to succeed than the British colonies of North America."[4]

What can explain this striking historical flip-flop?

The contrast between the United States, an exceptionally dynamic and successful society, and Latin America may be unfair. But a strikingly similar contrast has been illuminated by an Inter-American Development Bank study of a century of Scandinavian and Latin American economic development titled *Diverging Paths*.[5] The study makes little mention of culture and views the divergence as essentially a policy and institutional phenomenon. But if one asks, with respect to any number of policy or institutional issues, why the Scandinavians chose the right path while the Latin Americans chose the wrong one, the answer inevitably gravitates toward fundamental cultural differences. Keep that in mind, as mentioned in Chapter 2, the three Scandinavian countries—Denmark, Norway, and Sweden—along with Finland and Iceland, are the world champions of progress.

Natural Resources? Climate? Dependency?

The roots of the discrepant evolution of the United States and Canada on one hand and Latin America on the other are thus centuries deep. Can they be explained by natural resource endowment? Canada and the United States are blessed with vast extensions of arable land, but so are Argentina and Brazil, which is now among the world's largest exporter of soybeans. There is no clear advantage with respect to minerals. Canada and the United States have an advantage in navigable waterways, especially the Great Lakes, and the terrain of Mexico and the Central American and Andean countries is more severely interrupted by mountain ranges.

On balance, Canada and the United States may enjoy a somewhat more bountiful natural resource endowment, but Latin America is also very well off. Even if a rich resource endowment were a precondition of rapid development, an assumption challenged by successful resource-poor countries like Japan, Taiwan, South Korea, Switzerland, and Israel, the difference in resource endowment between the North and the South in the Western Hemisphere is insufficient to explain the gap. And the gap, after all, is not just in economic development. It is comparably vast with respect to democratic institutions and social justice. Yet Costa Rica demonstrates that you don't have to be rich to be democratic.[6] Alexis de Tocqueville correctly concludes, "Physical causes do not therefore affect the destiny of nations so much as has been supposed."[7]

Climate has to be considered. Early in this century, Ellsworth Huntington, like Montesquieu two centuries before him,[8] argued that the differences between the temperate and tropical zones principally explain variations in human progress.[9] The early inhabitants of the temperate zones had to work harder in the shorter growing season to put something aside for the winter. They enjoyed a more invigorating, energy-inducing climate. Their shelters had to be substantial, and fuel had to be found and stored to protect against the cold. This placed a premium on work and saving but also may have encouraged cooperation.

Those who lived in the tropics enjoyed the luxury of growing crops—or picking food that grew naturally—year round. And shelters needed only protect against the rain. But that same ease of feeding and sheltering oneself nurtured indolence, as did the enervating climate. And the fecund environment also nurtured disease.

I have no doubt that climate has played a role in the diverse evolution of the North and the South in the Western Hemisphere, just as it has in the Eastern Hemisphere. Around the world, the vast majority of poor countries are found in the tropical zone, almost all rich countries in the temperate zones. But there are exceptions: all the countries of the former Soviet Union are in the temperate zone, but none have achieved First World status. Hong Kong and Singapore are both in the tropics. Moreover, all of Uruguay, almost all of Argentina, most of Chile, and much of Mexico and Paraguay are in the temperate zones. And many Latin Americans who live in "tropical" countries enjoy temperate climates because of the region's many elevated plateaus, as is the case with the capitals of Mexico, Guatemala, Honduras, El Salvador, Costa Rica, Colombia, Venezuela, Ecuador, Bolivia, and Brazil.

Dependency Theory dominated interpretations of Latin American underdevelopment in universities around the world—including the United States—in the 1970s and 1980s and is still alive and well in many Latin American universities today. It blamed the First World, and above all the United States, for "rigging" the world market to perpetuate Latin America's dependence on low-priced primary product exports while ensuring for itself the export of high-priced manufactured products. Economics merged with politics as the United States allegedly conspired with authoritarian Latin American leaders and oligarchs to preserve a status quo that ensured the continuation of dependency, that is, until the wave of democratization—supported by the United States—washed over the region in the 1980s and 1990s.

Political scientist Lucian Pye described Dependency Theory, very accurately in my view, as "demeaning and despairing."[10]

The gap between North America and Latin America is further underscored by contrasting structures of government in the United States and Canada: federalism, with states and provinces retaining substantial powers; and centralized power in Latin America. Keith Rosenn, professor of comparative law at the University of Miami, observes,

> Canada and the U.S. were colonized by Great Britain, which allowed its colonies substantial freedom in governing themselves. In both countries, federalism was perceived as a useful technique for integrating substantially autonomous colonies into a single nation. Latin America, on the other hand, was colonized by Spain and Portugal, whose heavily centralized regimes permitted their colonies little freedom to govern their own affairs. . . .

Both the U.S. and Canada, with the exception of Québec, were products of colonizations that synthesized Protestantism, Locke's social compact theory, and the natural rights of Englishmen. This North American inheritance of theology and political theory was far more conducive to the structured dispersal of power among many regional centers than Latin America's inheritance of the central-ized hierarchical organization of Roman Catholicism and Bourbon absolutism. It should not be surprising, therefore, that power in all the Latin American coun-tries is far more centralized than in Canada or the United States.[11]

Latin America's chronically poor policies and weak institutions—and what may appear as persistent poor judgment—are principally cultural phe-nomena flowing from the traditional Ibero-Catholic system of values and attitudes. Traditional Ibero-Catholic culture focuses on the present and the past at the expense of the future; it focuses on the individual and the family at the expense of the broader society; it nurtures authoritarianism; it propa-gates a flexible ethical code; it enshrines orthodoxy; and it is disdainful of work, creativity, and saving.

It is that culture that chiefly explains why, as we enter the second decade of the twenty-first century, Latin America lags so far behind the United States and Canada. And it is the very different Anglo-Protestant system of values, at-titudes, and institutions that chiefly explains the success of those two countries.

Tocqueville on Culture

Tocqueville's *Democracy in America* is filled with wisdom that extends be-yond his incisive analysis of American democracy that, for example, antici-pated some of Gunnar Myrdal's analysis a century later of the racial dilemma of the United States.[12] In a discussion of the relation between religion and progress, Tocqueville foreshadowed Max Weber's analysis of Protestantism some seventy years later: "British America was peopled by men who, after having shaken off the authority of the Pope . . . brought with them into the New World a form of Christianity which I cannot better describe than by styling it a democratic and republican religion. This contributed powerfully to the establishment of a republic and a democracy in public affairs."[13]

But few are aware that the transcendental message Tocqueville wished to communicate to his readers was the overriding importance of culture in shaping societies. He is very clear:

The customs of the Americans of the United States are, then, the peculiar cause which renders that people the only one of the American nations that is able to support a democratic government. . . . Thus the effect which the geographical position of a country may have upon the duration of democratic institutions is exaggerated in Europe. Too much importance is attributed to legislation, too little to customs. These three great causes [geography, laws, customs] serve, no doubt, to regulate and direct American democracy; but if they were to be classed in their proper order, I should say that physical circumstances are less efficient than laws, and the laws infinitely less so than the customs of the people. I am convinced that the most advantageous situation and the best possible laws cannot maintain a constitution in spite of the customs of a country; while the latter may turn to some advantage the most unfavorable positions and the worst laws. The importance of customs is a common truth to which study and experience incessantly direct our attention. It may be regarded as a central point in the range of observation, and the common termination of all my inquiries . . . if I have hitherto failed in making the reader feel the important influence of the practical experience, the habits, the opinions, in short, of the customs of the Americans upon the maintenance of their institutions, I have failed in the principal object of my work.[14]

Tocqueville is also very clear about what he means by customs, and it is essentially what I mean by culture. He says, "I here use the word customs with the meaning which the ancients attached to the word mores; for I apply it not only to manners properly so called—that is, to what might be termed the habits of the heart—but to the various notions and opinions current among men and to the mass of those ideas which constitute their character of mind. I comprise under this term, therefore, the whole moral and intellectual condition of a people."[15]

Although Tocqueville focused his attention on the United States, he was not oblivious to conditions in Latin America (in the 1830s):

If the welfare of nations depended on their being placed in a remote position, with an unbounded space of habitable territory before them, the Spaniards of South America would have no reason to complain of their fate. And although they might enjoy less prosperity than the inhabitants of the United States, their lot might still be such as to excite the envy of some nations in Europe. There are no nations upon the face of the earth, however, more miserable than those of South America. . . . The inhabitants of that fair portion of the western Hemisphere seem obstinately bent on the work of destroying one another.[16]

Catholicism and the Grondona Typology

Mariano Grondona is an Argentine of Italian extraction who had in mind Argentina, and by extension Latin America, when he devised that half of his typology that analyzes progress-resistant (low cultural capital) cultures.

For our purposes here, three of the twenty-five factors of the typology are particularly relevant.

Work

Work is central to the good life in progressive societies, a source of satisfaction and self-respect, the foundation of the structure of daily life, and an obligation of the individual to the broader society. Work is viewed as noble and indispensable in the Protestant, Jewish, and Confucian ethics; in many Third World cultures, including the Ibero-Catholic, work is viewed as a necessary evil, and real satisfaction and pleasure are attainable only outside the workplace. Attitudes about work are, of course, intimately linked to achievement and entrepreneurship, on which economic development importantly depends.

Education

Education is the key to progress in dynamic societies. In contrast to traditional Catholicism, which interposed the priest as the interpreter of God's scripture to the faithful, both Protestantism and Judaism have stressed the importance of literacy so that each follower can read the Bible. And education is also central to Confucianism; witness the high level of Japan's literacy relative to Western Europe in the nineteenth century. In traditional societies, education is seen as an extra by the masses, an entitlement of the elites. Substantial illiteracy still exists in Latin America, and in several Latin American countries, half or more of high-school-age children do not attend secondary school.

Ethics

The rigor of the ethical code influences political and economic performance. Weber believed that the Roman Catholic emphasis on the afterlife, and, particularly, what he perceived as a more flexible ethical system, put Catholics at a disadvantage to Protestants in this life. "The God of Calvinism demanded of his believers not single good works, but a life of good works combined into a unified system. There was no room for the very human Catholic cycle of sin, repentance, atonement, release, followed by renewed sin."[17]

An anecdote will help make the point. The limits culture places on institutions, in this case legal institutions, is apparent from a conversation Keith Rosenn had with an Argentine lawyer. Since the nineteenth century, the Argentine Constitution has authorized trial by jury and the use of oral testimony by witnesses. But no jury trial has ever taken place. Instead, a cumbersome system of written depositions has prevailed (as has been the case throughout Latin America) with the verdicts the responsibility of judges.

Rosenn asked the Argentine lawyer why this was so. The latter replied, "We are a Catholic country, and everybody knows that it would be easy for a witness to lie, confess to a priest a few days later, and be absolved."[18]

The Challenge of Evangelical and Pentecostal Protestantism

David Martin is a sociologist and theologian who has focused his attention in recent years on the rise of Evangelical and Pentecostal Protestantism, particularly in Africa and Latin America. He is also an ordained Anglican priest. Evangelicalism and Pentecostalism are linked—"two phases of a faith based on change of heart and thoroughgoing revision of life."[19] The principal distinction, often blurred, is the greater emotionalism of Pentecostalism, which may express itself in unintelligible utterances ("the gift of tongues") and faith healing.

Martin estimates the global number of the two branches at about 500 million, with about 200 million in Africa, 100 million in Asia, 100 million in North America, and 50 million in Latin America. But the numbers are growing in Latin America. Perhaps as many as half of all Guatemalans are now Evangelical or Pentecostal, and the Brazilians who have converted (see below) already constitute a political force in that country.

At least in Latin America, Evangelical and Pentecostal Protestantism are seen by the poor, including many indigenous peoples, as avenues to family stability and upward mobility via the Weberian virtues symbolized by Benjamin Franklin. Martin observes, "In discussing how these virtues work out in practice, one needs to remember that these men of God are mostly women. Pentecostalism is a movement of women determined with God's help to defend home and family against machismo and the seductions of the street and the weekend. They represent female nurture and order over male 'nature' and disorder."[20]

These Protestant churches also provide a social structure that eases the adaptation from life in small villages to life in the intimidating chaos of big cities. Martin believes that the values engendered by Evangelicalism and Pentecostalism will lead to better lives for the converts and that the demonstration effect will sustain the momentum of conversion. Anecdotal evidence, for example, the image of Protestant honesty and reliability held by other Latin Americans, points in the same direction.

The 2010 census in Brazil supplies an important indicator (the 2000 census showed 26 million Brazilian Protestants of the total 170 million—about 15 percent). David Martin related the dramatic news in an as yet unpublished column:

BRAZIL A PROTESTANT COUNTRY BY 2020?

The startling news that the 2010 Census shows a doubling of the Protestant population in Brazil over a decade from 15 to 30 percent suggests that Brazil could become a predominantly Protestant country by the next census, in 2020. In the middle of the twentieth century, Protestants accounted for about one percent of Brazil's population.

This startling news is part of a wider global trend. Two thirds of the Protestants in Brazil are Pentecostal, and a very large proportion of the Protestant surge globally belongs to one of innumerable Pentecostal churches.

Brazil is a country of almost two hundred million people that was for centuries almost entirely Catholic. It is now wide open to religious pluralism and competition. There is reason to believe that Brazil's economic development will benefit from an injection of the Protestant work ethic. Insofar as it rejects alcohol, tobacco, and the weekend spree and weakens the hold of macho attitudes, Protestantism is also bound to strengthen family bonds.

Politically, Protestants have moved away from traditional acceptance of the status quo to participation; so that numerous Evangelical/Pentecostal candidates have been successful in national elections.

Needed: A Second Reformation

The continuing inroads being made by Evangelical/Pentecostal Protestantism on its heretofore substantial monopoly are one telling indicator of grave problems for the Catholic Church in Latin America. But the conversions are not the only unsettling consideration for the Church. Latin America's economic development, in terms of growth but particularly with respect to equity, has been generally disappointing. Finally, Latin America has not escaped the pandemic of sexual abuse by priests and nuns.

Economic Development

In an essay that appears in *Developing Cultures: Essays on Cultural Change*, Michael Novak, the prominent and prolific lay Catholic scholar, notes that there are now more than a billion Catholics around the world, with the largest contingent in Latin America. Moreover, the Church is growing, particularly in Africa, and he expects that the number of Catholics will increase to almost 1.5 billion by 2025.

Novak observes that the Church came late to the support and promotion of democracy, in part because political liberalization in Europe in the nineteenth and twentieth centuries was often accompanied by secularization and anticlericalism. But in the second half of the twentieth century, the

Church dropped its support of authoritarian governments in favor of a pro-democratic stance that contributed to the wave of democratization in Latin America in the last decades of the twentieth century.

In this trend toward democratization, one hears echoes of an observation by Tocqueville:

> I think that the Catholic religion has erroneously been regarded as the natural enemy of democracy. Among the various sects of Christians, Catholicism seems to me, on the contrary, to be one of the most favorable to equality of condition among men. In the Catholic Church, the religious community is composed of only two elements: the priest and the people. The priest alone rises above the rank of his flock, and all below him are equal . . . no sooner is the priesthood entirely separated from the government, as is the case in the United States, than it is found that no class of men is more naturally disposed than the Catholics to transfer the doctrine of the equality of condition into the political world.[21]

The changed posture of the Church with respect to democracy is particularly apparent in the case of Spain. The Vatican sent a congratulatory message to Francisco Franco on his victory over the republicans in 1939. But a quarter century later, Cardinal Vicente Enrique y Tarancón played a key role in Spain's transition to democracy after Franco's death.

In his book *The Catholic Ethic and the Spirit of Capitalism*, Novak[22] refers to a minority Catholic crosscurrent favorable to free-market economics. He strongly advocates reconsideration by the Church of its ambivalence with respect to capitalism.

In most of the dimensions of progress, Protestant countries have outperformed Catholic countries:

- *Democracy*: Catholic countries have generally been slower to consolidate democratic institutions than Protestant countries, and democracy remains fragile in Latin America.
- *Prosperity*: Catholic countries, particularly those in Latin America, lag economically. The first Catholic country to appear on the World Economic Forum's 2010–2011 Competitiveness Index is highly secularized France, ranked at fifteenth, preceded by ten Protestant and four Confucian countries. Rapid economic development in Italy, Spain, Ireland, and Québec has been accompanied by processes of secularization that have led to labeling these societies "post-Catholic." An article in *The Economist* a few years ago announced, "It used to be spoken of as Catholic Spain. Not these days."[23] Subsequently, Marlise Simons noted

in the *New York Times* that "of Spain's 43 million people, only one in five consider themselves practicing Catholics."[24]

- *Income distribution*: Some of the most inequitable income distribution in the world is found in Latin America. In 2004, the richest 10 percent in Brazil accounted for 45 percent of income, the poorest 10 percent for only 0.9 percent. The data for Chile, Latin America's fastest developing economy, were 45 percent for the top 10 percent, 1.2 for the bottom 10 percent. By comparison, the richest 10 percent in the United States—the most inequitable of the advanced democracies—accounted for 29.9 percent of income in the 2000 census, the poorest 10 percent for 1.9 percent. Denmark is the world champion of income equitability: the bottom 10 percent of Danes receives 2.6 percent, the top 10 percent received 22.4 percent.[25]

    The highly inequitable income distribution found in Latin America is profoundly ironic: the Catholic Church has long championed the poor—remember Matthew's judgment that "it is easier for a camel to go through the eye of a needle than for a rich man to enter into the kingdom of God." The irony is compounded by Calvinist Protestantism's preference for the rich: *the poor are proportionately fewer and less poor in Protestant countries than in Catholic countries.*

- *Trust*: Trust is significantly lower in Catholic societies than in Protestant ones.

- *Corruption*: Corruption is significantly higher in Catholic societies than in Protestant ones.

Michael Novak signals a key reform goal for Catholicism: a wholehearted commitment to market economics, coupled, of course, with democratic politics. Catholic doctrinal ambivalence about economics may be in part responsible for Latin America's dalliance with socialism/statism, the related chimera of dependency theory, and Marxist-Leninist–inspired Liberation Theology. Some Church leaders have advocated "Third Way" solutions to poverty and social injustice, presumably with the Nordic countries in mind. But the advanced Nordic welfare programs have been made possible by their essentially capitalist economies, which have produced high levels of prosperity, so the Third Way is another chimera.

Another key reform goal concerns ethical standards in Catholic countries. I believe that there is truth in Weber's contrast of "a life of good deeds" Protestantism with the "very human" Catholic cycle of sin/confession/absolution/renewed sin. The more flexible Catholic ethical code contributes to shorter radiuses of identification, lower levels of trust, and higher levels of corruption in Catholic countries. (A particularly egregious example of the latter is Nicaragua's Cardinal Miguel Obando y Bravo, who became embroiled in the corruption case of former President Miguel Alemán Valdés—on Alemán's side.)

The flexible ethical code probably also contributes to high levels of crime, exemplified by the disconcertingly common incidence of kidnappings in Latin America today. UNDP data on homicides show ten Latin American countries having among the twenty highest homicide rates in the world in the period 2000–2004. Colombia was at the bottom of the 121-country listing.[26]

To be sure, the Church's influence, at least in Europe and Latin America, is not what it once had been. The proportion of practicing Catholics has declined precipitously—a similar trend has occurred in the mainline Protestant denominations—and many tens of millions of Latin American Catholics have converted to Protestantism. But the Church retains substantial influence, and through reform of its economic doctrine and a more aggressive stance on issues of morality and ethics, it could make a critical contribution to modifications in traditional values that would enhance the chances for greater progress in Catholic countries. Reform could also arrest and possibly even reverse the drift away from Catholicism in Latin America.

A Relevant Anecdote

An Irish-Catholic friend, born and raised in New England and quite successful in his business, posed the following question upon reading the manuscript for this book:

> I wonder how my own development survived an extremely traditional Catholic upbringing now anathema to me: Authoritarian, afterlife-oriented, hostile to upward mobility, unreceptive to new ideas, and the rest.

To which I replied,

> How about the same way as my two sons-in-law, Jeff Grady and John Donnelly, survived—by growing up in an Anglo-Protestant culture.

To which he replied,

> Touché. An Anglo-Protestant wife didn't hurt either.

Urgently Needed: An End to Celibacy

The Catholic Church's sex scandal has become pandemic, as inevitably it would. Why? Because the Church's celibacy policy flies in the face of human nature and human needs. Moreover, there is no solid scripturally based reason for celibacy—the policy took hold over the years importantly because of the inheritance problems posed by the children of popes, bishops, and lesser priests.

As late as the mid-fifteenth century, Pope Felix V fathered and recognized a child. Eleven popes during the period from the fourth through the eleventh centuries were sons of popes or other clergy. During the fifteenth and sixteenth centuries, six popes fathered illegitimate children. But this problem within the church did not end then.

I recently met a woman who had worked for a Catholic educational institution for several years. She judged that about one-third of the priests were homosexuals and had consensual gay relationships; one-third were heterosexual and had consensual relationships with women; and the final third lived, ostensibly at least, celibate lives. I said that I assumed that the third category masturbated, to which she replied, "Of course."

I must state the obvious: this is a very narrow sample for reaching broad conclusions. But whether the proportions are equally one-third, or 20-40-40 or 40-20-40 percent—or any other numbers that leave a measurable percentage in each of the three groups—the overarching conclusion still holds: the celibacy policy flies in the face of human nature and human needs.

Surely a disproportionate number of homosexuals are drawn to the priestly vocation, importantly because of its maleness. And clearly the abuse of boys is more the result of homosexuality than of pedophilia. If the latter were the case, then girls and boys would, at the least, be equally victimized. Moreover, the vast majority of victims have been adolescents, not prepubescent children.

The pandemic first came to light in 2002 in the United States, in the Boston archdiocese. Cardinal Bernard Law bore the brunt of the intense criticism, which ultimately led to his reassignment to the Vatican. I remember thinking at the time how the priestly culture must have sympathized with the perpetrators. After all, virtually *all* had to grapple with sexual pressures and find release in some form or another.

It is noteworthy that the pandemic had surfaced only in the advanced democracies until recent years. But those of us who have lived in the Third World are aware that it is rife, for example, in Latin America, where many priests are widely believed to have live-in women. In Latin America, one hears less of homosexual activity among priests, perhaps because having a live-in woman is relatively common. Recently, and particularly in Argentina, Brazil, and Chile, numerous cases have made the headlines.[27]

On June 5, 2012, the *New York Times* printed the following note in its "World Briefing" section:

Paraguay: President Acknowledges Fathering Second Child as Bishop

By REUTERS

President Fernando Lugo, left, . . . admitted Tuesday to having fathered a second child when he was a Roman Catholic bishop, in an apparent effort to limit damage from the latest paternity scandal. Mr. Lugo, 61, confessed in 2008 to having fathered a child before he quit the church to enter politics. The second case came to light when a 42-year-old nurse told a newspaper that Mr. Lugo was the father of her youngest child, a 10-year-old boy. Mr. Lugo will not seek re-election next year because of term limits.[28]

Nuns: Victims and Victimizers

Very little attention has been paid to the Catholic female clergy—the nuns. However, it is clear that they have frequently been used—or abused—sexually by priests. Nuns have also engaged in abuse:

Rape and sexual molestation were "endemic" in Irish Catholic church-run industrial schools and orphanages, a report revealed today [May 20, 2009]. The nine-year investigation found that Catholic priests and nuns for decades terrorized thousands of boys and girls in the Irish Republic, while government inspectors failed to stop the chronic beatings, rape, and humiliation.[29]

The Catholic Church in Kerala, India, which has barely recovered from the Sister Abhaya murder case, allegedly murdered by two priests and a nun, now finds itself in another controversy. Fifty-two-year-old Sister Jesme, a former nun from Kerala, has blown the whistle on the alleged sexual abuse that nuns have to face in convents. Sister Jesme has written a book that talks about the sexual harassment that she faced in the convent at the hands of both priests and nuns.[30]

So, nuns are, after all, human beings like the rest of us, with desires and needs. This assertion gathers strength from the Vatican's scolding of Sister Margaret A. Farley, a past president of the Catholic Theological Society of America and an award-winning scholar who teaches at the Yale Divinity School. Sister Farley wrote the book, *Just Love: A Framework for Christian Sexual Ethics*, "that attempted to present a theological rationale for same-sex relationships, masturbation and remarriage after divorce."[31]

The aura of power and respectability that attaches to priests and nuns leaves them largely invulnerable to criticism, not to mention legal action, in many poor countries. It is unlikely that any poor, unconnected Catholic would seek legal remedy for clergy sexual abuse. And even if someone did summon the courage to report abuse to the authorities, the judicial systems are so weak and the influence of the Church so strong in many and perhaps most Third World predominantly Catholic countries that the plaintiff would run the risk of being laughed out of court.

Within the toll of victims of the Vatican celibacy policy, one must also count those priests and nuns who have left their orders, many of whom have subsequently married. In my years with USAID in Latin America, I encountered several priests who left the priesthood to marry and who continued their work in development as lay professionals.

Finally, in the wake of the pandemic, Catholicism is suffering from a massive loss of interest by young men who might otherwise have become priests. The *New York Times* of June 13, 2012, presented an article titled "For One New Priest, a Lonely Distinction," citing the class of 2012 in New York Diocese consisted of only the Rev. Patric D'Arcy.[32]

I have to conclude that the policy of celibacy—and priestly maleness—has been a costly, if predictable, failure. It should be rescinded.

CHAPTER 9

~

Latino Immigration
into the United States

The problem in which the current immigration is suffused is, at heart, one of numbers; for when the numbers begin to favor not only the maintenance and replenishment of the immigrants' source culture, but also its overall growth, and in particular growth so large that the numbers not only impede assimilation but go beyond to pose a challenge to the traditional culture of the American nation, then there is a great deal about which to be concerned.

—Richard Estrada, late columnist for the *Dallas Morning News*, letter to L. Harrison, January 13, 1991

President Barack Obama has encouraged Americans to start laying a new foundation for the country—on a number of fronts. He has stressed that we'll need to have the courage to make some hard choices. One of those hard choices is how to handle immigration. The United States must get serious about the tide of legal and illegal immigrants, above all from Latin America.

I don't think I am overstating it when I say that the nonacculturation of Latinos is now the chief social problem of our country—and that it will become the chief *national* problem before too many more years. Samuel Huntington was on the mark once again in his final book, *Who Are We? The Challenges to America's National Identity*, in which he points directly at immigration from Latin America as the principal threat to our unity as a nation

147

because Latin America's Ibero-Catholic value system is incompatible with the Anglo-Protestant system that is our bedrock.

Moreover, Huntington was gravely concerned by the evidence that Latinos were not "melting"—and by the related phenomenon of the Spanish-language challenging English, as we appear to be becoming, willy-nilly, a bilingual country, with all the divisiveness that phenomenon implies.

Thus, it's not just a short-run issue of immigrants competing with citizens for jobs, with unemployment currently near 8 percent, or the number of uninsured straining the quality of health care. Heavy immigration from Latin America threatens our cohesiveness as a nation.

In his new book *Coming Apart: The State of White America*,[1] Charles Murray presents a well-documented case that America is coming apart at the seams—seams of class, not ethnicity. My concerns are focused on ethnicity, specifically Latino ethnicity. The political realities of the rapidly growing Latino population are such that President Obama may be the last president who can avert the permanent, vast underclass implied by a Census Bureau projection that predicts Latinos will constitute almost *one-third* of our population by 2050[2]—and which virtually ensures the United States will become a bilingual country.

Sound like the concerns of a right-wing "xenophobe" or "nativist"? Of course, I'm not. I'm a lifelong Democrat; an early and avid supporter of President Obama; the grandson of Eastern European Jewish immigrants—and a member, along with several other Democrats, of the advisory boards of the Federation for American Immigration Reform (FAIR) and Pro English.

Moreover, although I am gravely concerned about the flood of immigrants from Mexico, and Latin America more generally, and mindful of the requirement for periodic assessments of need, I *welcome* immigrants from China, Korea, Japan, Vietnam, and India, whose swift acculturation and hugely disproportionate contribution to our progress contrasts strikingly with that of Latino immigrants. The Asians' rapid upward mobility is evidenced by their numbers at our most prestigious universities. Comprising about 5 percent of the US population, Asians constitute 41 percent of undergraduates at the University of California at Berkeley, 27 percent at MIT, 24 percent at Stanford, and 18 percent at Harvard.

Comparable numbers for Latinos are depressing: At 16 percent of the total population, and constituting three times the Asian population, Latinos account for a fraction of the Asian numbers at these universities (e.g., 7 percent of MIT students).

Latinos: The OECD Program for International Student Assessment

The Organisation for Economic Co-operation and Development (OECD) comprises thirty-four countries: the members of the European Union; the United States, Canada, Australia, and New Zealand; Japan and South Korea; Israel; and Chile, Mexico, Slovenia, and Turkey. The OECD is the home of the Program for International Student Assessment (PISA), which assesses mathematical literacy, scientific literacy, reading literacy, and problem solving for students in its member countries every three years starting in 2000.

The results of the 2009 PISA ranked the United States twenty-fifth in math and twenty-first in science, precipitating a lot of handwringing on the part of the media, government officials, and educators. However, analysis of the 2006 PISA results for science disaggregated by white and Asian, Hispanic, and black students presents a strikingly different picture.[3]

US white and Asian students ranked *seventh*, with 523 points (the OECD average was 500 points), after Finland, Canada, Japan, New Zealand, Australia, and the Netherlands. But the US white and Asian students were *ahead* of South Korea, Germany, the United Kingdom, and several other high-income countries including Switzerland, Austria, Belgium, and the other four Nordic countries (excluding Finland).

However, US black students were at the bottom of the list, after Greece, Turkey, and Mexico, and the increasingly numerous US Hispanic students were fourth from the bottom, behind Greece. When the three American groups were combined, the national total fell to 489 points—twenty-first of thirty.

Traditional Concerns of the Democratic Party

Concerns about the impact of immigration on low-income Americans preoccupied the distinguished Democrat Barbara Jordan when she chaired the congressionally mandated US Commission on Immigration Reform during the 1990s. The principal beneficiaries of our current immigration policy are affluent Americans who hire immigrants at substandard wages for low-end work.

Harvard economist George Borjas has estimated that US workers lose $190 billion annually in depressed wages caused by the constant flooding of the labor market at the low-wage end. I might add that remittances to Mexico in 2010 approximated $21 billion, and to Latin America about $59 billion.

The health care costs of the illegal workforce are especially burdensome and are subsidized by taxpayers. To claim Medicaid, you must be legal, but as the Health and Human Services inspector general found, forty-seven states allow self-declaration of status for Medicaid. Many hospitals and clinics are going broke treating the constant stream of uninsured, many of whom are the estimated 12 million to 15 million illegal immigrants, a large majority of whom are from Latin America, the large majority of those from Mexico. This translates into reduced services, particularly for lower-income citizens.

The Burgeoning Latino Population—and Its System of Values
The Pew Hispanic Center reports,

> The 2010 Census counted 50.5 million Hispanics in the United States, making up 16.3% of the total population. The nation's Hispanic population, which was 35.3 million in 2000, grew 46.3% over the decade, and even more sharply in many Southeastern states. Overall, growth in the Hispanic population accounted for most of the nation's growth—56%—from 2000 to 2010. Among children ages 17 and younger, there were 17 million Latinos, representing 23% of this age group, up from 17% in 2000.[4]

I should point out that the Latino population is probably greater, and possibly substantially greater, reflecting the reluctance illegal immigrants must feel about getting involved in the official census.

Population growth is the principal threat to the environment via natural resource use, sprawl, and pollution. And population growth is fueled chiefly by immigration. Consider what this, combined with worrisome evidence that Latinos are not melting into our cultural mainstream, means for the United States. Latinos have contributed some positive cultural attributes, such as multigenerational family bonds, to US society. But the same traditional values that lie behind Latin America's difficulties in achieving democratic stability, social justice, and prosperity are being substantially perpetuated among Hispanic Americans.

Several prominent Latin Americans have concluded that traditional values are at the root of the region's development problems, among them Peruvian 2010 Nobelist in literature Mario Vargas Llosa; Mexican Nobelist author Octavio Paz; Teodoro Moscoso, architect of Puerto Rico's successful Operation Bootstrap; Ecuador's former president Osvaldo Hurtado; and Costa Rican ex-president Oscar Arias, Nobel Peace Prize Laureate in 1987. Vargas Llosa has this to say:

The culture within which we live and act today in Latin America is neither liberal nor is it altogether democratic. We have democratic governments, but our institutions, our reflexes and our *mentalidades* are very far from being democratic. They remain populist and oligarchic, or absolutist, collectivist, or dogmatic, flawed by social and racial prejudices, immensely intolerant with respect to political adversaries, and devoted to the worst monopoly of all, that of the truth.[5]

Octavio Paz answers the question "What lies behind the contrasting experiences of Mexico and the United States (and Canada, the third of the NAFTA partners) with respect to broad-based democratic development?"

One [society], English speaking, is the daughter of the tradition that has founded the modern world: the Reformation, with its social and political consequences, capitalism and democracy. The other, Spanish and Portuguese speaking, is the daughter of the universal Catholic monarchy and the Counter-Reformation.[6]

In 1966, Teodoro Moscoso, architect of Puerto Rico's Operation Bootstrap and the first US coordinator of the Alliance for Progress—and at the outset highly optimistic about the prospects of the Alliance—wrote,

The Latin American case is so complex, so difficult to solve, and so fraught with human and global danger and distress that the use of the word "anguish" is not an exaggeration. The longer I live, the more I believe that, just as no human being can save another who does not have the will to save himself, no country can save others no matter how good its intentions or how hard it tries.[7]

Moscoso, who had been my boss once-removed when I started to work in the Latin American Bureau of USAID in 1962, had a sign on the wall in his office on the sixth floor of the State Department that read, "PLEASE BE BRIEF. WE ARE TWENTY YEARS LATE!"

Osvaldo Hurtado's article, "Know Thyself: Latin America in the Mirror of Culture," appeared in the January–February 2010 issue of *The American Interest*. In it, he cites the writings of the Venezuelan author Carlos Rangel:

Latin Americans now largely accept the idea that our position of inferiority *vis-à-vis* the United States is due . . . to that country's exploitation of our subcontinent through the mechanisms of imperialism and dependency. Thus we have fallen prey to the most debilitating and pernicious of several myths through which we have tried to explain our destiny. This myth is debilitating because it attributes all that is wrong in Latin America to external factors. . . . A sincere, rational, scientific examination of North American influence on Latin

America's destiny would have to . . . keep open the possibility that the United States' overall contribution may have been positive.[8]

Hurtado goes on to say, "Rangel concluded that at the root of Latin America's problems is neither dependency nor exploitation, but a set of cultural values that impede the consolidation of democratic institutions, the advance of social justice and the achievement of economic development. I am convinced that he was and remains correct, and that cultural change is indispensable to the region's long-term, sustainable progress."

In its January–February 2011 issue, *Foreign Affairs* published as its lead article an essay by Costa Rican ex-president Oscar Arias titled, "Culture Matters: The Real Obstacles to Latin American Development." Arias, who had won the Nobel Peace Prize in 1987 for his efforts at promoting peace in Central America, wrote,

> Instead of a culture of improvement, [Latin Americans] have promoted a culture of preservation of the status quo. Constant, patient reform—the only kind of reform compatible with democratic stability—is unsatisfying; the region accepts what exists, while occasionally pining for dramatic revolutions that promise abundant treasures only one insurrection away.

Ernesto Caravantes, whose parents immigrated to the United States from Mexico, had this to say in the preface to his 2010 book *From Melting Pot to Witch's Cauldron: How Multiculturalism Failed America*:

> I was at one of my book signings some time ago when a woman raised her hand to speak. She was a Mexican immigrant, and she told me that she had a 13-year-old son, whom she is raising here in southern California. In other words, her son is an American citizen by virtue of his birth. She said she makes it a point to tell her son of all the virtues and wonderful aspects of Mexico. She wanted her son to be proud of his Mexican heritage.
>
> What she said gave me pause. Presumably, this woman and her husband had immigrated to the United States in search of a better life for their family. Mexico had failed them on multiple levels. The United States was seen as the country most able to offer educational and occupational opportunities. Why, then, would they have left a failed country to come to the United States to raise their children and then exalt Mexico, a country which they were only too willing to leave behind? . . .
>
> This stands in stark distinction to the European immigrants who flocked to this country in the 19th century. Upon landing on the eastern seashores, they cut all ties with their mother country, and immediately began to forge for them-

selves an American identity. They did not force feed their children the language of the mother country, be it Danish, Norwegian, or Dutch. Yes, perhaps they did lose a part of their cultural identity, yet that loss was quickly replaced by a new forward-reaching identity: an American identity. Their quick adoption of an American identity, combined with industriousness and hard work inspired by their Protestantism, quickly allowed them to begin prospering and building metropolises that have become so iconic in the American landscape.[9]

Samuel Huntington captured the cultural implications for immigration from Latin America into the United States when he wrote, in his last book, *Who Are We?*, "Would America be the America it is today if it had been settled not by British Protestants but by French, Spanish, or Portuguese Catholics? The answer is no. It would not be America; it would be Québec, Mexico, or Brazil."[10]

Low Latino Priority for Education

Latin America's cultural problem is apparent in the persistent Latino high school dropout rate—30 percent in California, according to a recent study[11]—and the high incidence of teenage pregnancy, single mothers, and crime. The perpetuation of Latino culture is facilitated by the Spanish language's growing challenge to English as our national language. It makes it easier for Latinos to avoid the melting pot and for education to remain a low priority, as it is in Latin America—a problem highlighted in recent books by former New York City deputy mayor Herman Badillo, a Puerto Rican, and Mexican Americans Lionel Sosa and Ernesto Caravantes.

In his 2006 book, *One Nation, One Standard: An Ex-Liberal on How Hispanics Can Succeed Just Like Other Immigrant Groups*, Badillo stresses "The distressingly low level of educational achievement among Latin Americans in their own countries."[12] See Table 9.1, which outlines these data.

Based on a broad survey, the Pew Hispanic Center produced data for 2007 that showed that 50.6 percent of foreign-born age twenty-five and older Latino immigrants had dropped out of school before completing high school; 23.5 percent of Latinos born in the United States had dropped out. This compares with 19.8 percent of African Americans and 10.5 percent of white Americans.[13] The *Washington Post* reports, "Second-generation Hispanics have the highest high school dropout rate—one in seven—of any U.S.-born racial or ethnic group and the highest teen pregnancy rate. These Hispanics also receive far fewer college degrees and make significantly less money than non-Hispanic whites and other second-generation immigrants."[14]

Table 9.1. Education Achievement: Latin America and the United States

Years of Country Completed	"Compulsory" Education (years)	Average Education (years)
Argentina	9	8.8
Bolivia	8	5.6
Brazil	8	4.9
Chile	12	10.1
Colombia	10	11.0[1]
Costa Rica	10	6.0
Ecuador	10	6.4
El Salvador	9	5.2
Guatemala	11	3.5
Haiti	6	2.8
Mexico	10	7.2
Nicaragua	6	4.6
Peru	11	8.9
Uruguay	10	7.6
Venezuela	7	6.6
United States	12	12.0[2]

1. I suspect an error here: the 2010 UNDP human development report indicates that 30 percent of Colombian high school age students do not graduate.
2. Herman Badillo, *One Nation, One Standard: An Ex-Liberal on How Hispanics Can Succeed Just Like Other Immigrant Groups* (New York: Sentinel, Penguin Group, 2006), pp. 40–41.
Source: Herman Badillo, *One Nation, One Standard: An Ex-Liberal on How Hispanics Can Succeed Just Like Other Immigrant Groups* (New York: Penguin Group, 2006), pp. 40–41.

A University of California, San Francisco, study in 2002 concluded that improvement over the generations is spotty:

Just over half (56%) of 16–24 year old foreign-born Latinos are in school or have finished high school; this figure increases sharply to 80% for second generation youth and to 84% for third generation Latino youth. The generational pattern of college completion among adults, however, is not linear. About one in ten (9%) foreign-born Latino adults (ages 25–44) has a college degree, increasing to 18% of second-generation Latinos. For third generation Latino adults, however, this figure falls to 11%. . . .

Latino high school graduates are less likely to go to college than non-Latino white or African American graduates. Almost half (46%) of non-Latino whites and two-fifths (39%) of African Africans who graduated from high school attend college. In comparison, one-third (33%) of Latino high school graduates go on to college. One-fifth (19%) of Latino young adults, ages 18–24, are enrolled in college, as opposed to 30% of African Americans and four in ten (39%) non-Latino whites.[15]

The troublingly low level of educational achievement of Latinos brings with it several other problems:

High teenage birth rate: "Latinas have the highest teen birth rate of all major racial/ethnic groups in the U.S., resulting in an increasing number of young Latina mothers and children who are especially vulnerable to poverty, lack of health care, and welfare dependence. . . . Latinas had the highest teen birth rate of all major racial/ethnic groups in the United States, 83 births per 1,000 teenage women aged 15–19 in 2002, a rate nearly twice as high as the national rate of 43. Birth rates were highest for Latinas of Mexican descent (94.5), followed by those of Puerto Rican descent (61.4)."[16]

High incarceration levels: "[A] study, conducted by the Pew Center on the States, found that among Latino men, one in every 36 is incarcerated. One in every 15 black men is incarcerated . . . compared to one in every 106 white men."[17]

Welfare dependency: Department of Health and Human Services data for 2005 show 6.7 percent of whites, 24.9 percent of African Americans, and 14.6 percent of Latinos who receive some sort of welfare assistance.[18]

The contrast between Latinos and African Americans must be kept in a perspective that magnifies the Latino problem: In the 2000 census, Latinos numbered 35.3 million, or 12.5 percent of a total population of 281.4 million; African Americans numbered 34.7 million, or 12.3 percent. In the 2010 census, Latinos numbered 50.5 million, an increase of 16 million that raised their share to 16.3 percent, while African Americans grew only by 4.3 million, with a share of 12.6 percent. Moreover, the latest Census Bureau projections for 2050 would bring the Latino segment of the population to 132.8 million, or 30 percent of the total, compared to an African American segment of 65.7 million, *one-half the size of a Latino segment to which it was equal in the 2000 census.*[19]

A Bilingual United States

We are becoming, willy-nilly, a bilingual country; witness the experience of calling a business and hearing, "If you wish to speak in English, press one; *si quiere hablar en Español, oprima el botón número dos.*" Never in our history has an immigrant language acquired the power to compete with English anywhere in the nation. As Samuel Huntington points out in *Who Are We?*,

The continuing growth of Hispanic numbers and influence has led some Hispanic advocates to set forth two goals. The first is to prevent the assimilation of Hispanics into America's Anglo-Protestant society and culture, and instead create a large, autonomous, permanent, Spanish-speaking, social and cultural

Hispanic community on American soil. Advocates, such as William Flores and Rina Benmayor, reject the idea of a "single national community," attack "cultural homogenization," and castigate the effort to promote the use of English as a manifestation of "xenophobia and cultural arrogance" . . .

The second goal of these Hispanic advocates follows from the first. It is to transform America as a whole into a bilingual, bicultural society. America should no longer have the core Anglo-Protestant culture plus the ethnic subcultures that it has had for three centuries. It should have two cultures, Hispanic and Anglo, and, most explicitly, two languages, Spanish and English. A choice must be made "about the future of America," the Duke professor Ariel Dorfman declares: "Will this country speak two languages or merely one?" And his answer, of course, is that it should speak two.[20]

Huntington goes on to point out that Latinos in large metropolitan areas like Los Angeles, New York, Miami, and Chicago can live their lives substantially in a Spanish-speaking environment. Heretofore *all* immigrant groups made sure that their US-born offspring were native speakers of English, which usually resulted in the native language being substantially lost to the third generation.

Now, a Spanish-language television network, Univisión, competes with the major US networks. My friend since college days and colleague Reese Schonfeld, the first president of CNN and the media person on the Cultural Change Institute's executive committee, periodically brings to my attention such information as the following:

ADULTS ARE BEATING A PATH TO UNIVISIÓN, AND WE'RE BEATING THE OTHER NETWORKS.

- We've beaten NBC 64 out of 112 nights with adults 18–49 in primetime . . .
- We deliver more bilingual Hispanics 18–49 than *American Idol, Dancing with the Stars* or *Modern Family.*
- 18 of the top 25 shows with bilingual Hispanics are on Univisión.

The game has changed. If you want to win with the Hispanic consumer, click here.[21]

I am, I guess, a fairly good example of the heretofore typical language acculturation pattern of immigrant groups in the United States. My Yiddish-speaking grandparents learned English as adults; both of my parents spoke Yiddish but were native speakers of English—and they often spoke Yiddish so that my brother and I wouldn't understand what they were saying. The result is, sadly, that I know some Yiddish words and expressions but can't understand it or speak it. (I say "sadly" because Yiddish is a dying language, even though it has contributed many words to modern American English, e.g., bagel, lox, nosh, schlep, schmooze, tush.)

Huntington cites Senator S. I. Hayakawa of Hawaii on Spanish's unique supporters:

> Why is it that no Filipinos, no Koreans object to making English the official language? No Japanese have done so. And certainly not the Vietnamese, who are so damn happy to be here. They're learning English as fast as they can and winning spelling bees all across the country. But the Hispanics alone have maintained there is a problem. There [has been] considerable movement to make Spanish the second official language.[22]

One need only look at other bilingual countries (e.g., Canada, Belgium) to sense what divisiveness may be in store for the United States, above all as the Latino component of our population soars toward one-third. But in those two cases, the competing languages are spoken by high cultural capital cultures: English and French in Canada, Flemish (Dutch) and French in Belgium.[23] In the new American bilingualism, one culture is progress prone, the other progress resistant.

Language and Culture

Language is the conduit of culture. Consider that there is no word in Spanish for "compromise" ("*compromiso*" means "commitment") nor for "accountability," a problem that is compounded by a passive reflexive verb structure that converts "I dropped (broke, forgot) something" into "it got dropped" ("broken," "forgotten").

As the USAID mission director during the first two years of the Sandinista regime in Nicaragua, I had difficulty communicating "dissent" to a government minister at a crucial moment in our efforts to convince the US Congress to approve a special appropriation for Nicaragua. The minister was the scion of an upper-class Nicaraguan family who had studied at a US university. Yet he was buffaloed by the concept of dissent as a legitimate, even indispensable, democratic concept. After an extended effort on my part to explain, his face brightened, and he exclaimed, "Now I understand what you are talking about—civil disobedience!"

I was later told by a bilingual, bicultural Nicaraguan educator that when I used the word "dissent," what my Nicaraguan colleague understood was "heresy." "We are, after all, children of the Inquisition," he added.

In his letter to me in 1991, Mexican American columnist Richard Estrada addressed the consequences of bilingualism: Estrada believes that, in the long run, the language problem in the southwest may prove to be greater than in the case of Québec:

[F]or Québec . . . does not lie contiguous to France. . . . The Southwest, on the other hand, shares a 2000-mile long border with a Spanish-speaking country of at least 85 million people [in 1990; 112 million in 2010], hundreds of thousands of whom yearly move to the US, or who reside with one foot in one country the other in the other. The twin factors of geographic contiguity and rate of immigration must give pause. No one can witness the growth of Spanish-language media in this country and fail to believe that things are headed in the direction of a parallel culture. And that is the point: bilingualism has generally militated against assimilation. It has promoted a parallel culture instead of a subordinate one.[24]

Huntington poses the problem in even stronger terms, with which I agree:

Despite the opposition of large majorities of Americans, Spanish is joining the language of Washington, Jefferson, Lincoln, Roosevelts, and Kennedys as the language of America. If this trend continues, the cultural division between Hispanics and Anglos will replace the racial division between blacks and whites as the most serious cleavage in American society. A bifurcated America with two languages and two cultures will be fundamentally different from the America with one language and one core Anglo-Protestant culture that has existed for over three centuries.[25]

Jaime "Jim" Ruvalcaba's Mission

Jaime "Jim" Ruvalcaba was, in 2004, a US Marine major in the master's program at Tufts University's Fletcher School when he first participated in my seminar, "Cultural Capital and Development." I arranged for him to meet with Samuel Huntington. We stayed in touch after he returned to the Marine Corps, and, after retiring from the Corps as a lieutenant colonel, and as a student at Harvard's John F. Kennedy School, he participated in my seminar once again in the fall of 2011.

Jim retired from the military because he wants to dedicate his life to encouraging Latino immigrants to acculturate to the US value system, above all by giving heavy emphasis to education. Ultimately, he is thinking of running for Congress from California, his home state. What follows is derived from his term paper, "The Economic and Social Impact of Latino Immigration."

Growing up as an indigent migrant farm worker in California and living among legal and illegal immigrants confirmed to him that Latino families (especially those of Mexican ethnicity) focus much more on family than on community and the broader society. Furthermore, their dominant focus on the present and past, and the absence of role models, preclude many Latinos from visualizing the benefits of investing in education.

One particularly noxious result of these cultural obstacles to progress has been the emergence of Latino gangs. The Department of Justice National Gang Center estimated that, in 2009, there were 731,000 gang members of all types operating in the United States, 367,000—more than 52 percent—were Latinos. Although the total number of gang members declined by over 115,000 in thirteen years, the proportion of Latino involvement in gangs increased by 5 percent, while that of black and white Americans both decreased.

Gangs also expose their family members to emotional and psychological trauma, injury, and death. Ruvalcaba can attest to the emotional pain and trauma associated with losing a family member to the corrosive gang lifestyle. His closest brother was involved in gangs from the age of sixteen. During his six-year involvement in gangs, he dropped out of school, was in and out of juvenile hall and prison, fathered two children by age eighteen, and was engaged in violent gang activity (i.e., shootings, stabbings), and heavy drug use. Because of this dangerous lifestyle, Ruvalcaba's brother did not live to see his twenty-second birthday.

Ruvalcaba finishes his presentation with a clarion call to replace multiculturalism with the US national cultural mainstream:

> Samuel Huntington was absolutely correct in addressing the important issues regarding the slow or non-assimilation of the massive flow of Latinos into mainstream American society. Although there are many productive Latinos in the U.S. who are fully assimilated into the American culture, we have to pay attention to the alarming current indicators and trends among Hispanic Americans that validate Huntington's warning.
>
> After analyzing the Latino legal and illegal immigration flows, education levels, welfare utilization, gang involvement, incarceration rates, and the costly, parasitic . . . subculture that prevents Latino youth from assimilating into mainstream society, I conclude that it is of the highest national priority that assimilation of Latinos be vastly accelerated. The social and economic costs are too high to continue to tackle this challenge piecemeal. Accordingly, the government, religious organizations, media, corporate sector, and, first and foremost, Latino families must come together to address this threat to Latino youth—and to American identity.

The motto on our national seal reads "E Pluribus Unum" (From Many One). This motto needs to be the guiding theme for our immigration policy and especially our assimilation philosophy—not the multiculturalism that is without core values. Although I acknowledge the value of ethnic diversity, we must exercise caution in espousing the multiculturalist perspective that states that all cultures are equal—regardless of evidence to the contrary, and the costs with which it burdens society.

The multiculturalist viewpoint is not only costly to our society's present and future; it tolerates the status quo (low or non-assimilation) as an acceptable level of comportment. Our national identity and political integrity depend on a unified vision—a national creed. We can and should do better: E Pluribus Unum!

The National Council of La Raza; the League of United Latin American Citizens (LULAC); and the Mexican-American Legal Defense Fund (MALDEF) are all committed to the multicultural vision—and are receiving support from the Ford and Rockefeller Foundations. A new pro-acculturation organization might be a crucial actor. And what better person to lead it than Jim Ruvalcaba? One possible name: LATUSA—Latinos for the USA.

What We Must Do

- We must end illegal immigration by enforcing the laws on employment and strengthening our control of our southern border.
- We should calibrate legal immigration annually to (1) the needs of the economy and (2) past performance of immigrant groups with respect to acculturation and contribution to our society.
- We should declare our national language to be English and discourage the proliferation of Spanish language media.
- We should end birthright citizenship, limiting citizenship by birth to children with at last one parent who is a citizen.
- We should provide immigrants with easy-to-access educational services that facilitate acculturation, including English language, citizenship, and culture.

CHAPTER 10

~

African Americans

The election of Barack Obama to the presidency transformed the issue of race in the United States, and indeed throughout the world. It was the ultimate assertion of racial equality. I can imagine the dual impact on most, and perhaps all, African Americans: first, that I *am* an American, and second, that I can *do* anything—or *be* anyone—that I wish. The latter must also apply to blacks everywhere.

That the election of Obama has enhanced his position throughout the world is undeniable:

> Opinion polls in the region show that Mr. Obama's election has . . . improved Latin American countries' opinion of the United States as a whole. Among Brazilians, those with a favorable view increased by 16 percentage points from 57 percent in 2008 to 73 percent in 2009, according to Latinobarometro, a polling company in Santiago, Chile.[1]

> The excitement, aroused by the news that Obama had been elected the 44th president of the United States, in Africa and especially in his father's birth country Kenya . . . probably surpassed that in the US. People went on the streets cheering and dancing; newspapers and websites were overflowing with articles singing his praises, while African heads of state lost no time to congratulate him; and the Kenyan government took one step further by declaring Nov 4 a public holiday.[2]

> India's prime minister, Manmohan Singh: Obama's "extraordinary journey to the White House will inspire people not only in your country but also around the world."[3]

One would expect that President Obama's election would in a major way diminish—if not end—the self-view of US blacks as "victims" of racism and discrimination, thereby facilitating a refocus on cultural factors as explanatory of African American underachievement. This explanation of the slow progress of African Americans relative to most other American groups (excepting Latinos and Native Americans) is captured by Governor Richard Lamm in his book *Two Wands, One Nation*:

> Let me offer you, metaphorically, two magic wands that have sweeping powers to change society. With one wand you could wipe out all racism and discrimination from the hearts and minds of white America. The other wand you could wave across the ghettos and barrios of America and infuse the inhabitants with Japanese or Jewish values, respect for learning and ambition. But alas, you can't wave both wands. Only one.[4]

Governor Lamm opts for the latter.

"Skip" Gates: Victim of Victimology

His strong sense of being victimized by white America was, I feel certain, what drove the behavior of Harvard professor Henry Louis Gates, Jr., widely known as "Skip," that led to his arrest at his home in Cambridge, Massachusetts, shortly after midnight on July 16, 2009.

I have participated with Gates in two conferences on race relations in the United States that took place on Martha's Vineyard, where I reside; the first in the early 1990s, the second in September 2008, two months prior to the election of President Obama. In each, it was clear to me that he views himself as a victim of US racism, in a manner less strident but nonetheless reminiscent of the prominent black movie producer Spike Lee, a summer Vineyard resident.

Lee, who believes that he has been so discriminated against in the United States that he refuses to stand (or at least refused to stand until Obama's election) when "The Star Spangled Banner" is played, has a summer home on the eighteenth hole at Farm Neck Golf Club from which, further endearing himself to most Vineyarders, he flies a New York Yankees flag.

In his important book *Losing the Race*, John McWhorter, an African American senior fellow at the Manhattan Institute, who teaches linguistics at Columbia University, argues that "victimology" is a major obstacle to blacks entering, and enjoying the fruits of, the US cultural mainstream.

Gates has made his way professionally as a genteel guru of victimology—although it's difficult to detect his victimhood as a chaired, senior Harvard professor.

The September 2008 conference—on the eve of the election of the first black president in US history—amounted to an orgy of victimology. Gates was there. I was the only white panelist, invited by Charlayne Hunter Gault, the moderator, when Stanley Crouch, the prominent antivictimology African American, was unable to participate. Charlayne knows me and was aware (1) that I was an avid Obama supporter and (2) that I believed that the black subculture, not racism and discrimination, was the principal cause of black underachievement.

I became an instant pariah at that conference. It will become apparent why when I tell you that one of the speakers, Melissa Harris-Lacewell of Princeton University, described the United States as a "white supremacy society"—this, to repeat, on the eve of the election of Barack Obama. Professor Harris-Lacewell is a colleague of Cornel West, with whom I had participated in the Vineyard conference of the early 1990s. West, after supporting President Obama's candidacy, has been taking potshots at him and First Lady Michelle Obama because, according to Boston Globe columnist Derrick Z. Jackson, "he supported the Obama campaign hoping for a progressive White House but has since felt politically betrayed and personally snubbed." Jackson goes on to say, "While criticizing Obama's policies is fair game, it is despairing to see an Ivy League professor of rare privilege himself succumb to a jealous attempt to humiliate fellow achievers."[5]

And Deborah Gray White of Rutgers University insisted that she and other African Americans were entitled to an official apology for slavery, racism, and discrimination—in the form of "reparations" payments. (I suspect that Professor White's net worth is several times my own.)

Harris-Lacewell's and White's comments were roundly applauded by the audience, and, presumably, by Skip Gates.

Another View: Keith Richburg

The Washington Post's current New York bureau chief, Keith Richburg, who is black, was based in Kenya as the Post's Africa bureau chief from 1991 to 1994. Richburg traveled throughout Africa reporting on wars, famines, mass murders, and the corruption of African politics. Unlike many African Americans who romanticize Africa, Richburg concludes that he is simply an American, not an African American.

The *New Yorker* staff writer William Finnegan had this to say about Richburg's book *Out of America* in the *New York Times Book Review*:

> To his credit, Mr. Richburg lays out his own confusion and guilt about saying some of the things he does . . . he is candid about his gratitude that his ancestors made it to America. Mr. Richburg lambastes whites in the West who, for fear of appearing racist, hesitate to place responsibility for Africa's woes on African shoulders, and then he extends this criticism to white Americans who are allegedly afraid to hold black Americans responsible for their own woes.[6]

The Other Cambridge Scenario

Think of how John McWhorter might have handled the Skip Gates episode in Cambridge:

> Cambridge Police Sergeant James Crowley: "May I see some identification, sir?"
>
> McWhorter, smiling and producing the necessary identification: "I'm aware that more than half of all robberies in the United States are perpetrated by African Americans, officer . . ."
>
> Sergeant Crowley: "That may or may not be true, sir, but it is irrelevant to my request for your identification. A neighbor reported suspicious activity at this house . . ."
>
> McWhorter, again with a smile: "Fair enough, officer."
>
> End of incident.

Thomas Sowell: Disaggregating Blacks

In his pioneering 1981 book *Ethnic America*,[7] the black economist and columnist Thomas Sowell makes a compelling case for acculturation of blacks into the US mainstream. He divides US blacks into three groups: (1) "free persons of color"; (2) slaves freed by the Emancipation Proclamation; and (3) immigrants from the West Indies.

The first blacks arrived in Virginia in 1619. They were not slaves but, like so many whites, indentured servants who, in due course, earned their freedom. Slavery was not introduced in the colonies until the second half of the seventeenth century, by which time there was already an appreciable number of "free persons of color." The number grew as a result of the freeing of slaves by masters, often following sexual liaisons; the purchase of freedom by slaves who enjoyed a salary or other income; or escape via the underground railway to the North.

By the outbreak of the Civil War, the number of "free persons of color" approached 500,000, more than 10 percent of the total black population at the time. Many lived in the North, but large and dynamic free black (principally mulatto) communities also sprang up in New Orleans, where a third of "free colored" families owned slaves, and Charleston, South Carolina. By the Civil War, most free blacks were literate and self-sufficient. Almost all black slaves were illiterate, since most slave owners believed that education would ultimately precipitate slave uprisings.

Free blacks were increasingly acculturated to the white cultural mainstream. In many cases, white fathers of mulattos facilitated their access. Their self-image—and expectation of upward mobility—had to be far more positive than that of the slaves. Sowell adds, "As workers, blacks had little sense of personal responsibility under slavery. Lack of initiative, evasion of work, half-done work, unpredictable absenteeism, and abuse of tools and equipment were pervasive under slavery, and these patterns did not suddenly disappear with emancipation."[8]

Thus, most black leadership and achievement in the nineteenth century and in the first decades of the twentieth century came from the descendants of "free persons of color," who got a head start on acculturation to the US mainstream. The first great black leader, Frederick Douglass, had escaped from urban slavery in the South and lived for many years as a freeman in the North, married to a white woman. In 1870, free persons of color established the first black high school in the United States, Dunbar High in Washington, D.C., whose students scored higher than any white high school in citywide tests in 1899 and for years thereafter—and which also sent three-fourths of its graduates on to college.

W. E. B. Du Bois was a descendant of free blacks. So were Ralph Bunche, Thurgood Marshall, Andrew Young, Clifford Alexander, and Julian Bond. Sowell notes that, through the first half of the twentieth century, descendants of free persons of color constituted the majority of black professionals and were far better educated and had smaller families than descendants of emancipated slaves. Sowell concludes, "As with other groups around the world, historic advantages in acculturation had enduring consequences for generations to come."[9]

Further evidence of the significance of culture in black achievement is furnished by West Indian immigrants in America. Substantial West Indian immigration started in the early years of the twentieth century, principally from Jamaica, Barbados, Trinidad, and the Bahamas. Sowell observes that, by 1920, one-quarter of Harlem's population was West Indian, although West Indians represented only about 1 percent of the national black population.[10] That 1 percent has produced an extraordinary number of leaders and achievers: Marcus Garvey, Stokely Carmichael, Malcolm X, James Farmer, Roy Inness, Congresswoman Shirley Chisholm, Kenneth B. Clarke, Sir W. Arthur Lewis, Sidney Poitier, Harry Belafonte, Godfrey Cambridge, ex-Ford Foundation president Franklin Thomas, and General Colin Powell.

Sowell concludes, "The contrast between West Indians and American Negroes was not so much in their occupational backgrounds as in their behavior patterns. West Indians were more frugal, hard-working, and entrepreneurial. Their children worked harder and outperformed native black children in school."[11]

Orlando Patterson's Cultural Analysis

I know of no better structure for analysis of how cultural obstacles have impeded African American progress than that of Orlando Patterson, a professor of sociology at Harvard whose roots lie in Jamaica. Patterson presented his analysis at the "Culture Matters" symposium at Harvard in 1999. I subsequently used it in *The Central Liberal Truth*. I apologize for the repetition here to readers of either or both.

The Patterson Model

Patterson employs African American history to illustrate how his model works. The behavioral outcome he focuses on is the current high rate of paternal abandonment of children by African American males (Figure 10.1).

Point A, the "Transmitted Cultural Model," is the condition of male-female relationships in slavery. Those relationships discouraged the sense of paternal responsibility because "most men did not live regularly with their partners." Many such relationships were formed between partners who lived on different plantations, "and a third [of the male slaves] had no stable unions."[12] Paternal responsibility was further undermined by the African tradition of "matrifocality," which placed higher value on the mother–child relationship than the father–child relationship, which persisted through slavery, and by the related tradition of female independence, which also persisted through slavery. Finally, in Patterson's words, "slave men lacked the one thing that all other men primarily relied on for their domination of women: control of property."[13]

The pattern of male irresponsibility with respect to children was perpetuated (Point B) during the Jim Crow period when vast numbers of former

**Socio-Cultural
Determinants**

**Individual
Outcomes**

Transmitted
Cultural Models

A.

B.

Modified
Cultural Models

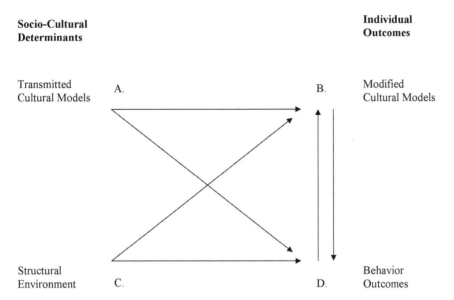

Structural
Environment

C.

D.

Behavior
Outcomes

Figure 10.1 Interactions among cultural models,
the structural environment, and behavioral outcomes.

male slaves became sharecroppers. Their income depended on the amount of labor they could apply to their land, and virtually their sole source of labor was the children they sired. Viewing children chiefly as an economic resource did not enhance the paternal instinct. Moreover, Patterson believes that the demeaning treatment of black males—at the extreme, castration and lynching—established a psychological environment in which the only way that African American males could "prove their worth" was through sexual conquest. One result was the strengthening of bonds among African American women and between the women and their children.

Point C in the diagram is the structural environment: "Unemployment, low income, and the neighborhood effects of segregated habitats, as well as ethnic and gender discrimination in employment."[14] Patterson also mentions the impact of welfare programs; the profound influence of successful black athletes on the value system of African American males; and the influx of low-skilled immigrants as contributing structural factors.

Patterson concludes,

> Thus we have A and C leading to . . . variants of B, leading to a . . . model of sexuality of and paternity among young men, expressed in D, which, in turn encourages attitudes toward mainstream society and work (DB) and a ghetto

lifestyle that reinforces . . . predatory sexuality and unsecured paternity. In this context of opposition to mainstream norms, the likelihood of the modified sexual and paternal models being actualized in D is even greater. . . . It is reasonable to conclude that among a large number of urban, Afro-American lower-class young men, these models are now fully normative and that men act in accordance with them whenever they can.[15]

Patterson's analysis strongly evokes John McWhorter's Culture Matters Research Project essay, "Scene from a Fast-Food Restaurant: Signs of the Times in Black America and the Path Beyond."[16]

In his controversial book *Losing the Race*,[17] McWhorter argues that African Americans are pursuing a self-destructive strategy by promoting a "victim" self-image, racial separatism, and the view that education doesn't matter. His essay starts in a fast-food restaurant in New York City, where he observed a group of African American boys, around fourteen years old, apparently skipping school and misbehaving, to the consternation of the manager, a black woman. "They seemed to consider themselves inherently exempt from observing public norms of behavior. They gave a sense of having begun checking out of mainstream society."

McWhorter continues,

Since the 1960s, Black America has been infected by an equation, sometimes explicit but usually tacit, that the core of black identity is rebellion and disaffection. . . . Misbehavior and criminality are not the only ways this is expressed. Even the most educated blacks with the most assimilated demeanors get their "black authenticity" stripes to the extent that they subscribe to the notion that being black remains a battle forty years after the Civil Rights Act. . . .

The development of black identity among teens often entails learning to process mainstream America as an alien realm, deserving of contempt rather than engagement.[18]

He concludes,

The boys at the restaurant were victims indeed—not of "racism" but of an ideological detour that the sociological history of black America has conditioned. That detour would perplex the black Americans who worked so hard before the 1960s to pave the way for blacks to make the best of themselves in an imperfect world. Realizing that culture is the main problem now rather than racism or societal inequity, our task is to pull black America out of that detour, freeing us from the self-fulfilling prophecies of recreational indignation and returning us to a clear-eyed, proactive race leadership that will allow us to truly "get past race" for good.[19]

I am convinced that Barack Obama, both by virtue of his election and the distinguished conduct of his office, will prove to be the Moses who leads his people out of the sterile land of victimology into the enriching US mainstream. This will not happen overnight: cultural change almost never does. It will probably not be apparent by the end of his first term. But sooner or later, Barack Obama will displace the rappers and the athletes as role model for blacks, above all black kids.

CHAPTER 11

~

What to Do

On May 16, 2006, a book party was held at the Oxford University Press headquarters in Manhattan to mark the publication of *The Central Liberal Truth*. Among those present was Marin Strmecki, senior vice president and director of the Smith Richardson Foundation, which had provided some assistance to the Culture Matters Research Project (CMRP), on which *The Central Liberal Truth* was based.

Marin suggested that I consider developing a proposal for an institute at the Fletcher School dedicated to promoting cultural change. A year later, on April 24, 2007, the Cultural Change Institute (CCI) was inaugurated, with financial support from the Smith Richardson, John Templeton, and Sidney Swensrud Foundations. Its sphere of action was largely governed by the "Guidelines for Progressive Cultural Change," the concluding chapter in *The Central Liberal Truth*.

Early on, we formed an executive committee, comprised of experts for each of the following "avenues" of approach to cultural change:

Childrearing: Jerome Kagan, developmental psychologist, Harvard University
Education: Fernando Reimers, Graduate School of Education, Harvard University
Religion: Peter Berger, sociologist, Boston University
Media: Reese Schonfeld, first president of CNN

Political leadership: Richard Lamm, former governor of Colorado

Development assistance: Andrew Natsios, former administrator of USAID

Economics: James Fox, former chief economic advisor, Latin American Bureau, USAID

Legal reform: Octavio Sánchez, chef de cabinet, current Honduran government

Private sector: Rob Kleinbaum, former head of General Motors internal evaluation unit

Data collection/interpretation: Matteo Marini, University of Calabria, Italy

Conclusion: Guidelines for Progressive Cultural Change

I want to stress that what follows should not be viewed as a prescription for certain success, a judgment confirmed in the four years that CCI had been operating. All CMRP members agreed that the cultural dimension of human progress has been neglected by the government officials and development institutions that bear the principal responsibility for guiding the policies and programs whose goal is the greater freedom and well-being of humankind. The same is true of other institutions, particularly religions, educational institutions, and the media, that influence popular values, beliefs, and attitudes. None of us believed that the integration of cultural factors into policies and programs will bring about instant development. But we do believe that by incorporating culture into the mix of factors that shape development, the *pace* of progress can be accelerated.

I also want to restate a basic CMRP premise: cultural change, like democracy and market economics, cannot be imposed from the outside, except in the most extraordinary circumstances (e.g., in Japan after its unconditional surrender in 1945). Progress endures only when it is driven chiefly from within. Thomas Friedman got it exactly right in his *New York Times* June 26, 2011, column titled "It Has to Start With Them," the lead paragraph of which reads as follows:

> When President Obama announced his decision to surge more troops into Afghanistan in 2009, I argued that it could succeed if three things happened: Pakistan became a different country, Pres. Hamid Karzai of Afghanistan became a different man and we succeeded at doing exactly what we claim not to be doing, that is nation-building in Afghanistan. None of that has happened, which is why I still believe our options in Afghanistan are: lose early, lose late, lose big or lose small. I vote for early and small.[1]

Openness to the ideological, political, technological, and institutional lessons learned by more advanced societies is also a precondition. But until a critical mass of awareness emerges in a society, external pressures for change are likely to be resisted. As Daniel Latouche emphasized in his CMRP paper on Québec, "there can be no cultural transformation without the widely-accepted belief that there is indeed something 'wrong' with the [culture] and without widespread discussion of how to fix it. For culture to matter, there must [first be] a realization that it needs fixing."[2]

I also want to stress the intimate relationship between cultural change and "development," as it has come to be defined over the past half century. Initiatives to promote cultural change are likely to promote political, economic, or social development; and initiatives designed to promote development in the traditional sense may also promote progressive cultural change. As an example, Francisco Franco's decision to open up the Spanish economy toward the end of the 1950s has proven to have had profound cultural change effects.

Finally, the evidence strongly suggests that a single instrument of cultural change (e.g., Ecuador's aborted punctuality campaign)[3] is unlikely to divert the powerful momentum of culture. What is necessary is a coordinated program that may involve, among other things, childrearing, religion and religious reform, education and education reform, the media, legal reform, reform of business culture, and political leadership committed to the democratic capitalist model.

The only conceivable exception is religious reform. In virtually all cultures, religion is the principal source of values, beliefs, and attitudes. Just as the Reformation drove progress in the Protestant countries, a sweeping reform of religion may be sufficient to bring about significant cultural change in a single country. Brazil's movement toward conversion from a virtual Catholic monopoly to a predominantly Protestant country warrants careful study in this regard.

The following are the avenues to cultural change that our research and experience suggest.

I. Childrearing and Education
A. End illiteracy
Illiteracy is the single greatest obstacle to progressive cultural change. It enshrouds the human capacity to learn to change and it nurtures the perpetuation of traditional culture. Human progress lags the most in societies, above all in Islamic countries and Africa, where illiteracy levels are highest. In most of these countries, female literacy is sharply lower than male literacy.

Yet in terms of cultural change, it can be argued that female literacy is more important than male literacy because of the crucial role women play in childrearing, as the Aga Khan, among others, has emphasized. It is relevant that females are more literate than males in Botswana, a leading sub-Saharan African democracy.

The argument that low literacy levels are an inevitable consequence of generalized poverty is not convincing. Its relative poverty notwithstanding, Scotland was the most literate country in the world by the end of the eighteenth century. High levels of literacy were also achieved by the Nordic countries while they were still poor. Japan had substantially eliminated illiteracy by the early years of the twentieth century, long before it could be considered affluent. Chilean men and women were more literate than other Latin Americans in the nineteenth century.

I am confident that, given high priority by governments in poor countries and the international development institutions, illiteracy could be substantially eliminated in a generation, two at the most. Ending illiteracy must embrace plans to ensure first a complete primary education for everyone. Because poor parents often keep their children out of school either to earn money or help at home, government grants to parents to keep their children in school may be necessary. Such a program was instituted by the Luiz Inácio da Silva government in Brazil with apparent success.[4]

Then the goal must be a complete secondary education for everyone; and finally, access for everyone to postsecondary education.

B. Modify childrearing techniques

Traditional childrearing patterns are sustained from generation to generation, in large measure because the only preparation most young parents have is the recollection of the way their parents raised them. Yet, as Costa Rican child psychologist Luis Diego Herrera suggests in his CMRP essay,[5] traditional childrearing may inculcate values, beliefs, and attitudes that are obstacles to the progress of the individual and the society, not only through *what* the parent teaches the child but also through *how* the parent relates to the child.

Jerome Kagan suggests what parents can do to strengthen the values that facilitate democracy, social justice, and prosperity:

> In order to promote **the ethic of democracy**, the family must encourage a sense of personal agency in their children by providing experiences that allow sons and daughters to feel they have some power to affect the family. Put simply, consulting the child, asking her opinions, and when appropriate taking the child's preferences into account, should strengthen the child's sense

of agency. Psychologists call parents who adopt these practices authoritatively democratic.

The assumption that all members of a community should have equal power to decide on the future of the community is harder to promote than a sense of agency because this premise requires the child to understand the difference between economic gain and symbolic signs of status, on the one hand, and political privilege, on the other. . . . Unlike a sense of agency, which can emerge before age 7, this more abstract idea has to wait until the years before puberty, when the maturing cognitive abilities make it possible for youth to understand that the vitality of the community should sometimes have priority over the desires of the individual. Promotion of this goal requires conversation . . . and is accomplished less easily through parental rewards and punishments. Parents have to be clever and detect when a context is appropriate to teach this lesson.

Nature awarded all children, save a very small proportion with a special biology, the ability to empathize with those in physical or psychic distress. An empathic concern over a whining puppy or a crying infant comes easily to all children. This sentiment, which Hume assumed was the foundation of human morality, represents a significant foundation on which the teaching of **social justice** rests.

If children are reminded regularly of the deprivation experienced by disen-franchised citizens, they should, by adolescence, create a concern for strangers in need. It helps, of course, if the parents not only promote this ethic in con-versation, but also display it in their behavior.

The attainment of **economic prosperity** requires an ethic that celebrates the intrinsic value of personal accomplishment; that is, a work ethic in which individual accomplishment brings virtue. . . . This standard, common in North America and parts of Europe, requires suppressing worry over "being better than another."[6]

CCI Experience with Reform of Childrearing Practices

The CCI has sponsored three pilot projects aimed at modifying traditional childrearing practices: one in Costa Rica; a second in East Boston, Massachu-setts; the third in Brazil. Each has involved intensive coaching of mothers of two- to three-year-old children. Results of the Costa Rican pilot project were disappointing, with few of the mothers responding to the opportunity. Results of the East Boston project were more promising, with 40 percent of the mothers responding positively. However, Martha Julia Sellers, a senior development psychologist who did her doctoral work at Harvard with Jerome Kagan, was deeply involved in the project, and we are concerned about the cost-effectiveness of the approach.

The three above-mentioned pilot projects are all focused on Latina mothers. We have a strong expression of interest from the College of Charleston, South Carolina, in a similar approach focused on African Americans. We are awaiting the results from Brazil and a final evaluation of the East Boston project before seeking funding for the Charleston project.

C. Reform education

In their CMRP paper "Schooling Open Societies in Latin America," Fernando Reimers of the Harvard Graduate School of Education and Eleonora Villegas-Reimers of Wheelock College suggest six objectives for educational reform in Latin America that will strengthen the values that make democracy work. Their paper has substantial relevance for Africa, the Islamic world, and other lagging areas. The six objectives apply principally to primary and secondary education:

1. a broad commitment to educating all children at high levels;
2. schools that are themselves open communities;
3. stronger relationships between schools and communities;
4. teachers who are well prepared; who can serve as democratic models; and who value freedom and diversity;
5. civic education curriculum (see also the CMRP paper of Richard Niemi and Steven Finkel[7]); and
6. microlevel experiences to learn well and to learn to make choices.[8]

A seventh objective is the integration of character education into curricula, an initiative discussed by Thomas Lickona in his CMRP paper "Character Education: Restoring Virtue to the Mission of Schools."[9]

Finally, I would urge independent assessments of the way that universities are succeeding or failing to meet their responsibilities to produce the leaders, professionals, and technical experts that modern democratic capitalist societies need. I appreciate that this will not be easy in Latin America, where universities are extremely protective of their autonomy. But many of these universities do not serve their societies well—Marxism-Leninism is alive and well in many of them—and good universities are crucial to progress.

In 2007 and 2008, Fernando Reimers led a civic education pilot project in Mexico designed to change the essentially antidemocratic value system of eighth graders in Acapulco and Oaxaca. The project emphasized practical work outside the classroom, usually in groups, to solve common problems. Value profiles were developed for all participants both before and after the pilot project. Significantly more democratic values were apparent in the wake of the project.

D. Learn English

The Singaporean and Irish miracles and India's recent economic surge owe a lot to their English-language capabilities. US capital has dominated the heavy flow of foreign investment into Ireland in recent decades, and this was partly due to Ireland's being a nation of native speakers of English. India's dynamic outsourcing sector has been made possible by the large number of Indians who now speak English. In his CMRP paper "India: How a Rich Nation Became Poor and Will Be Rich Again," Gurcharan Das makes the point and underscores the irony:

> Ever since the British left, Indians constantly complained against the English language. But in the 1990s this carping seemed to die, and quietly, without ceremony English became one of the Indian languages. . . . Young Indians in the new middle class think of English as a skill, like Windows.[10]

A similar irony is found in Québec. In their zeal to protect the French language, the Québecois separatist leaders have promoted a campaign to suppress English. Yet the English facility of many Québecois is a valuable resource, for example, in the expansion of trade with and tourism from the neighboring United States, not to mention Anglophone Canada.

That most people in the Nordic countries are fluent in English has facilitated the access of those countries to the world market in goods and ideas. The recent left-of-center government of Chile led by Michelle Bachelet announced a program to make Chile bilingual in Spanish and English. The *New York Times* quotes Bachelet's minister of education Sergio Bitar: "We have some of the most advanced commercial accords in the world, but that is not enough. We know our lives are linked more than ever to an international presence, and if you can't speak English, you can't sell and you can't learn."[11]

English is a resource for both economic development *and* cultural change. If learning from the experience of more advanced societies is crucial to progressive cultural change, command of English today is extremely valuable.

II. Religious Reform

The condition of the three main religions, Roman Catholicism, Orthodox Christianity, and Islam, have already been discussed in some detail in Chapter 2. Some general further comments about Hinduism, Buddhism, and African animist religions follow:

Hinduism

As Pratap Bhanu Mehta stresses in his CMRP essay on Hinduism,[12] the religion is a good deal more flexible and diverse than many critics appreciate, and it has demonstrated a considerable capacity for change. Moreover, India's democratic politics have had a powerful influence on Hindu practice, for example, in breaking down the caste system.

Nonetheless, Hindu leaders might ponder the typology with a view to doctrinal modifications that support India's quest for modernity.

Buddhism

"Buddhist theory for the most part remains resolutely a theory about individual life and practice. In a strictly formal sense, Buddhism and democracy are mutually independent. Buddhism neither precludes nor entails liberal democracy; liberal democracy neither precludes nor entails Buddhism," observes Jay Garfield of Smith College.[13] Yet there are elements in Buddhist doctrine and practice that are clearly compatible with democracy, above all the egalitarian nature of the *sangha*, the ideal Buddhist community in which seniority matters but not class, caste, wealth, or prestige.

Christal Whelan, in her CMRP paper on Buddhism,[14] emphasizes the vast variety of Buddhist interpretations and practices, some supporting modernization, others resisting it. That variety is reflected in the performance of Buddhist nations: Freedom House ranks Myanmar (Burma) with the "least free" countries like North Korea and Cuba. Yet Mongolia and Thailand are listed as "free" countries. Of the seven Buddhist countries included in the Whelan analysis, only Thailand has experienced rapid economic development, and that is disproportionately attributable to Thailand's Chinese minority.

There is, of course, a major question as to the extent of contemporary Buddhist influence on politics and economics, considering that so many other forces, globalization among them, are also in play. It seems reasonable to conclude that "reform" of Buddhism is unlikely—and unlikely to have much influence on the paths followed by the countries in which the religion predominates.

African animist religions

In his chapter in *Culture Matters*, Daniel Etounga-Manguelle says: "A society in which magic and witchcraft flourish today is a sick society ruled by tension, fear, and moral disorder. Sorcery is a costly mechanism for managing conflict and preserving the status quo, which is, importantly, what African culture is about."[15] Animist religions, in which what happens in life is determined by a pantheon of capricious spirits, present an extreme case of progress-resistant culture, as we have seen in Haitian Voodoo, the roots of which are in Africa. Animist religions are most widely practiced in Africa, although they are also found in the Western Hemisphere both in Haitian Voodoo and Brazilian Santería.[16]

The guideline with respect to animism is to encourage conversion of those practicing animist religions to more progress-prone religions. Given the current condition of Islam and Catholicism, the religion of preference is Protestantism.

III. Governments
A. *Raise awareness of the key role of culture*
Political leaders should be mindful of the implications of their policies, programs, and public appearances for the strengthening of progressive values. Harold Caballeros's campaign for the presidency of Guatemala in the 2011 elections is a case in point—his party is ViVa, an acronym for Visión con Valores (Vision with Values). (Caballeros lost, but he was subsequently named foreign minister by the winner, Otto Pérez Molina.) Leaders should educate the public on the key role progressive values play in the achievement of the goals of a society, and they should sustain a continuing dialogue with the media on its role in promoting progressive values.

B. *Look for historic/mythical precedents for cultural change*
As the cases of Botswana, Georgia, Novgorod, and Québec in *The Central Liberal Truth* demonstrate, it will be easier to strengthen progressive values if the initiative involves at least an appearance of continuity—"the creation of new mythologies based on selective memories taken from the past," in Daniel Latouche's words.[17]

C. *Be alert to developments in other societies that may be applied beneficially at home*
Develop an institutionalized means of keeping in continuing touch with global advances in science, technology, policies, institutions, and cultural change.

D. *Give high priority to education and education reform* (see I. above)

E. *Pursue open economic policies and encourage foreign investment*
Several of the transformations (e.g., Spain and Ireland) were either driven or facilitated by open economic policies. Such policies should produce more

rapid economic development. Higher, steadily growing levels of prosperity are reflected not only in higher standards of living and more effective government action (for example, in education reform), but they also help to create a national psychology of optimism and opportunity that sap the strength of fatalism and strengthen the entrepreneurial vocation so central to development. Foreign investment not only produces economic benefits (most of the time) but also often transfers new technologies, new ideas, and new values.

F. Build a competent, honest, respected civil service
Aside from the performance benefits that attend competence and honesty in the public sector, an efficient, professional civil service plays an important role in extending a society's radius of identification and trust—in government and in the broader society. High-quality bureaucracies have contributed much to the success of Sweden, Botswana, Chile, and Singapore, among others.

G. Encourage and facilitate home ownership
Home ownership played a key role in the transformations of Spain and Singapore. In both cases, housing policies were consciously designed to give people a stake in the society, to create a middle class, and to strengthen the family.

H. Regularize property ownership
The advantages that attend Hernando de Soto's emphasis in *The Mystery of Capital*[18] on real property security through legalized registration programs that facilitate market transactions are not only economic. Security and marketability of property are also likely to nurture optimism, sap the strength of fatalism, and strengthen the entrepreneurial vocation.

I. Institutionalize periodic surveys of values, beliefs, and attitudes
The CCI has created a survey instrument that enables the development of a national value profile tied to the twenty-five-point typology. Periodic resurveys will permit assessments of cultural change that should be helpful in guiding public policy decisions.

J. Reform legal institutions
It was around 1987 or 1988 when I received a letter from Octavio Sánchez Barrientos, a Honduran who was thirteen years old at the time. He had read my first book, *Underdevelopment Is a State of Mind: The Latin American Case*,

and liked it. (I assume that he had read a Spanish edition because the letter was in Spanish.) As I recall, we corresponded from time to time until the mid-1990s, when a speaking engagement brought me to Tegucigalpa, where we met for the first time. As I recall, Octavio was then studying law at the University of Honduras.

He must have graduated near or at the top of his class, because a few years later, he was doing graduate work at the Harvard Law School. During the year he was at Harvard, he visited my wife, Pat, and me at our home on Martha's Vineyard several times.

Octavio then arranged for a year at the University of Arizona Law School, where he worked closely with an old friend from my second tour in Costa Rica (1969–1971), Boris Kozolchyk, director of the National Law Center. With the election of Ricardo Maduro in 2002, he was first named as a presidential advisor and then as minister of culture.

Given his background, it was natural for Octavio to gravitate toward a broad view of the role of legal institutions as a reflection of, and influence on, culture. He presented a paper at the 2008 "Culture Matters, Culture Changes" conference at Tufts that begins:

> Latin America's failure to develop economically is largely due to the fact that we are prisoners of a medieval mentality, which sees law as a series of dogmas and not as a malleable instrument of justice, social change, and commerce. . . . The law in developed countries is flexible in that it promotes innovation and the creation of wealth not only by adopting modern regulation, but also by staying away from regulating certain areas that best develop through market practice.[19]

Two initiatives have followed in the wake of the Sánchez paper. First, former CCI deputy director Miguel Basáñez, a lawyer as well as a political scientist, designed and administered a CCI program that brought 120 Mexican judges to the United States, Chile, and Colombia to help implement a broad-scale legal reform program of the Mexican government.

Second, Octavio Sánchez, at the age of thirty-five, was named cabinet chief of the Honduran government by President Porfirio Lobo Sosa. In this capacity, Octavio has led the design of a program that will establish areas of Honduras where investment-friendly laws will reign rather than Honduran law. Mary O'Grady, the Wall Street Journal's editorial board expert and columnist on Latin America, commented favorably on the initiative,[20] and Mike Gibson, a columnist for Let a Thousand Nations Bloom, compared Octavio to John James Cowperthwaite, the British diplomat widely credited for Hong Kong's boom.[21]

IV. Development Assistance Institutions

A. Confront culture

Most development assistance institutions, both multilateral and bilateral, have thus far failed to address cultural change, chiefly because anthropologists and other social scientists committed to cultural relativism have dominated policy. That some cultures are more prone to progress than others is a message that goes down very hard in development circles, all evidence to the contrary notwithstanding. This obstacle is magnified by the politics of the international institutions, where both donors and recipients have a voice and where it is much more interpersonally comfortable, and less threatening to self-esteem, to view the countries lagging behind as either the victims of the more successful countries or as merely having failed so far to find the proper content and mix of policies, incentives, and institutions. Evidence of this intellectual/emotional obstacle is the response to the two UNDP Arab Human Development Reports, both of which focus on the need for cultural change and have provoked outspoken criticism from many Arabs.

I can only hope that the persistent, widespread dissatisfaction and frustration with the sluggish pace of progress in most poor countries will cause development professionals to ponder the message that culture matters. The considerable intelligence, creativity, and dedication of development professionals over the past half century have not succeeded in transforming the large majority of poor, authoritarian societies. Where transformations have occurred, they have usually either been nurtured by cultures that contain progress-prone elements (e.g., the Confucian societies of East Asia) or been cases where cultural change was central to the transformation (e.g., Spain, Ireland, Québec).

B. Integrate cultural change analysis into research programs, strategies, and project design

Development assistance institutions should acquire the doctrine and staff that will enable them to help countries integrate cultural change into their policies and programs. They should be prepared to provide technical assistance for baseline value, belief, and attitude surveys that can subsequently be reiterated to assess change; and they should integrate cultural change into their research agenda. The development-assistance institutions should examine the impact that the projects they support will have on values, beliefs, and attitudes and be mindful of such impacts in project design. Project evaluations should address the impact on culture along with the other objectives of a project.

C. *Consider establishing a network of quality universities under international institution auspices*

The positive impact of US and other universities overseas, in terms both of quality education and cultural change, suggests the desirability of establishing a network of universities, dedicated to excellence, in lagging areas. Such a network might be particularly helpful in the Islamic world and Africa. The United Nations would be one possible home for the network, the World Bank and International Monetary Fund another.

V. Universities

A. Confront culture

Like the development institutions, universities around the world have avoided addressing culture, again because of the dominance of cultural relativism in the social sciences. The *Culture Matters* view is politically incorrect and often associated—incorrectly—with a right-wing agenda. I am aware of only four courses that address the relationship between culture and development: one that was offered by Samuel Huntington at Harvard; another by Harvey Nelson at the University of South Florida; another by Robert Klitgaard at Claremont Graduate University; and the one that I offer at the Fletcher School at Tufts. On the other hand, *Culture Matters* and *The Central Liberal Truth* are in use in universities throughout the United States, and there may be other such courses, or parts of courses, that address the issue.

It should be crystal clear from *The Central Liberal Truth* that the CMRP agenda is *not* conservative. I know of no one associated with the CMRP who believes in cultural determinism—that culture is immutable, perhaps even genetically rooted. All of us believe that culture is acquired, that it changes, and that cultural change may offer a vehicle for accelerated progress toward the elimination of tyranny, injustice, and poverty. If we are right, it behooves the universities, like the development institutions, to take culture and cultural change seriously. That means developing courses and research programs on the role of culture and cultural change in human progress. Childrearing is one of several aspects of the CMRP in which universities should take the lead.

VI. The Media

The power of the media, above all television, to influence not only the views and opinions of people but also their values is enormous. The degree of objectivity with which news is presented is a central issue. Because reporters and editors are human, complete objectivity is unattainable, and the substance of news stories and the prominence given to them will inevitably reflect bias. The problem becomes acute when bias becomes policy and the television channel or newspaper pursues an ideological "line" that confounds objectivity and may reinforce both prejudice and error. This is the case in my judgment with respect to the Fox Network in general and the *New York Times'* "open borders" approach to the immigration issue in particular.

Reese Schonfeld describes Al Jazeera in his CMRP essay on entertainment media as "respectable but slanted."[22] Al Jazeera's reporting—not to mention the violently anti-American, anti-Semitic, anti-Israel programming of al Manar, a Hezbollah network recently banned in France and the United States—reinforces the prevalent Arab "victim" self-image that presents such a huge obstacle to progress in the Arab world, and in doing so, runs contrary to the thrust of the UNDP "Arab Human Development" reports. In sharp contrast, as Schonfeld observes, are highly popular talent shows broadcast by Lebanon's Future TV and the Lebanon Broadcast Company in which viewers participate through voting to decide the winners. The message of these shows is one of modernity, upward mobility, and participation.

A similar competition in values is found today in China. The domination of the media by the government is threatened by all the foreign channels beamed through satellites, not to mention the Falun Gong's New Tang Dynasty Television (NTDT) network, which "features Hollywood movies from the thirties through the fifties, partly because they are affordable but, more importantly, because they conform to NTDT's avowed intention to promote democratic cultural change [so that] 'more people can enjoy peace and freedom and live harmoniously among different races and beliefs.'"[23]

What about the advanced democracies? In Britain, Germany, Sweden, and Japan, public networks still dominate television viewing. In other Western countries, they have been increasingly marginalized. The tendency is toward more privatization and more competition, which is surely consistent with the sacrosanct principle of freedom of the press. There are, however, risks that either public or private television may be sending messages that undermine the values that nurture democracy, prosperity, and justice. One possible innovation: an institutionalized continuing dialogue on the role and impact of the media on values involving people concerned about national well-being and progress from government, the private media, universities and research institutions.

VII. The Private Sector

Late in January 2009, I received an email from Rob Kleinbaum that caught my attention, in part because he linked General Motors' crisis to the company culture, but also because of the acronym of his company: RAK, my beloved wife, Pat's, maiden name. I subsequently learned that the acronym combined Rob's name with that of *his* wife, Aviva.

Rob had written a paper that thrust culture squarely into the private sector. It started:

> GM is currently engaged in developing a plan, owed to Congress, which demonstrates long run viability. The company is looking at its products, brands, manufacturing footprint and capacity, health care, and "structural costs," while negotiating with the UAW to further reduce labor costs. All this is well and good but it is almost certain that GM is not addressing an issue that, in the long run, could be more important than all these others: its culture.

I was reminded of Geert Hofstede's pioneering work in business culture, *Culture's Consequences*,[24] in which Hofstede examined the varying values and attitudes of IBM offices around the world and concluded that culture matters—and that indeed some cultures are more apt to promote success than others.

Kleinbaum's message circulated widely and was mentioned by David Brooks in his *New York Times* column. The net result has been for the CCI to incorporate business culture into its portfolio, with Rob Kleinbaum representing business in the CCI executive committee.

There are two other opportunities for the private sector to play a part in the promotion of progressive values: philanthropy and participatory management.

A. Philanthropy

Philanthropy has made a huge contribution to progress in the United States, through, for example, financial support of universities, libraries, hospitals, and museums. But philanthropy also has an important cultural effect by reinforcing the national social fabric. Philanthropic traditions encourage the affluent to reflect and act on their sense of obligation to the broader society and its values, for example, by making a university education, and the upward mobility it implies, possible for people who would otherwise not be able to afford it. On the other hand, the beneficiaries of philanthropy see new horizons opening up to them that reinforce their sense of identification with the society and its values.

In February 1999, Harvard University sponsored a workshop on philanthropy in Latin America. As the report of the workshop notes, "Philanthropy, as it is understood in North America, has little solid tradition in Latin America. Typically, philanthropy in Latin America is . . . 'passive' . . . limited to charitable, clientelistic, or paternalistic practices. Rarely is philanthropy associated with any structured or sustained effort to relieve poverty, or with institutionalized forms of corporate citizenship. . . . The Latin American historical tradition has left a weak, fragile, and poorly organized civil society, although with democratization there are now infinitely more opportunities for participation."[25]

The findings and recommendations of the workshop include the following:

- Enhance awareness of philanthropic practices through mobilization of the media.
- Work toward better legal frameworks that provide incentives for philanthropy.
- Strengthen alliances among government, business, and nongovernmental organizations. "Many countries suffer from an extraordinary lack of trust in public institutions and in their provision of services . . . [and] tax evasion."[26] (A reminder of the importance of an honest and efficient civil service.)
- Encourage civic engagement through "policies that promote a culture of generosity and civic participation. There was unanimous agreement that working to create a more favorable environment for philanthropy requires major cultural and psychological change. . . . It was generally accepted that one should start young."[27]

B. Participatory management

In most poor countries, the authoritarianism found in government is repeated in all human relationships. That is particularly true of relationships in the workplace. The boss's word is law, and anything other than blind obedience can result in severe consequences.

Modern participatory management, of the kind we now associate with Japanese industry's Toyota, for example, can precipitate cultural change. The manager who explains rather than commands, who encourages communication in his organization, who encourages and rewards initiative, can create an environment in which:

[W]orkers feel they are recognized by their superiors; responsibilities and a certain degree of autonomy are . . . delegated by all levels of management; all levels of personnel identify with their jobs, the enterprise, and its goals; workers willingly cooperate with each other and with all levels of management in the pursuit of personal, but common, advantages; individuals are free to discuss problems arising from their jobs with superiors and workmates and willingly take advantage of such opportunities.[28]

We are reminded of Rob Kleinbaum's diagnosis of General Motors' cultural problem.

Urgently Needed: A "Laboratory" to Make the Case

Since it was inaugurated in 2007, the CCI tried on five occasions to establish a "laboratory" where a comprehensive cultural change program could be mounted and evaluated. For a variety of reasons, not one has yet materialized.

The California Teachers' Association (CTA)

In July 2007, I received the following email from Yale Wishnick, an official of the California Teachers' Association, which represented 350,000 teachers as the California affiliate of the National Education Association:

> We have been using your research as a framework for high school change; more specifically, to create a High School Culture of Success.
>
> As part of a grant from the Gates Foundation, we have interviewed the highest performing African American, Latino and Native American students and their parents from our most underperforming high schools in California. Using Appreciative Inquiry as our approach and methodology, we have developed seven general categories for creating a culture of high school success. Based on these categories we have developed 33 guiding principles.
>
> Until such time as we are willing to deal with what makes up a culture of success (values, beliefs and attitudes) we will not close the achievement gap for so many of our students.
>
> Because our efforts are based on your wonderful work, I was curious if you might be interested in our findings and recommendations.

I of course responded positively and with alacrity. A few months later, several members of the CCI executive committee and I, as well as some invited guest speakers (e.g., Ronald Ferguson, Harvard's expert on closing the minority achievement gap; Peter Cook, teacher at a charter school in Los Angeles that had succeeded in graduating almost all of its Latino high school students), put on a program for approximately one hundred CTA teachers and supervisors. The program was generally well received.

The CTA leadership requested a second similar program, but this time, several of its board members, including African Americans and Latinos, attended. Their reaction was anything but positive: I was subsequently told—curtly—that the CTA no longer had interest in our approach. And Yale Wishnick was fired.

Haiti

The second opportunity was Haiti, where some positive serendipity—in the form of Janet Ballantyne, old friend and USAID colleague who was the acting USAID assistant administrator for Latin America and the Caribbean—led me to Secretary of State Hillary Rodham Clinton's chief of staff, Cheryl Mills. Adding to the positive serendipity was my long-standing friendship with Peace Corps director Aaron Williams and his chief of staff, Stacy Rhodes, forged when we worked together in Haiti in the late 1970s.

Haiti being Haiti, the positive serendipity was soon overwhelmed by negative serendipity, in this case, the horrifyingly destructive earthquake of January 12, 2010, which may have taken as many as 300,000 lives. For the foreseeable future, US government resources would have to be dedicated to reconstruction.

East Timor

The USAID office in Timor Leste contacted the CCI after the program officer read *The Central Liberal Truth*. Timor Leste, which translates from Portuguese into "East Timor," is a former Portuguese colony occupying roughly half of the island of Timor, the closest to Australia of the Indonesian archipelago. It was claimed by force by Indonesia in 1975 after the Portuguese left but, with Australia's help, regained its independence in 2002 after much bloodshed.

Miguel Basáñez guided the use of the twenty-five factor questionnaire, with interesting results: the East Timorese were predictably low in the economic factors but unpredictably high in the political factors.

I had the opportunity to spend four days in Dili, the capital of East Timor, in July 2010, following a conference of the International Association for Cross-Cultural Psychology in Melbourne, where I spoke. My excellent guides were two young Timorese, Ivo Rangel and Eduardo Soares, both of whom had worked with Miguel on the survey.

I had the opportunity to meet with several Timorese leaders and the head of the USAID operation, Mark Anthony White. All were supportive of a broad-scale program of cultural change focused on the economic dimension. The design phase would have involved all the members of the CCI executive committee, with Michael Novak substituting for Peter Berger because of the predominance of the Catholic religion. The proposal also included Judith Tendler, the MIT development economist, because of her long-standing familiarity with another, if larger, former Portuguese colony, Brazil.

The interest of the Timorese leaders and the USAID people in Dili notwithstanding, I found no interest in pursuing the initiative in Washington.

Perm, Russia

In May 2010, I was in Moscow as cohost with Evgeny Yasin of a symposium on cultural values, cultural change, and economic development dedicated to the memory of Samuel Huntington. Yasin, who is the academic dean of the State University School of Higher Economics, had served as Boris Yeltsin's minister of economy.

Among the many distinguished participants in the symposium were Nobel Peace Prize winner Oscar Arias, whose presentation was subsequently converted into the lead article in the January–February 2011 issue of *Foreign Affairs*. Other symposium participants included Nobel Prize–winning economists Douglass North and Eric Maskin; Russian filmmaker Andrei Konchalovsky; Josef Joffe, editor-publisher of the German weekly newspaper *Die Zeit*; and prominent academics, journalists, and development practitioners from around the world. I subsequently learned that Oleg Cherkunov, the governor of Perm Oblast, had read and been impressed by my second book, *Who Prospers?* Perm is about one thousand miles east of Moscow and has a unique history as a way-station for those headed for the Gulag. Cherkunov had decided to set up a conference on culture, which included high and pop culture as well as cultural change, in September 2010. I was invited to give one of the keynote addresses, and several CCI colleagues also spoke.

The evening after the conference closed, I met with Cherkunov, who expressed enthusiasm for a comprehensive program of cultural change, along the lines of the programs CCI had designed for Haiti and East Timor. So we developed a proposal, substituting Christopher Marsh, director of the Institute of Church–State Studies at Baylor University and a Russia expert, for Peter Berger/Michael Novak.

The proposal was transmitted early in October, and we soon received word that a high-level official had been assigned by the governor to follow-up. However, by January 2011, momentum was lost, as were communications with the Perm government.

Trinidad and Tobago

I received the following email in January 2011:

> Your work on culture and its effect on development is invaluable, indeed you have found the key responsible for the progress of any nation. As a result

of your understanding and invaluable work, your presence is requested in Trinidad and Tobago so as to do a full presentation for the Government of the country, as well as other Caribbean nations.

It was signed by Bernard Marshall, interestingly, a police official of the government of Trinidad and Tobago. The conference has been postponed on three occasions, and I am currently awaiting word on its rescheduling.

These four-and-a-half setbacks (I consider the Trinidad and Tobago opportunity still open, although with some reservation) and simultaneous acute funding problems have taken the wind out of the sails of the CCI. But interest continues to grow in culture to explain variations in human progress—prominently stimulated by Republican presidential candidate Mitt Romney's comments in Israel—and in cultural change as an implement to accelerate progress. I have also recently received inquiries from Argentina, Latvia, and Serbia.

In Conclusion

Culture does matter, particularly in the long run. But Daniel Patrick Moynihan was right: politics, in the sense of policies and programs, *can* change culture, enabling more rapid progress. Societies *can* be substantially transformed within a generation. We have also been reminded that numerous other factors are in play, geography and natural environment prominent among them, and that culture can be trumped, for example, by adverse ideologies, as in the case of North Korea. But we are aware of how powerful culture can be, both as a facilitator of, or an obstacle to, progress.

I can think of no better way to conclude this book than with the words that concluded *Culture Matters*, echoed in *The Central Liberal Truth*:

> An important and promising . . . current focused on culture and cultural change is flowing throughout the world that has relevance for both poor countries and poor minorities in rich countries. . . . It offers an important insight into why some countries and ethnic groups have done better than others, not just in economic terms but also with respect to consolidation of democratic institutions and social justice. And those lessons of experience, which are increasingly finding practical application, may help to illuminate the path to progress for the substantial majority of the world's people for whom prosperity, democracy, and social justice have remained out of reach.

~

Notes

Introduction

1. Alexis de Tocqueville, *Democracy in America* (London: David Campbell Publishers/Everyman's Library, 1994), pp. 322–323.

2. In *A History of the Jews* (New York: Harper & Row, 1988), Paul Johnson dates Judaism from the time of Abraham, about 2000 BC. The Hebrew calendar year, in early 2009 as this is written, is 5769—the starting date is Creation, which means that something like 1,750 years passed before Abraham.

3. Ronald Inglehart, Miguel Basáñez et al., eds., *Human Beliefs and Values: A Cross-Cultural Sourcebook Based on the 1999–2002 Values Surveys* (Mexico City: Siglo Veintiuno, 2004). In the 1990 questionnaire, 52 percent of Americans and Canadians responded "Yes" to the question "Can most people be trusted?" In 2000, 36 percent of Americans and 39 percent of Canadians answered "Yes." The most trusting societies in 2000 were Denmark and Sweden, with respectively 67 percent and 66 percent of respondents saying "Yes." The least trusting was Brazil, where 3 percent of respondents said "Yes."

4. Harvard Kennedy School, Robert Putnam on Immigration and Social Cohesion, March 20, 2008, www.hks.harvard.edu/news-events/publications/insight/democratic/robert-putnam.

5. Landes used the word "toxic" in a conference, "Culture Counts," sponsored by the World Bank in Florence in the summer of 2000. That comment, and *Culture Matters* (New York: Basic Books, 2000), which contains a chapter by Landes and was a bestseller at the World Bank bookstore, may have contributed to the World Bank's decision to publish *Culture and Public Action* (Palo Alto, Calif.: Stanford Social Sciences, 2004).

6. National Security Strategy of the United States of America. The President's Report to Congress on a New National Security Strategic Doctrine for the U.S.A. by President George W. Bush, September 20, 2002.

7. Quoted in Renato Rosaldo, "Of Headhunters and Soldiers," *Issues in Ethics* 11, 1 (Winter 2000).

8. Placide David, *L'Heritage Colonial en Haiti* (Madrid: publisher unknown, 1959).

9. William Easterly, *The White Man's Burden: Why the West's Efforts to Aid the Rest Have Done So Much Ill and So Little Good* (New York: Penguin, 2006); the World Bank and the International Monetary Fund, *Finance and Development*, March 1994, p. 51.

10. From an email to me dated January 28, 2009.

11. Washington D.C, The Federal Reserve Board: Remarks by Chairman Alan Greenspan at the Woodrow Wilson Award Dinner of the Woodrow Wilson International Center for Scholars, New York, June 10, 1997.

12. United Nations International Children's Emergency Fund, "Afghanistan: Statistics," www.unicef.org/infobycountry/afghanistan_statistics.html.

13. Francis Fukuyama, *The End of History and the Last Man* (New York: Harper Perennial, 1993).

14. Oscar Arias, "Culture Matters," *Foreign Affairs* (January–February 2011).

15. Lionel Sosa, *The Americano Dream* (New York: Dutton Adult, 1998).

16. Herman Badillo, *One Nation, One Standard* (New York: Sentinel (Penguin) 2006).

17. Ernesto Caravantes, *From Melting Pot to Witch's Cauldron: How Multiculturalism Failed America* (Lanham, MD: Hamilton Books, 2010).

18. Ernesto Caravantes, *Clipping Their Own Wings: The Incompatibility between Latino Culture and American Education* (Lanham MD: Hamilton Books, 2006).

19. Ernesto Caravantes, *The Mexican-American Mind* (Lanham MD: Hamilton Books, 2008).

20. Osvaldo Hurtado, "Know Thyself: Latin America in the Mirror of Culture," *American Interest* (January–February 2010): Vol. 5.

21. Census Bureau, National Population Projections 2008: Projections of the Population by Sex, Race, and Hispanic Origin for the United States: 2010 to 2050; www.census.gov/population/www/projections/summarytables.html

22. Samuel Huntington, *Who Are We? The Challenges to America's National Identity* (New York: Simon & Schuster, 2004), p. 59.

23. Throughout this book, I will use "Confucianism" as shorthand for the several currents of Chinese culture of which Confucianism is but one, albeit the most influential.

Chapter 1

1. Mariano Grondona, with Irakli Chkonia, Ronald Inglehart, Matteo Marini, and Lawrence Harrison, "Typology of Progress-Prone and Progress-Resistant Cultures," in

Lawrence Harrison, *The Central Liberal Truth: How Politics Can Change a Culture and Save It from Itself* (New York: Oxford University Press, 2006) Table 2.1, 37–38.

2. Geert Hofstede, Gert Jan Hofstede, and Michael Minkov, *Culture's Consequences: Intercultural Cooperation and Its Importance for Survival* (New York: McGraw-Hill, 2010), p. 6.

3. Pierre Bourdieu and Jean-Claude Passeron, "Cultural Reproduction and Social Reproduction," in Richard K. Brown (Ed.), *Knowledge, Education and Cultural Change* (London: Tavistock, 1973).

4. http://en.wikipedia.org/wiki/Cultural_capital.

5. P. Bourdieu, "The Forms of Capital," in J. Richardson, ed., *Handbook of Theory and Research for the Sociology of Education* (New York: Greenwood), pp. 241–258.

6. Mariano Grondona, *Las Condiciones Culturales del Desarrollo Económico* (The Cultural Conditions of Economic Development) (Buenos Aires: Grupo Editorial Planeta, 1999).

7. Mariano Grondona, "A Cultural Typology of Economic Development," in Lawrence E. Harrison and Samuel P. Huntington eds., *Culture Matters: How Values Shape Human Progress* (New York: Basic Books, 2000) pp. 44–55.

8. Memo from Robert Hefner to author, April 28, 2004.

9. Ronald Inglehart, "Testing the Progress Typology," presented at the final Culture Matters Research Project conference at the Fletcher School, Tufts University, March 27–28, 2004, p. 10.

10. Ibid., p. 6.

11. Alexis de Tocqueville, *Democracy in America* (London: David Campbell Publishers, 1994), p. 300. Tocqueville goes on to assert that Catholicism is also nurturing of democracy so long as it is separated from the state.

12. Bassam Tibi, "Political Innovation in the Gulf: Society and State in a Changing World," presented at the ninth annual conference of the Emirate Center for Strategic Studies, Abu Dhabi, January 10–13, 2004.

13. Inglehart, "Testing the Progress Typology," Table 5.

14. Quoted in Max Weber, *The Protestant Ethic and the Spirit of Capitalism* (London and New York: HarperCollins Academic, 1992), p. 175.

15. Tibi, "Political Innovation in the Gulf," p. 13.

16. *The Economist*, November 22, 2003, p. 38.

17. James Surowiecki, "The Financial Page: Punctuality Pays," *New Yorker*, April 5, 2004.

18. George M. Foster, "Peasant Society and the Image of the Limited Good," in Jack M. Potter, May N. Diaz, and George M. Foster, eds., *Peasant Society: A Reader* (Boston: Little Brown, 1967), p. 304, emphasis in the original.

19. Bernard Lewis, "The West and the Middle East," *Foreign Affairs* (January–February 1997), p. 121.

20. David Landes, "Culture Makes Almost All the Difference," in *Culture Matters*, p. 7.

21. Weber, *The Protestant Ethic*, pp. 48–50.

22. Ibid., p. 117.

23. Hara Hiroko and Managawa Mieko, "Japanese Childhood Since 1600," English manuscript version of a chapter in *Zur Sozialgeschicte der Kindhet*, eds. Jochen Martin and August Nitschke (Freiburg/Munchen: Verlag karl Alber, 1985), p. 176.

24. Gary Becker, Library of Economics and Liberty, "The Concise Encyclopedia of Economics: Human Capital," www.econlib.org/library/Enc/HumanCapital.html, emphasis added.

25. Inglehart, "Testing the Progress Typology," Table 5.

26. The World Bank, *World Development Indicators 2003*, Table 3.15.

27. Joseph A. Schumpeter, *Capitalism, Socialism, and Democracy* (New York: Harper, 1950), p. 132.

28. Ibid.

29. Hernando De Soto, *The Mystery of Capital: Why Capitalism Triumphs in the West and Fails Everywhere Else* (New York: Basic Books, 2000).

30. John L. Stephens, *Incidents of Travel in Central America, Chiapas and Yucatan* (New York: Dover Publications, 1969), Vol. II, p. 13.

31. Grondona, "A Cultural Typology of Economic Development," in *Culture Matters*, p. 49.

32. Today the Catholic populations of the Netherlands and Switzerland may outnumber the Protestants, but the value systems of both societies have been largely shaped by Protestantism. What matters, as Ronald Inglehart points out in his chapter, "Culture and Democracy," in *Culture Matters* (p. 91) is "the historical impact . . . on the societies as a whole."

33. Inglehart, "Testing the Progress Typology," in *Culture Matters*, p. 4.

34. Ibid., p. 2.

35. From a *Washington Post* article, "Putting the Good in Good Government," November 1, 1998, p. C5. The writers of the report included Rafael LaPorta, Florencio López de Silanes, and Andrei Schleifer of Harvard and Robert Vishny of the University of Chicago.

36. David Hackett Fischer, *Albion's Seed: Four British Folkways in America* (New York and Oxford: Oxford University Press, 1989), p. 24.

37. Edward Banfield, *The Moral Basis of a Backward Society* (New York: Free Press, 1958).

38. Roberto DaMatta, *A Casa e a Rua* (São Paolo: Editora Brasiliense, 1985), p. 40.

39. Robert Putnam, *Making Democracy Work* (Princeton, NJ: Princeton University Press, 1994).

40. Robert Putnam, *Bowling Alone* (New York: Touchstone Books by Simon & Schuster, 2001).

41. Cited by Francis Fukuyama in *Trust: The Social Virtues and the Creation of Prosperity* (New York: Free Press, 1995), p. 10.

42. Robert Putnam, *Making Democracy Work*, p. 170.

43. José Ortega y Gasset, *Invertebrate Spain* (New York: Norton, 1937), pp. 152–153.

44. Daniel Etounga-Manguelle, "Does Africa Need a Cultural Adjustment Program?," in *Culture Matters*, p. 71.

45. Tu Weiming, "Multiple Modernities: A Preliminary Inquiry into the Implications of East Asian Modernity," in *Culture Matters*, p. 264.

46. Magnus Blomström and Patricio Meller, *Diverging Paths* (Washington, D.C.: Inter-American Development Bank, 1991).

47. Dag Blanck and Thorleif Pettersson, "Strong Governance and Civic Participation: Some Notes on the Cultural Dimension of the Swedish Model," in Lawrence Harrison and Peter Berger, *Developing Cultures: Case Studies* (New York: Routledge, 2006) 486.

48. Email to author, April 28, 2004.

49. Alfred Stepan, *Arguing Comparative Politics* (Oxford and New York: Oxford University Press, 2001), p. 217.

50. Yilmaz Esmer, "Turkey Torn Between Two Civilizations," in *Developing Cultures: Case Studies*, p. 227.

51. World Bank, *World Development Indicators 2003*, Table 2.14.

52. Alicia Hammond, "Heterosexism and Cultural Development in Jamaica," term paper prepared for the Culural Capital and Development Seminar, The Fletcher School, Tufts University, Fall 2010.

Chapter 2

1. Daniel Etounga Manguelle, "Does Africa Need a Cultural Adjustment Program?" in Lawrence Harrison and Samuel Huntington, *Culture Matters: How Values Shape Human Progress* (New York: Basic Books, 2000) 65–77

2. Daron Acemoglu and James A. Robinson, *Why Nations Fail* (New York: Crown Business, 2012).

3. Ibid., p. 57.

4. Ibid., p. 73.

5. Douglass North, *Institutions, Institutional Change and Economic Performance* (Cambridge, UK: Cambridge University Press, 1990), pp. 36–37, emphasis added.

6. Inglehart, "Culture and Democracy," in *Culture Matters*, p. 91.

7. Angus Maddison, *The World Economy in the 20th Century* (Paris: OECD, 1989), Table 1.3.

8. The U.S. Census Bureau calculated median income for white families at $60,088 in 2009 (in the 2010 census, whites accounted for 63.7 percent of the American population); median family income for Asians in the United States (Asians accounted for 4.8 percent of the total population in 2010) such was $75,027; median income for black families (blacks accounted for 12.6 percent of the total population in 2010) was $38,409; median income for Hispanic families (Hispanics accounted for 16.3 percent of the total population in 2010) was $39,730. www.census.gov/compendia/statab/2012/tables/12s0695.pdf

9. "France's Protestants—Prim but Punchy," *The Economist*, April 18, 1998, p. 48.

10. *Washington Post*, November 1, 1998, p. C5.

11. Published by the World Economic Forum on October 13, 2004 .

12. www.haaretz.com/print-edition/news/israel-ranks-fourth-in-the-world-in-scientific
-activity-study-finds-1.4034.

13. Centre for Global Development and *Foreign Policy Magazine*, website of latter,
October 2004.

14. Roger Doyle, "Civic Culture," *Scientific American* (June 2004), p. 34.

15. Nikolas Gvosdev, cited in Lawrence E. Harrison, *The Central Liberal Truth:
How Politics Can Change a Culture and Save It From Itself* (New York: Oxford University Press, 2006), pp. 107–108.

16. Irakli Chkonia, "Timeless Identity versus Final Modernity: Identity Master
Myth and Social Change in Georgia," in Lawrence E. Harrison and Peter Berger eds.,
Developing Cultures: Case Studies (New York: Routledge, 2006), p. 354.

17. Nikolas Gvosdev, "Reimagining the Orthodox Tradition," in Lawrence Harrison and Jerome Kagan, eds., *Developing Cultures: Essays on Cultural Change* (New
York: Routledge, 2006), p. 206.

18. The fertility data in Table 1 were drawn from the UN's *Human Development
Report 2002*; the *Human Development Report 2003* contains the 2000–2005 estimates.

19. World Values Survey (WVS) data for trust in 2000 in the Islamic countries
contain two apparent anomalies that substantially increase the Islamic averages:
65 percent of Iranians (the same as Norwegians) and 38 percent of Egyptians (2 percent higher than the United States) believe that most people can be trusted. We
are reminded of the fallibility of WVS data, particularly in authoritarian societies,
where people may respond to questions not with what they really believe but what
they believe the government wants them to say. However, the WVS data for 2006
made major adjustments: Iran dropped fifty-four points to 11 percent, by far the largest drop; and Egypt dropped by twenty points to 18 percent, the second largest drop.

20. Iraq is ranked 175, Afghanistan tied with Burma (Myanmar) at 176. Somalia
is in last place.

21. http://en.wikipedia.org/wiki/Jewish_population.

Chapter 3

1. Steven L. Pease, *The Golden Age of Jewish Achievement: The Compendium of a
Culture, a People, and Their Stunning Performance* (Sonoma, Calif.: Deucalion, 2009),
p. 15.

2. Malcolm Gladwell, *The Outliers* (New York: Little, Brown, 2008), the quote
appears on pp. 142–143.

3. For a listing of prominent Canadian Jews, see http://en.wikipedia.org/wiki/
List_of_Canadian_Jews. Among them are a deputy prime minister, several cabinet
ministers, many members of parliament, and mayors of Toronto, Vancouver, Quebec
City, Halifax, and Edmonton.

4. Farrukh Saleem, "Why Are the Jews So Powerful?," Ibnmahadi's Blog, January 12, 2009, http://ibnmahadi.wordpress.com/2009/01/12/why-are-the-jews-so-powerful-by -dr-farrukh-saleem-the-writer-is-a-pakistani-an-islamabad-based-freelance-columnist/.

5. Steven Silbiger, *The Jewish Phenomenon: Seven Keys to the Enduring Wealth of a People* (Atlanta: Longstreet, 2000), back cover.

6. Plinio Apuleyo Mendoza, Carlos Alberto Montaner, and Álvaro Vargas Llosa, *Guide to the Perfect Latin American Idiot* (Lanham, MD: Madison Books, 2001).

7. Plinio Apuleyo Mendoza, Carlos Alberto Montaner, and Álvaro Vargas Llosa, *El Regreso del Idiota* (Mexico City: Grijalbo Publisher, 2007).

8. Email, Montaner to Harrison, July 7, 2008.

9. Max Weber, *The Protestant Ethic and the Spirit of Capitalism* (London and New York: Routledge, 2000), chap. 1, n. 5, pp. 188–189.

10. Silbiger, *The Jewish Phenomenon*, p. 121.

11. Jewish Virtual Library, "Jewish Population of the World, 2010," www.jewish-virtuallibrary.org/jsource/Judaism/jewpop.html.

12. Interestingly, in terms of the percentage of the Jewish population to the total, Uruguay stands first at 0.53%.

13. www.liveincostarica.com.

14. Samuel Stone, *La Dinastía de los Conquistadores* (San José, Costa Rica: Editorial Universitaria Centroamérica, 1975), p. 71.

15. For more on Zemurray see Lawrence Harrison, *The Pan-American Dream* (New York: Basic Books, 1997), pp. 96–100.

16. See Gonzalo Trejos Chacón, *Costa Rica Es Distinto en Hispano América* (San José: Imprenta Trejos Hermanos, 1969).

17. http://en.wikipedia.org/wiki/Luis_Carvajal_y_de_la_Cueva.

18. Jewish Virtual Library, "Virtual Jewish History Tour," www.jewishvirtualli-brary.org/jsource/vjw/Mexico.html.

19. Everett Hagen, "The Entrepreneur as Rebel Against Traditional Society," *Human Organization* 19, 4 (Winter 1960), pp. 185–187.

20. House of Inquisition Museum in Cartagena, Colombia, www.learnnc.org/lp/multimedia/2780. In "The Dawn of the Sephardic Revival" www.ifmj.org, Rabbi Haim Levi has this to say: "The story of my family's Sephardic Jewish roots begins in Medellin, Colombia, where a colony of Sephardic Jews from Spain, Holland, and Portugal settled in the late 1500s."

21. Preston E. James, "Expanding Frontiers of Settlement in Latin America," *Hispanic American Historical Review* 21, 2 (May 1941), pp. 183–185.

22. Ibid., p. 24.

23. Ibid., p. 170.

24. Ibid., p. 177.

25. Ibid., p. 178.

26. Paul Johnson, *A History of the Jews* (New York: Harper & Row, 1988), 283.

27. http://en.wikipedia.org/wiki/Heinrich_Heine.

28. Jews constituted around 35 percent of Brookline's population in 2002. (http://en.wikipedia.org/wiki/Brookline,_Massachusetts). My sense is that the percentage was even higher in the 1940s and 1950s.

29. Jewish Virtual Library, www.jewishvirtuallibrary.org.

30. Samuel Huntington, *Who Are We? The Challenges to America's National Identity* (New York: Simon and Schuster, 2004), p. xvi.

31. Richard J. Herrnstein and Charles Murray, *Bell Curve: Intelligence and Class Structure in American Life* (New York: Free Press, 1994).

32. See, for example, William Saletan, "Jewgenics," *Slate*, November 1, 2007, www.slate.com/id/2177228/.

33. Paul Johnson, *A History of the Jews*.

34. Quoted in J. H. Hertz, ed., *The Pentateuch and Haftorahs* (London: Soncino Press, 1961), p. 196.

35. Cited in Lawrence Harrison, *Who Prospers?* (New York: Basic Books, 1992), p. 149.

36. Silbiger, *The Jewish Phenomenon*, pp. 193-94.

37. Silbiger, *The Jewish Phenomenon*, p. 186.

38. One is reminded of the Calvinist doctrine of "calling" that humans are put on earth to do something to enhance the glory of God—and of Eric Liddell's motivation in the 1924 Olympics.

39. Jim Lederman, "The Development of the Jews," in Lawrence E. Harrison and Jerome Kagan (eds.), *Developing Cultures: Essays on Cultural Change* (New York: Routledge, 2006), pp. 157–175 passim.

40. Silbiger, *The Jewish Phenomenon*, p. 186.

Chapter 4

1. www.google.com/search?client=safari&rls=en&q=Korea+is+more+Confucian+than+China&ie=UTF-8&oe=UTF-#q=Korea+is+more+Confucian+than+China&hl=en&client=safari&rls=en&prmd=imvns&ei=9WUdUOC1JoXf0QH17oCYCQ&start=10&sa=N&bav=on.2,or.r_gc.r_pw.r_qf.&fp=74d00b0500df2a74&biw=998&bih=1007 ILHYUNG LEE, UNIVRSITY OF MISSOURI-COLUMBIA

2. Ruth Benedict, *The Chrysanthemum and the Sword* (North Clarendon VT: Charles E. Tuttle, 1954).

3. For a comprehensive analysis of the role of Confucianism in Vietnam, see William Ratliff, "Confucianism and Development in Vietnam," prepared for the Culture Matters, Culture Changes conference at the Fletcher School, October 24–26, 2008.

4. The Navy Department Library, "The Religions of Vietnam," April 1968, www.history.navy.mil/library/online/religions.htm#viet. Ambrose Y. C. King and Michael H. Bond observe, "While we fully appreciate that Chinese culture is a far from homogeneous system, it seems to us that Confucian values have played a

predominant role in molding Chinese character and behavior." ("The Confucian Paradigm of Man: A Sociological View," in Wen-Shing Tseng and David Y. H. Wu, eds., *Chinese Culture and Mental Health* [Orlando, Fla.: Academic Press, 1985], p. 29.)

5. A collection of essays presented at a 2008 conference at Tufts University dedicated to Samuel Huntington, currently under consideration for publication. I am the editor.

6. Pham Duy Nghia, "Confucianism and the Conception of the Law in Vietnam," in John Gillespie and Pip Nicholson, eds., *Asian Socialism & Legal Change: The Dynamics of Vietnamese and Chinese Reform* (Canberra: Asia Pacific Press at the Australian National University, 2005) p. 86.

7. Confucius was the principal but far from the only architect of the system. Most prominent among his many disciples through the ages was Meng-tsu (Latinized as Mencius), who lived some 200 years later.

8. Edwin O. Reischauer and John K. Fairbank, *East Asia: The Great Tradition* (Boston: Houghton Mifflin, 1960), p. 70.

9. Ibid., p. 30.

10. Ibid., p. 28.

11. Roy Hofheinz, Jr., and Kent Calder, *The Eastasia Edge* (New York: Basic Books, 1982), p. 121.

12. Reischauer and Fairbank, *East Asia*, p. 74.

13. Ibid., p. 72.

14. Lucian Pye, "Tiananmen and Chinese Political Culture—The Escalation of Confrontation from Moralizing to Revenge," *Current Asian Survey* 30, 4 (April 1990), pp. 331–347.

15. Ibid.

16. Government Information Office, Republic of China (Taiwan), Income Distribution in Taiwan," www.gio.gov.tw/info/taiwan-story/society/edown/table/table-1 .htm.

17. The post–World War II economic success of Italy, Spain, and Ireland has also been cited as evidence of a fundamental flaw in Weber's belief that Catholicism provides an unpropitious value setting for economic dynamism. Readers will recall that the "miracle" of all three—and the Province of Quebec—involved secularization to the point that one hears the term "post-Catholic" applied to each.

18. Max Weber, *The Religion of China* (New York: Macmillan, 1951), pp. 18, 20, 76.

19. Malcolm Gladwell take note—see the concluding comment in this chapter.

20. Weber, *The Religion of China*, pp. 33, 79, 76.

21. Ibid., p. 81, emphasis added.

22. Edwin O. Reischauer and John K. Fairbank, *East Asia: The Modern Transformation* (Boston: Houghton Mifflin, 1965), p. 93.

23. Weber, *The Religion of China*, p. 80.

24. Lucian Pye, *Asian Power and Politics* (Cambridge, Mass: Belknap Press of Harvard University Press), p. 60.

25. Pye, *Asian Power and Politics*, p. 160.

26. Edward S. Mason, Mahn Je Kim, Dwight H. Perkins, Kwang Suk Kim, and David C. Cole, *The Economic and Social Modernization of the Republic of Korea* (Cambridge, Mass., and London: Harvard University Press), pp. 284–285.

27. From an unpublished 1987 paper, "The Transformation of Confucianism in the Post Confucian Era," prepared for the 2008 conference at the Fletcher School.

28. Tu Weiming, "A Perspective on Confucian Democracy in Cultural China, " in *Culture Matters, Culture Changes*.

29. UN Food and Agriculture Organization, "Rice Paddy: Production," www.fao .org/docrep/004/ad452e/ad452e0f.htm.

Chapter 5

1. Michael Novak, *The Catholic Ethic and the Spirit of Capitalism* (New York: Free Press, 1993).

2. John Nicholas Murphy, in *Ireland Industrial, Political, and Social* (New York: Longman, Green, 1870), estimates that 76.5 percent of Ireland's land—15.5 million acres—is arable compared to 22.3 percent of Scotland's—4.4 million acres.

3. It is doubtful that any man of the cloth in the sixteenth century would have considered women on the same footing as men. On the other hand, the emphasis on literacy extended to women as well as men.

4. Arthur Herman, *How the Scots Invented the Modern World* (New York: Three Rivers Press, 2001), pp. 23, 25.

5. Alexis de Tocqueville, *Democracy in America* (New York: Harper Perennial, 1969), p. 288.

6. Ibid., p. 117.

7. Napoléon Roussel, *Catholic and Protestant Nations Compared* (Lenox, Mass.: Hard Press, 2007[1854]), pp. 90–91.

8. Washington State University, Paul Brians, "The Enlightenment," March 11, 1999, www.wsu.edu/~brians/hum_303/enlightenment.html.

9. http://www.newschool.edu/het//schools/scottish.htm.

10. General Register Office for Scotland, "Registrar General's Review of Scotland's Population 2004," July 29, 2005, www.gro-scotland.gov.uk/press/news2005/ registrar-generals-review-of-scotlands-population.html.

11. Wesley Johnston, "Settlement in Ireland," www.wesleyjohnston.com/users/ ireland/geography/settlement.html.

12. Oracle Education Foundation: ThinkQuest, "Immigration: The Journey to America," http://library.thinkquest.org/20619/Irish.html.

13. Dick Spring, "Ireland as the Celtic Tiger: How Did It Happen?" in Lawrence Harrison and Peter Berger, eds., *Developing Cultures: Case Studies* (New York and London: Routledge, 2006), pp. 419–424.

14. Nikolas Gvosdev, "Reimagining the Orthodox Tradition: Nurturing Democratic Values in Orthodox Christian Civilization," in Lawrence E. Harrison and

Jerome Kagan eds., *The Developing Cultures: Essays on Cultural Change* (New York: Routledge, 2006), pp. 195–208.

15. In the article "Civic Culture" in *Scientific American* (June 2004), Rodger Doyle writes, "Political scientists Tom W. Rice of the university of Iowa and Jan L. Feldman of the University of Vermont have measured civic culture among ancestry groups in the U.S. They find that Americans of Scandinavian and British descent have the highest levels of civic culture."

16. Dag Blanck and Thorleif Pettersson, "Strong Governance and Civic Participation," in Lawrence Harrison and Peter Berger, eds., *Developing Cultures: Case Studies*, pp. 483–498.

17. Ibid., p. 489.

18. Quoted in ibid., p. 9.

19. Samuel Huntington, *Who Are We? The Challenges to America's National Identity* (New York: Simon and Schuster, 2004), p. 59.

20. Ibid., p. 75.

21. Gunnar Myrdal, *An American Dilemma* (New York: Harper, 1944), Vol. 1, p. 495.

22. Huntington, *Who Are We?*, p. 71.

23. Ibid., pp. 68–69.

24. Ibid., p. 79.

25. Robert Woodberry, National University of Singapore, "The Missionary Roots of Liberal Democracy," *American Political Science Review*, May 2012, pp. 244-74, passim.

Chapter 6

1. Steven L. Pease, *The Golden Age of Jewish Achievement* (Sonoma, Calif.: Deucalion Press, 2009).

2. François Depons, *Viaje a la Parte Oriental de la Tierra Firme en la América Meridional* ("Trip to the Eastern Part of South America") (Caracas: Central Bank of Venezuela, 1960).

3. Ibid., p. 84.

4. Ibid., p. 85.

5. Ibid., p. 105.

6. http://en.wikipedia.org/wiki/Basque_people.

7. Ibid. A range of 1.6 million to 4.5 million is cited.

8. Arnold J. Bauer, *Chilean Rural Society* (Cambridge, UK: Cambridge University Press, 1975), pp. 6, 24.

9. Ibid.

10. The team was a major step toward an early John F. Kennedy administration National Security Action Memorandum that established support of civic action as a US policy. My participation led to my shifting from OSD to USAID in May 1962.

11. David Hojman, "Economic Development and the Evolution of National Culture: The Case of Chile," in Lawrence Harrison and Peter Berger, eds., *Developing Cultures: Case Studies* (New York and London: Routledge, 2006), p. 281.

12. Ibid., p. 271.

13. The Basque Museum and Cultural Center, http://www.basquemuseum.com/content/Echevarria_Ramon.

14. Kikim Media, "Company History," www.kikim.com/xml/aboutUsCompany History.php.

Chapter 7

1. Edward Banfield, *The Moral Basis of a Backward Society* (New York: Free Press, 1958), p. 17.

2. See, for example, Park Romney, *The Apostasy of a High Priest* (West Conshohocken, Pa.: Infinity Publishing); Park Romney is a second cousin of Mitt Romney.

3. For a particularly funny address to the issue of baptism of dead Jews, see Stephen Colbert's February 23, 2012, segment on *The Colbert Report*, "Posthumous Mormon Baptism,": www.colbertnation.com/the-colbert-report-videos/409086/february-23-2012/posthumous-mormon-baptism.

4. All About Mormons, "Famous Mormons," www.allaboutmormons.com/famous_mormons.php.

5. *The Central Liberal Truth*, p. 53.

6. The Church of Jesus Christ of the Latter-Day Saints, "The Family: A Proclamation to the World," September 23, 1995, www.lds.org/ensign/1995/11/the-family-a-proclamation-to-the-world.

7. Islamic Insights, Sumayya Kassamali, "Why Canada Doesn't Need an Islamic Art Museum," June 8, 2010, www.islamicinsights.com/news/opinion/why-canada-doesn-t-need-an-islamic-art-museum.html.

8. Stephen Pinker, *The Better Angels of Our Nature: Why Violence Has Declined* (New York: Viking Adult, 2011), pp. 363–364.

9. Bernardo Vega, "We Got Bad Marks in Davos," in the 2010–2011 Global Index of Competitiveness. Unpublished, n.d.

10. Alexis de Tocqueville, *Democracy in America* (London: David Campbell Publishers/Everyman's Library, 1994), pp. 322–323.

11. Thomas Friedman, "Facebook meets Brick-and-Mortar Politics," *New York Times*, June 10, 2012. www.nytimes.com/2012/06/10/opinion/sunday/friedman-facebook-meets-brick-and-mortar-politics.html?_r=2&ref=thomaslfriedman

12. UN Development Program and Arab Fund for Economic and Social Development, *Arab Human Development Report 2002* (New York: UNDP, 2002), p. 8.

Chapter 8

1. Carlos Rangel, *The Latin Americans: Their Love-Hate Relationship with the United States* (New Brunswick, N.J.: Transaction, 1987), p. 182.

2. Excerpted from a speech made in the Faculty of Law and Social Sciences of Buenos Aires.

3. Quoted from Daniel R. Miller, "Protestantism and Radicalism in Mexico from the 1860s to the 1930s," www.calvin.edu/henry/research/symposiumpapers/Symp08 Dmiller.pdf.

4. Rangel, *The Latin Americans*, p. 67.

5. Magnus Blomström and Patricio Meller, eds., *Diverging Paths* (Washington, D.C.: Inter-American Development Bank, 1991).

6. For an explanation of Costa Rica's democratic evolution, see Lawrence E. Harrison, *Underdevelopment Is a State of Mind—The Latin American Case* (Lanham, Md., and London: Center for International Affairs, Harvard University, and University Press of America, 1985), chap. 3.

7. Alexis de Tocqueville, *Democracy in America* (London: David Campbell Publishers/Everyman's Library, 1994), p. 320.

8. Charles de Secondat, Baron de Montesquieu, *The Spirit of the Laws* (Cambridge, UK, and New York: Cambridge University Press, 1989).

9. Ellsworth Huntington, *Civilization and Climate* (New Haven, Conn.: Yale University Press, 1915). For a more recent argument on the impact of climate on culture, see Thomas Sowell, *Race and Culture: A World View* (New York: Basic Books, 1994).

10. Lucian Pye, with Mary Pye, *Asian Power and Politics: The Cultural Dimensions of Authority* (Cambridge, Mass.: Belknap Press of Harvard University Press, 1985), p. 4.

11. Keith Rosenn, "Federalism in the Americas in Comparative Perspective," *Inter-American Law Review* 26, 1 (Fall 1994).

12. Gunnar Myrdal, *An American Dilemma* (New York: Harper, 1944), chap. 18.

13. Tocqueville, *Democracy in America*, p. 300. Tocqueville also concludes, presciently, that secularization of Catholic societies will make them more susceptible to democracy (p. 301).

14. Ibid., pp. 322–323.

15. Ibid., p. 299.

16. Ibid., pp. 320, 231–232.

17. Max Weber, *The Protestant Ethic and the Spirit of Capitalism* (London and New York: Routledge, 2000), p. 117.

18. Rosenn told me the anecdote in an October 1995 conversation in his office.

19. David Martin, "Evangelical Expansion and 'Progressive Values' in the Developing World," in Harrison and Kagan, eds. *Developing Cultures: Essays on Cultural Change*, Vol. I collection of essays, pp. 117–36.

20. Ibid., p. 11.

21. Tocqueville, *Democracy in America*, pp. 300–301.

22. Michael Novak, *The Catholic Ethic and the Spirit of Capitalism* (New York: Free Press, 1993).

23. "Contradictions," *The Economist* (April 12, 2003), p. 48.

24. Marlise Simons, "Spain Is Seeking to Integrate Growing Muslim Population," *New York Times*, October 24, 2004.

25. World Bank Organization, "2007 World Development Indicators: Distribution of Income or Consumption," http://siteresources.worldbank.org/DATASTATISTICS/Resources/table2_7.pdf.

26. United Nations Development Programme, "Intentional Homicides per 100,000 People, 2000–2004: Ranked Lowest to Highest," www.photius.com/rankings/murder_rate_of_countries_2000-2004.html.

27. http://en.wikipedia.org/wiki/Catholic_sexual_abuse_scandal_in_Latin_America.

28. www.nytimes.com/2012/06/06/world/americas/paraguay-president-acknowledges-fathering-second-child-as-bishop.html.

29. Henry McDonald, "'Endemic' Rape and Abuse of Irish Children in Catholic Care," The Guardian, May 20, 2009, www.guardian.co.uk/world/2009/may/20/irish-catholic-schools-child-abuse-claims.

30. Dance with Shadows, "Amen—Autobiography of a Nun, by Sister Jesme, Alleges Sexual Abuse and Corruption in Kerala's Catholic Church," February 20, 2009, www.dancewithshadows.com/politics/amen-autobiography-of-a-nun sister-jesme/.

31. Margaret A. Farley, Just Love: A Framework for Christian Sexual Ethics (New York and London: Continuum Books, 2006). It was number sixty-seven on Amazon Books as of June 10, 2012.

32. Sharon Otterman, "For New York Archdiocese's One New Priest, a Lonely Distinction," New York Times, June 12, 2012, www.nytimes.com/2012/06/13/nyregion/patric-darcy-is-ny-archdioceses-only-new-priest.html?pagewanted=all.

Chapter 9

1. Charles Murray, Coming Apart: The State of White America (New York: Crown Publishing, 2012).

2. Steven Ceasar, "Hispanic Population Tops 50 Million in U.S.," Los Angeles Times, March 24, 2011, http://articles.latimes.com/2011/mar/24/nation/la-na-census-hispanic-20110325. I have worked with another Census Bureau projection that predicts that 24.4 percent of our population will be Hispanic in 2050, so I called the Census Bureau on June 16, 2011, and was told that the "current" projection is the one in the LA Times report.

3. The Daily Howler, "The Three Americas," October 4, 2010, www.dailyhowler.com/dh100410.shtml.

4. Pew Research Center, Pew Hispanic Center, "Immigration," http://pewhispanic.org/topics/?TopicID=16.

5. Mario Vargas Llosa, "América Latina y la Opción Liberal," in Barry Levine, ed., El desafío neoliberal: El fin del tercermundismo en Amérca Latina (Bogotá, 1992), cited in Claudio Véliz, The New World of the Gothic Fox: Culture and Economy in English and Spanish America (Berkeley and Los Angeles: University of California Press, 1994), pp. 190–191.

6. Octavio Paz, El Ogro Filantrópico ("The Philanthropic Ogre") (Mexico City: Joaquín Mortiz, 1979), p. 55, my translation.

7. Teodoro Moscoso, "The Will to Economic Development," in L. Ronald Scheman, ed., *The Alliance for Progress—A Retrospective* (New York, Westport, Conn., and London: Praeger, 1988), p. 86.

8. Hurtado is referring to Carlos Rangel's *The Latin Americans: Their Love-Hate Relationship with the United States* (New Brunswick, N.J.: Transaction, 1987).

9. Ernesto Caravantes, *From Melting Plot to Witch's Cauldron: How Multiculturalism Failed America* (Lanham, Md.: Hamilton Books, 2010), pp. vii, x.

10. Samuel Huntington, *Who Are We?: The Challenges to America's National Identity* (New York: Simon and Schuster, 2004), p. 59.

11. Nanette Asimov, "California High School Dropout Rate Far Higher than Expected," *San Francisco Chronicle*, July 17, 2008, http://articles.sfgate.com/2008-07-17/bay-area/17174438_1_dropout-rate-students-ethnic-groups.

12. Herman Badillo, *One Nation, One Standard: An Ex-Liberal on How Hispanics Can Succeed Just Like Other Immigrant Groups* (New York: Penguin Group, 2006), p. 40.

13. The Pew Hispanic Center, "Statistical Portrait of Hispanics in the United States, 2007: Table 21. Educational Attainment, by Race and Ethnicity: 2007," http://pewhispanic.org/files/factsheets/hispanics2007/Table-21.pdf.

14. N. C. Aizenman, "Second-Generation Latinos Struggle for a Higher Foothold," *Washington Post*, December 6, 2009, www.washingtonpost.com/wp-dyn/content/article/2009/12/06/AR2009120602775.html.

15. Center for Reproductive Health Research and Policy, Department of Obstetrics, Gynecology and Reproductive Sciences and The Institute for Health Policy Studies, University of California, San Francisco, "Fact Sheet on Latino Youth: Education," November 2002, http://bixbycenter.ucsf.edu/publications/files/Latino.edu.pdf.

16. Mary C. Dickson of the Population Resource Center and updated by Megan McNamara in March 2004, "Latina Teen Pregnancy: Problems and Prevention," www.prcdc.org/files/Latina_Teen_Pregnancy.pdf.

17. Diversity, Inc., www.niji.gov/journals/270/criminal-records.htm.

18. Department of Health and Human Services, 2008 Indicators of Welfare Dependence "Chapter II. Indicators of Dependence: Rates of Participation in Means-Tested Assistance Programs," http://aspe.hhs.gov/hsp/indicators08/ch2.shtml#ind4.

19. CNN U.S., "Minorities Expected to Be Majority in 2050," July 13, 2008, http://articles.cnn.com/2008-08-13/us/census.minorities_1_hispanic-population-census-bureau-white-population?_s=PM:US.

20. Samuel P. Huntington, *Who Are We?: The Challenges to America's National Identity* (New York: Simon & Schuster, 2004) p. 324.

21. Schonfeld email to Harrison, May 26, 2011.

22. Huntington, *Who Are We?*, p. 323.

23. German is also an official Belgian language, although it is spoken by only 1 percent of the inhabitants.

24. Huntington, *Who Are We?*

25. Ibid, p. 324.

Chapter 10

1. Clay Waters, "Obama: Now a Hero in Brazil, too, According to NY Times," NewsBusters, March 21, 2011, http://newsbusters.org/blogs/clay-waters/2011/03/21/obama-now-hero-brazil-too-according-ny-times.

2. TASAI, Togolese Association In Arizona, "Welcome to Jean-Pierre Kuegah," November, 18, 2008, http://usamonoafrica.com/wjpkuegah.html.

3. Peter Walker, "The World Reacts to the New US President," *The Guardian*, November 5, 2008, www.guardian.co.uk/world/2008/nov/05/barackobama-uselections2008.

4. Richard D. Lamm, *Two Wands, One Nation: An Essay on Race and Community in America* (Golden, Colo.: Fulcrum Publishing, 2006), p. 3.

5. Derrick Z. Jackson, "A Lesson for Cornel West," *Boston Globe*, May 28, 2011, p. A15.

6. William Finnegan, "Black Like Me," *New York Times Book Review*, March 30, 1997.

7. Thomas Sowell, *Ethnic America: A History* (New York: Basic Books, 1981).

8. Ibid., p. 200.

9. Thomas Sowell, *The Economics and Politics of Race* (New York: Quill, 1983), p. 128.

10. Sowell, *Ethnic America*, p. 216.

11. Ibid., p. 219.

12. Orlando Patterson, "Taking Culture Seriously: A Framework and an Afro-American Illustration," in Harrison and Huntington eds., *Culture Matters*, pp. 202–18.

13. Ibid., p. 212.

14. Ibid., p. 214.

15. Ibid., p. 217.

16. John McWhorter, "Scene from a Fast-Food Restaurant: Signs of the Times in Black America and the Path Beyond," in Lawrence Harrison and Peter Berger, eds., *Developing Cultures: Case Studies Developing Cultures: Case Studies* (New York and London: Routledge, 2006), pp. 409–18.

17. John McWhorter, *Losing The Race: Self-Sabotage In Black America* (New York: Harper Perennial, 2001).

18. Ibid., pp. 4–6.

19. Ibid., p. 21.

Chapter 11

1. Thomas Friedman, "It Has to Start With Them," *New York Times Sunday Review*, June 25, 2011, www.nytimes.com/2011/06/26/opinion/sunday/26friedman.html.

2. Daniel Latouche, "Culture and the Pursuit of Success," in Lawrence Harrison and Peter Berger, eds., *Developing Cultures: Case Studies* (New York and London: Routledge, 2006), pp. 12–13.

3. See in Lawrence E. Harrison, ed., *The Central Liberal Truth: How Politics Can Change a Culture and Save It from Itself* (Oxford: Oxford University Press, 2006), pp. 190–192.

4. See Celia W. Dugger, "To Help Poor Be Pupils, Not Earners, Brazil Pays Parents," *New York Times*, January 3, 2004, p. 1, www.nytimes.com/2004/01/03/world/to-help-poor-be-pupils-not-wage-earners-brazil-pays-parents.html?pagewanted=all&src=pm.

5. Luis Diego Herrera, "Parenting Practices and Governance in Latin America: The Case of Costa Rica," in Harrison and Kagan eds., *Developing Cultures: Essays on Cultural Change*, pp. 21–33.

6. Jerome Kagan, "Culture, Values, and the Family," in *Developing Cultures: Essays on Cultural Change*, pp. 3–19 passim [author's emphasis].

7. Richard G. Niemi and Steven E. Finkel, "Civic Education and the Development of Civic Knowledge and Attitudes," in Lawrence E. Harrison and Jerome Kagan, *Developing Cultures: Essays on Cultural Change*.

8. Fernando Reimers and Eleonora Villegas-Reimers, "Schooling Open Societies in Latin America," in *Developing Cultures: Essays on Cultural Change*, pp. 95–114, passim.

9. Thomas Lickona, "Character Education: Restoring Virtue to the Mission of Schools," in *Developing Cultures: Essays on Cultural Change*, pp. 57–76.

10. Gurcharan Das, "India: How a Rich Nation Became Poor and Will Be Rich Again," in *Developing Cultures: Case Studies*, p. 152.

11. James Brooke, "A Mongolian and His Nation, Evolving Together," *New York Times*, December 25, 2004, p. A4, reported on a Mongolian program to promote mastery of English. http://query.nytimes.com/gst/fullpage.html?res=9F06E4DA1E30F936A15751C1A9629C8B63&pagewanted=all

12. Pratap Bhanu Mehta, "Hinduism and Modernity," in *Developing Cultures: Essays on Cultural Change*, pp. 275–292.

13. Jay L. Garfield, "Buddhism and Democracy," www.buddhistinformation.com/buddhism_and_democracy.htm.

14. Christal Whelan, "Buddhist Economics in Asia," in *Developing Cultures: Essays on Cultural Change*, pp. 235–244.

15. Daniel Etounga-Manguelle, "Does Africa Need a Cultural Adjustment Program?," in *Culture Matters*, p. 73.

16. Animism also finds some adherents in Asia—see, for example, Robert Weller's CMRP paper on Taiwan, "Market Development, Political Development, and Taiwanese Political Cultures," in *Developing Cultures: Case Studies*, pp. 119–137.

17. Daniel Latouche, "Culture and the Pursuit of Success: The Case of Québec in the Twentieth Century," in *Developing Cultures: Case Studies*, p. 450.

18. Hernando de Soto, *The Mystery of Capital* (New York: Basic Books, 2003).

19. Octavio Sánchez, "Culture and Legal Dogmatism in an Era of Immaterial Wealth," presented at the 2008 "Culture Matters, Culture Changes" conference.

20. Mary O'Grady, "Honduras' Experiment With Free-Market Cities," *Wall Street Journal*, February 14, 2011, http://online.wsj.com/article/SB10001424052748703843004576139000748751220.html.

21. Mike Gibson, "More on Honduras's Charter City in the Making," *Let a Thousand Nations Bloom*, February 21, 2011, http://athousandnations.com/2011/02/21/more-on-hondurass-charter-city-in-the-making/.

22. Reese Schonfeld, "The Global Battle for Cultural Domination," in *Developing Cultures: Essays on Cultural Change*, pp. 306, 309–310.

23. Ibid., pp. 311–314, passim.

24. Geert Hofstede, Culture's Consequences: Comparing Values, Behaviors, Institutions and Organizations Across Nations (Thousand Oaks CA: Sage Publications, 2001).

25. David Rockefeller Center for Latin American Studies and Hauser Center for Nonprofit Organizations, Harvard University, "Strengthening Philanthropy in Latin America—Executive Summary," p. 4.

26. Ibid., pp. 11, 12.

27. Ibid.

28. Tomás Roberto Fillol, *Social Factors in Economic Development* (Cambridge, MA: MIT Press, 1961), 97.

Index

~

About the Author

L awrence E. Harrison directed USAID Missions in five Latin American countries—the Dominican Republic, Costa Rica, Guatemala, Haiti, and Nicaragua—between 1965 and 1981. Convinced that culture was a crucial, and largely ignored, factor behind Latin America's development problems, he retired from USAID in 1982 and spent eight years at Harvard University's Weatherhead Center for International Affairs, which copublished his first book, *Underdevelopment Is a State of Mind: The Latin American Case.*

Jews, Confucians, and Protestants is the fifth book he has authored, following, most recently, *The Central Liberal Truth: How Politics Can Change a Culture and Save It from Itself* (2006).

Harrison has also coedited three collections: *Culture Matters*, with Samuel Huntington; *Developing Cultures: Essays on Cultural Change*, with Jerome Kagan; and *Developing Cultures: Case Studies*, with Peter Berger.

Harrison started teaching at Tufts University's Fletcher School in 2002. In 2007 he inaugurated the Cultural Change Institute, which he directed at Fletcher through 2011.